In Search of the Unitive Vision

Letters of Sri Madhava Ashish to an American Businessman 1978-1997

Compiled with a Commentary by Seymour B. Ginsburg

New Paradigm Books Boca Raton 2001

22783 South State Road 7
Suite 97
Boca Raton, FL 33428
The New Paradigm Books Web Site address is:
< http://www.newpara.com >

IN SEARCH OF THE UNITIVE VISION:
LETTERS OF SRI MADHAVA ASHISH TO
AN AMERICAN BUSINESSMAN, 1978-1997

The author is grateful for permission to reproduce the following articles: Sri
Madhava Ashish, "The Guru as Exemplar of and Guide to the Term of Human
Evolution," Time and the Philosophies, UNESCO (1977), pp. 211-236 © UNESCO
1977; Sri Madhava Ashish, "The Value of Uncertainty," The American Theosophist, Vol. 67, No.1 (January 1979), pp. 10-13, © The Theosophical Society in
America, P. O. Box 270, Wheaton, IL 60189-0270; Sri Madhava Ashish, "What
Can be Taught," The American Theosophist, Vol. 77, No. 2, (March/April, 1989),
pp. 51-53, © The Theosophical Society in America, P. O. Box 270, Wheaton, IL
60189-0270; Sri Madhava Ashish, "A Return to Intelligent Inquiry" (paper
presented at the Conference of the Indo-European Neuro-Surgeons, New Delhi,
India, November, 1992), reprinted with permission of Sri Dev Ashish and Dr.
Brahm Prakash, publisher of the proceedings of the International Congress of
Neuro Sciences, at New Delhi.

Cover design by Knockout Design
< http://www.directcon.net/kodesign >

First New Paradigm Books Quality Paperback Edition: October 15, 2001
New Paradigm Books ISBN No. 1-892138-05-0
Library of Congress Preassigned Control No. 2001 132675

10 9 8 7 6 5 4 3 2 1

In the unitive vision the identity of the individual with the universal is experienced, and it is perceived that this identity encompasses all being as an eternally valid fact. It has not come into being with the seer's attainment to the vision, but simply is. What comes into being, or, more truly, is developed in the seer, is the seer's capacity to perceive the identity. In this context it seems meaningless to say that any individual man ever attains anything. The spirit raises its human vehicle out of its own being and, through this vehicle, achieves knowledge both of the qualities it has made manifest to itself and of the undifferentiated and unmanifest being within which all qualities inhere. Our life is its life; our awareness is its awareness; our desire to live, to experience, and to know, is its desire. And the motivation which urges men to turn inwards to self-discovery is the driving motive behind the whole universe, a motive that seems to be as inherent to the nature of being as is consciousness itself.

TABLE OF CONTENTS

Acknowledgments

Because my association with Sri Madhava Ashish covered so extended a period of time, almost nineteen years, from 1978 to 1997, there were a great many people whom I met and who helped me during those years of search. This was long before there was any thought given to the project of publishing Madhava Ashish's letters to me.

The germ of the idea to publish the letters originated with Dev Ashish (née David Beresford), Madhava Ashish's successor as head of the Mirtola ashram. In November, 1997, after the death of Ashish, he wrote to me:

"I remember Ashishda saying to me, 'If Sy hadn't asked all those questions I would not have written any of it.' We've all heard him talk about the subjects, but not everyone has such a lot of written stuff. It looks like you may have the lion's share and we would be grateful and indebted to you if you could share it, leaving out the very personal things."

Several others, resident or associated with the ashram, helped me not only to form an understanding but also helped in one way or another to produce the resultant text of this book. Mahesh Sexena, a resident when I first visited, introduced me to the nature of an ashram, especially the Mirtola ashram and its history. He also gave me insight into Madhava Ashish's guru, Sri Krishna Prem, and into the relationship between these two men. Ann Mitchell, my companion for many years, strongly encouraged me to meet Madhava Ashish when I first thought about it in 1978. She accompanied me on several of the visits to Mirtola in support of my effort and in pursuit of her own quest. Herbert Klein and Jacqueline Litzenberg, fellow students of Gurdjieff's teaching, accompanied me on one of the visits to Mirtola, and Jacqueline was instrumental in translating the channeled talks referred to in the text. Chitra Iyer, who was a resident of the ashram for many years and whom Madhava Ashish looked upon almost as a daughter, helped to make my visits comfortable and helped me to understand what I witnessed during those visits. Others who were of influence include Patricia Finkle, Odette Petrequin, Shashi Puri, and Bobby and Mala Tandan with whom Madhava Ashish stayed while undergoing medical treatment in his final years. Mala recorded details of Madhava Ashish's passing.

Still others became specifically involved with the manuscript. Donald Eichert encouraged me to go forward with the publishing project at the outset and offered suggestions. Mike and Pramila Jackson, Kersy and Usha Katrak, Sean and Pervin Mahoney, Satish and Kamla Pandey, Rajeev and Madhu Tandan and later, Vini Kapur read drafts and offered suggestions. Ashish's sister, Penelope Phipps, shared personal notes and read an early draft, as did John and Veronica Donovan.

As the manuscript began to take shape, Dr. Sophia Wellbeloved edited a later draft. Her knowledge of and experience with the Gurdjieff teachings helped to shape the manuscript. Professor Paul Beekman Taylor, who knew Gurdjieff personally, read a still later draft and made significant suggestions.

My publisher and editor, John Chambers, was the force behind taking a collection of teaching letters and setting them into the form of the spiritual adventure set forth here, an adventure that I hope the reader will enjoy. John did much more than I would have expected from any publisher or editor. He familiarized himself with the history and teaching of the Mirtola gurus and G. I. Gurdjieff, and much of the text is owing to his efforts.

Although far too numerous to mention by name, many participants in the Gurdjieff work, many Theosophists and several others whom I met at or through Mirtola, helped form my understanding of concepts expressed throughout this text. I wish to thank them all.

Lastly, but far from least, my wife Dorothy Usiskin, who came back into my life just a month after I last saw Madhava Ashish in September, 1996, has been a force of persistence in keeping me at this project when I would have preferred to abandon it. I wrote to Ashish at the beginning of 1997, to tell him that Dorothy and I had renewed our relationship after a hiatus of more than twenty years and that we were planning to marry. He replied in his final letter, "This is wonderful news...You have as much to learn from her as she has from you." In his final words, Ashish asked me to remember one of his favourite Sufi quotes, "Love is the guide and love is the goal. Where e'er love's camels turn, the one true way is there." Ashish never met Dorothy, but he would have liked her. They are both balanced beings and she, like him, is not afraid to dig in the soil, the earthly soil and the soil of understanding.

Seymour B. Ginsburg and Sri Madhava Ashish in England, April, 1991.
This was Madhava Ashish's only visit to England since his having left
there almost fifty years before.

1

Encounter at Mirtola

M̲irtola via Panuanaula
District Almora, U.P. 263623
INDIA
18th Sept. 1978

Dear Seymour Ginsburg:
Thank you for your letter of Sept. 6, 1978. I shall certainly be glad to meet you when you come to India. Just where we shall meet may have to be decided nearer to the time when both our programs are more certain. I am usually here in January, but it sometimes happens that I have to be in Delhi during February...
Before meeting, you might care to read a collection of Sri Krishna Prem's articles, Initiation into Yoga.... The title article would give you a general idea of his approach to the spiritual path which, of course, I have largely inherited...
Yours sincerely,
Madhava Ashish

There was more, but these were the key lines in the letter. I was delighted. It was late September, the day of my departure by plane for India. Though as a businessman I had traveled extensively throughout the world, this would be my first trip to India and my first trip anywhere as a fledgling seeker on the spiritual path. And that very day—this morning—I had received this letter, unexpectedly, from Sri Madhava Ashish, the guru who lived at the Mirtola ashram, near Almora, in the Himalayan foothills of India.

A month earlier, I had written to Madhava Ashish praising his books of commentary on Theosophical Society founder Madame Helena Blavatsky's masterpiece, *The Secret Doctrine*—a book which I had found it extremely difficult to read. But somebody had given me Ashish's books of commentary, and they had helped me greatly. In my letter, I had asked him if I might meet him at some later date. Now I stuffed his letter into my pocket, thanking my good fortune that it had arrived only a few hours before my scheduled departure for India—just in time for me to receive it.

In actual fact, I had joined a group of travelers going to southern India to see Sathya Sai Baba, the guru celebrated, even notorious, in the West for his ability to apparently materialize physical objects out of thin air. I hadn't made any specific plans to visit Madhava Ashish, since I hadn't heard from him. But, with his letter in hand, I thought that somehow, before the trip was over, I would attempt to find him at his ashram in the north. I took the receipt of his letter just before my departure as a fortuitous occurrence that it would be unwise to overlook.

Thirty-six hours later, the journey was over. We were landing in New Delhi; soon our travel plans were taking our small group southward from Delhi to the Taj Mahal and other tourist sites. Soon we were on our way to Bombay, now called Mumbai. From Mumbai, our group proceeded to Bangalore and on to the ashram of Sathya Sai Baba in the small outlying village of Puttaparthi.

My journey in search of Sai Baba was hardly the sort of pilgrimage that, as a youth, or as a young man, I could have imagined myself making. Even less could I have imagined, in the relatively carefree days of my youth, the chain of life's circumstances—one of them tragic—which would eventually, and, it would seem, inevitably, set me upon this strange journey of a spiritual seeker that I had now undertaken.

True, there had been a time when, as a child, I had asked questions like: Who am I, what am I doing here, what happens when we die, what is God? But I had gotten no satisfactory answers from those people who presumed to be my teachers. I was told over and over again by the science teacher at my elementary school, by the family rabbi, by the priest who taught one of my good friends, that knowledge of God and of life and death was a matter of faith. But I had no faith. It hadn't taken my eleven-year-old mind long to figure out that these people knew no more than I did about these matters. My father, to his credit, simply called me a "free thinker" and encouraged me to keep asking the questions that interested me, though he could offer no answers.

What was most discouraging of all was that none of these people appeared to want to seriously inquire into these questions. I concluded then that all the stories about God, angels, heaven and all the rest had simply been made up throughout history by people who were desperately afraid of their own impending deaths. They needed children's fairy tales to comfort them, because in such matters they were themselves children—notwithstanding the exalted titles by which they knew each other: teacher, rabbi, priest. And so they made up stories. By age twelve, I was a confirmed atheist.

A career oriented around ruthless competition in the business world only added to my disenchantment. I graduated in law, then co-founded and ran a large chain of retail stores, a chain that would continue on to become a part of one of the premier retailing organizations in the world. Afterward, I tried my hand at creating an organization in the cutthroat world of commodity trading. But I noticed over the years that competitive accomplishments would give only an evanescent "high" that soon wore off. A new challenge was then required. This left in me a feeling of dissatisfaction and emptiness. The vainglorious strutting by politicians, entertainers and business people, myself included, the ongoing wars, and the whole litany of ills that plague humanity, caused a nagging feeling in me that something was very wrong.

Then, in 1971, a brutal event intervened to bring my feelings of disenchantment to a head and revive the questions about life and death that I had asked as a child. This event was the unexpected death of my young wife. With her death, all my dreams, all that I had striven for in terms of worldly success in family and

3

business, suddenly seemed unimportant. I found myself disenchanted with what life had to offer. I wondered if there was anything else. In the years from 1971 to 1978, I was taken up with raising my three children, two of whom had not even been teenagers when my wife had died. I muddled about for much of those years, going through the motions of being a businessman, but without the enthusiasm that had characterized my earlier years in business.

In 1978, the seeds of a need to pursue these ultimate questions—seeds that had been sown in childhood—suddenly sprouted. Perhaps it was because my children were now more or less grown up, and I could think more of myself. Perhaps it was my own continuing fear of death and annihilation, one exacerbated by the sudden death of my wife, that caused me to renew this inquiry. It could simply have been the intuition that there is, after all, something else.

Whatever the reasons, I looked about me with freshly inquiring eyes. On one side, there were the churches and synagogues all over the city where I lived. Plenty of intelligent people belonged to them and attended, if not regularly, than at least on occasion. This was true not just in my town, but throughout the world. Billions, not just millions, of people were involved in these religions. How could I have the hubris to proclaim them all children pretending to believe in fairy tales? On the other side, countless generations of human beings had lived and died on earth over the millennia, and there was no evidence so far as I knew of another reality, whether it was called heaven or by any other name. Or *was* there some evidence, however minuscule and vague? What about the psychic phenomena that I had read about over the years? What about the miracles that people reported? If there was another reality to which these things were clues, could that which veiled it be lifted, and answers found to the questions I had asked as a child and now asked again?

It was at about this time that I stumbled on Madame Blavatsky.

Perhaps "stumbled" is not quite the right word. I was about to become conscious of a world where, not chance, but meaningful coincidence and Jungian synchronicity, played a significant role. I had set about finding out, in a fairly systematic way, where I could glean current information about psychic phenomena and the like. A local "New Age" magazine led me to a meeting of the South Florida Theosophical Society taking place not far from Fort Lauderdale where, working to no fixed schedule, I now lived while commuting to Chicago for business. At this meeting, I first learned about the founder of the society, Madame Helena Petrovna Blavatsky, or H.P.B. as she was called by her friends, her disciples and even her enemies, who had lived from 1831 to 1891.

Whatever you think about Theosophy—or any "New Age"-related matter—Madame Blavatsky seemed to me a very remarkable woman. Born of a talented minor-nobility family in the Ukraine, she had mastered occult lore at an early age and become fluent in nine languages. She had traveled twice around the world, mastered piano and horseback riding, and apparently even fought on horseback alongside Mazzini at the Battle of Mentana in the Italian wars of independence, in 1867.

Most importantly, in 1873 H.P.B. had come to New York City where, in 1875, she created the modern theosophical movement. She did this by founding, with fifteen others, the Theosophical Society. This was an organization the purpose of which was to provide a forum for the investigation of spiritual/philosophical ideas that were at that time little known in the west. These included teachings from the eastern religions of Hinduism and Buddhism, along with the investigation of psychic phenomena. In 1879, Blavatsky moved the Society's headquarters to India. There she attracted the attention of British officials who were especially interested in her reputed psychical gifts.

This latter aspect of her character especially interested me. I had learned that H.P.B. was alleged to have extraordinary powers. Several writers had recounted claims that she had materialized rose petals and teacups, that invisible bells sounded in her presence, and that she could telepathically send and receive letters and messages. If this hugely intelligent if eccentric woman claimed to possess these gifts, then I thought she might be telling the truth.

H.P.B. had written two 1,000-page tomes supporting various doctrines of the Theosophical Society. The first, *Isis Unveiled*, had appeared in 1877; the second, *The Secret Doctrine*, published in 1888, was considered to be Madame Blavatsky's masterpiece. Many Theosophists believed that large parts of *The Secret Doctrine* had been "channeled"—that is, psychically communicated to H.P.B. from higher, purer, less material realms of reality.

I learned that *The Secret Doctrine* purported to be about an extremely ancient, even a primordial text called the *Stanzas of Dzyan*, which Madame Blavatsky said she had seen when she was studying with her "Masters" (discarnate or incarnate, I wasn't sure which) in Tibet—or perhaps she had seen this book in her mind's eye, that is, had "channeled" it from higher realms of reality; again, I wasn't quite sure. Blavatsky had spoken in very concrete terms, stating that "An Archaic Manuscript—a collection of palm leaves made impermeable to water, fire, and air, by some specific unknown process—is before the writer's eye." The *Stanzas of Dzyan* seemed to be the Holy Book of Holy Books, a kind of template or archetypal model of all the Holy Books that had come thereafter, the *Bhagavad Gita*, the *Egyptian Book of the Dead*, the Mayan *Popul Vuh*, all of them; it was even, somehow, the fount from which all of these books had been watered.

The *Stanzas of Dzyan* was apparently a description of nothing less than how the universe had come into being out of "nothingness," and how it would one day sink back into nothingness (the book seemed to treat this "being" and "unbeing" as a continuous process). I've since learned that a perennial question of philosophers is, Why does the universe exist at all? What is it that obliged and enabled something to come out of nothing in the first place? Or, Why did God, being by definition perfect, have to create the universe at all? How could He, She, or It, being perfect, have that need, which was imperfection?

H.P.B.'s *The Secret Doctrine* claimed that the "secret doctrine" in fact comprised the answer to this question and even explained the stages by which existence came about—and that the *Stanzas of Dzyan* contained the secret doctrine in its most pristine form.

I tried to read *The Secret Doctrine*. I found that, to support her thesis, the founder of Theosophy had pulled in every "secret doctrine" and Holy Book imaginable, from the highest and purest to the lowest and most bogus. If there was brilliance of imagination and intellect everywhere in the book, there was also, it seemed to me, no discrimination whatsoever. I could hardly make head or tail of the book, and I wondered if it were worth my while—or anyone else's—to try to penetrate this monstrous conglomeration of truths, half-truths, quarter-truths, and, I suspected, outright confabulation.

But Blavatsky's achievements were remarkable. Who was I to dismiss her esoteric masterpiece outright? I asked some Theosophists if there was a book that could help me understand Blavatsky's *Secret Doctrine*. "Of course," came the answer. I was handed two books that seemed to make up a set. One was called *Man, the Measure of All Things*, and the other, *Man, Son of Man*. The first was by "Sri Krishna Prem" and "Sri Madhava Ashish," the second by "Sri Madhava Ashish"only.

I looked through the books. Madame Blavatsky had divided *The Secret Doctrine* into two parts, the first called "Cosmogenesis," describing the creation of the universe, and the second "Anthropogenesis," taking up the story with the creation of mankind. I saw that *Man, the Measure of All Things* was a commentary on "Cosmogenesis," and *Man, Son of Man*, a commentary on "Anthropogenesis." I set about reading these two books in detail. I was much taken with the intelligence of the inquiry they expressed and with the light they shed on *The Secret Doctrine* and the questions I had begun to ask again. I wrote to Sri Madhava Ashish (I found out that Sri Krishna Prem, who had been Ashish's guru, had now passed away) in care of the publisher, wanting to know more about him and what he had found. That letter was sent on to India; for, as I've already said, I had received a reply from Ashish and stuffed it into my pocket just before my flight to India took off.

I had written to Sri Madhava Ashish because I was particularly interested in the various claims that H.P.B. had remarkable psychic powers. I thought these claims were nonsensical, but I was curious—and I wondered if a man who wrote as intelligently about the matters Blavatsky raised in *The Secret Doctrine* as did Sri Madhava Ashish, could have been hoodwinked into believing such nonsense. Were there really people who had such powers? If so, what significance could be attributed to the manifestation of those powers? I thought that perhaps the co-author of *Man, the Measure of All Things* and author of *Man, Son of Man* might be able to tell me.

But the primary purpose of my trip to India was nothing so subtle as an investigation into why and how the universe had unfolded. It hadn't taken me long, in the course of my investigation into paranormal phenomena, to find out that the most famous living person for whom claims of extraordinary paranormal powers could be made was Sathya Sai Baba. He was perhaps the best known of all the living Indian gurus, with devotees numbering in the millions. Because the vast majority of those millions lived in India, Sathya Sai Baba was relatively unnoticed in the West. But, even in the West, there were groups of Sai Baba devotees, who met regularly in cities in many countries.

Although Sathya Sai Baba's teachings were well respected, much of his fame stemmed from his purported ability to manipulate matter. He was apparently able to materialize objects or otherwise alter their shape and location through the use of his paranormal powers. Years earlier, I'd heard about the demonstration of such powers by the Israeli, Uri Geller, but had paid little attention; now I was in India with the goal of actually witnessing the powers of Sathya Sai Baba.

Our group had arrived at the ashram of Sathya Sai Baba, in the small outlying village of Puttaparthi. It was the occasion of Dusshera, the Hindu religious holiday. And here, at Puttaparthi, we did indeed see demonstrations by Sathya Sai Baba of psychic phenomena manifested through powers apparently at his command.

They proceeded along two lines. The first was the seeming materialization in the palm of his hand of a gray ash known as *vibuthi*, with alleged healing powers, which he passed out to the throngs of people who had come to see him. The second and more dramatic demonstration was the apparent materialization of two objects. At this demonstration, I witnessed the materialization by Sathya Sai Baba of both a metal necklace of silver color and an oblong stone.

The history of Sathya Sai Baba recalled an earlier guru of similar name, Sai Baba of Shirdi, who had lived in India in the mid-nineteenth century. He lived a simple life mostly in the courtyard of a Hindu temple and had become known as a healer. People had come from all over to see him, and in numerous instances he had been able to heal their afflictions. Among the techniques he used was the rubbing on them of ash taken from a fire he tended in the temple courtyard. Hence, the tradition of the giving of *vibuthi* by Sathya Sai Baba, who was claimed to be the reincarnation of Sai Baba of Shirdi.

In demonstrating his powers to the assembled crowd in which I sat, Sathya Sai Baba had wheeled in before him a metal bust of Sai Baba of Shirdi over which he stood. With the waving of his hands, he produced a metal necklace which he then proceeded to drape over the bust. Immediately following this demonstration, Sathya Sai Baba extended his fingers down his throat and extracted what appeared to be a stone about five inches in length. The stone was presumably a representation of the male phallus, the *lingam*; this is an important symbol in the Hindu tradition, representing the male generative force.

During each of these instances, the crowd of onlookers went wild, shouting, cheering, and in some cases sobbing in gratitude for having been present at so awesome a demonstration of power. To understand the impact of what I witnessed that day, you have to appreciate the setting in which it took place. As I have said, the occasion was Dusshera, one of the most important of Hindu religious festivals. The open-sided and roofed auditorium in which the demonstrations took place was crowded with several thousand devotees, sitting mostly cross-legged on the concrete floor. I estimated the size of the crowd that day to be about 10,000. They had come from all over India in expectation of witnessing such feats, and they were not to be disappointed.

The ceremonies of the day had begun some three hours earlier, with prayers and the chanting and singing of Hindu spiritual songs or *bhajans*. Our group, consisting of eight people from the South Florida area, had been seated at the front of the auditorium, along with perhaps another hundred Westerners who had traveled to Puttaparthi for the occasion. In front of us was a row of obviously sick people, some in wheelchairs, others on stretchers, who had come for the occasion and to receive Sathya Sai Baba's blessing and perhaps his healing. Our viewing site was excellent—about as good as could be expected in a crowd of that size. My immediate reaction to the demonstration was to be amazed by what I witnessed, and such was the reaction of my equally awed fellow travelers and the thousands of shouting and crying Indians. We had just witnessed a miracle.

It was only afterward, away from the frenzy of the crowd, that I began to reflect on what I had seen. In a different setting, a Las Vegas nightclub for instance, such a demonstration would not have been taken as a miracle. The assumption in that setting is that one is witness to the talents of a competent illusionist. But now, in India, I wanted to believe in the miraculous; and, caught up in a crowd of thousands of worshippers who like me wanted to believe, I was, for a few moments at least, a believer in having witnessed a miracle.

This is not to say that what I saw Sathya Sai Baba do was anything but what it appeared to be. I simply do not know, and since that time I have experienced other instances of paranormal phenomena. These have not been as dramatic as the demonstration of phenomena described above, and mostly fall into the category of synchronicities, the word coined by Carl Jung to describe an order of causality not within the realm of currently known scientific principles. Doubts remained in me about the reality of what I had seen at Sathya Sai Baba's ashram. After a few days I left our group of travelers, who remained at the ashram, apparently more captivated than I with the experience of Sathya Sai Baba.

I passed through the international headquarters of the Theosophical Society at Adyar, near Madras (today called Chennai), and chatted with a visiting scholar in residence there, Dr. Charles S. J. White, who had made a study of the Sai Baba movement. Dr. White seemed to have some plausible explanations for what I'd seen Sai Baba do, but I was still bewildered by the apparent mastery of paranormal power that Sathya Sai Baba seemed to have at his command. I wasn't willing to admit that what I had witnessed had been in any way fraudulent.

Although I witnessed, and was amazed at, the apparent powers at Sathya Sai Baba's command, my visit had hardly satisfied my craving for knowledge of what this was all about; in fact, it had merely intensified it. I flew north to New Delhi, determined to meet Sri Madhava Ashish. I thought that the man who had shed light on the *Stanzas of Dzyan*—however opaque that light might still be to my eyes—must surely be able to shed some light on what I had witnessed and on my inquiry in general. Once in Delhi, I arranged transportation with a taxi company, and the driver and I set off for the foothills of the Himalayas, in search of the Mirtola ashram and Madhava Ashish.

Getting to Mirtola for the first time was quite an experience. Westerners who have traveled in India know just how different it is, and how much more difficult it is to travel about than in the West, even when you stick to the established tourist routes. Mirtola is not on any ordinary tourist route and the best I could do in Delhi was to find a taxi driver who knew how to get to Almora. This was the city, locatable on a map and eleven hours by car from Delhi, that had been mentioned by Ashish in his letter.

The roadside scene for a traveler in India, especially when you are off the tourist routes, is incredible. On that first trip to Mirtola I saw, as I would on every subsequent trip, every sort of conveyance imaginable, from pushcarts to bicycles to elephants, along with thousands of people simply walking along the roadside. Not the least of a driver's problems is to avoid hitting someone or something, and on that trip we did hit a pushcart and knocked out one of our taxi's headlights in addition to damaging the cart. Subsequent trips involved many more roadside incidents, the most serious being once when I was in a taxi along with the driver and two other passengers on our way to the Mirtola ashram. On that occasion, the taxi driver, attempting to avoid an oncoming vehicle driving on the wrong side of the road, had to swerve, causing us to roll over. The car did one-and-a-half flips and landed on its roof. Luckily (or were we charmed?) the four of us crawled out the windows with no serious injuries. Getting to Mirtola was an adventure.

We arrived at Almora, a town of scattered bungalows facing the Himalayan peaks far off on the horizon. To the west stood Badrinath and Nilkanth, and on the eastern horizon the distant mountains of Nepal. In the center, Trisul and Nanda Devi—the latter a peak of 24,000 feet— rose above the foothills. Mirtola was still 18 miles away, on the other side of a deep valley, along a poorly graded graveled road. Peering at the horizon, we could just make out the ashram, a white spot high up on the wooded hills. My driver asked directions. Soon we were bumpily descending the nine miles down into the valley and then ascending the nine miles up the other, steeper, side. Around us, through the pine trees that changed to oak as we drew closer to Mirtola, we caught darting glimpses of plunging valleys and soaring mountains. The final half-mile of the journey was up a very steep dirt road with lots of switchbacks; then, suddenly, we burst into an ocean of flowering marigolds and cosmos that had been allowed to run wild and stood taller than a man. There rose up in front of us, out of this yellow undulating sea of flowers, the gray dome of a temple framed by a background of green trees. The dome was in the distance; in front of us, a mundane cowshed marked the entrance to Mirtola.

I will never forget my first sight of Madhava Ashish striding down the hillside path at the entrance to the ashram. Having seen the taxi approaching from down the mountain, he had come to see what stranger had arrived. I knew from his books that Madhava Ashish was British by birth, but I was not prepared for this six-foot two-inch tall, gangling *sadhu* of so fair a complexion, attired in the ochre robe of a monk, who in a moment stood before me.

Ashish was perhaps as surprised to meet me as I was to see him. Although he had received my September letter and replied to it, we had made no specific arrangements to meet. While many people, I learned, came to the Mirtola ashram during the course of a year to meet and to visit with the guru, the vast majority were Indians. In that respect a western visitor was unusual, although by no means unique. To just drop in as I did, without prior invitation, was even more unusual. I recall my attempt at a joke:

"Well, I was just in the neighborhood passing by [this after an eleven-hour car ride, the last hour of which was along a dusty graveled road], and thought I would stop in and say hello."

We both chuckled. His bright blue eyes seemed to peer right through me. We chatted. I detected in his voice the faintest whisper of a Scottish brogue. Ashish explained to me that it was a policy of the ashram to provide hospitality for up to two nights to any visitor. I was more than shown that hospitality: I was housed in a small stone cabin known as "Moti's cottage" after its first resident, Moti Rani, the daughter of the ashram's first guru, Sri Yashoda Mai. The taxi driver stayed in an annex to the cabin.

Ashish made me welcome, and over the next two days answered many of the questions I had begun to formulate about the "inner search." I noticed that the other residents of the ashram called him "Ashishda," and he suggested that I might like to call him that also.

"*Da*," he said, "means 'big brother.' It is a way for my pupils to name me without becoming overly absorbed in the niceties of addressing a Hindu holy man, which is what I seem to have become."

He told me that witnessing the Sai Baba phenomena would not satisfy me because I was not a devotional type. Certainly, he was right about that. I then asked him what he knew about G.I. Gurdjieff, the mystic whose name I'd heard for the first time from a fellow passenger on the flight over, during this very trip to India. Hearing this, Ashish proceeded to tell me, in tones of the greatest certainty, of the importance of Gurdjieff to my spiritual search.

"Gurdjieff's teaching is the way for you because it is a western way," he affably declared. "It is no accident that you came across the name of Gurdjieff on your visit to see me. These things are, in some way that we do not understand, planned and connected. Jung would have called them 'synchronicities.' If you want to pursue

13

in a western way the path that we follow here at Mirtola, you need to study and work with the Gurdjieffian teaching. That is why Gurdjieff was sent in—to bring the teaching to the West."

I was astonished that, having just met me, he should make such an emphatic pronouncement about who my spiritual teacher should be.

But then, I had noticed that he seemed to be the shrewdest of men, quite capable of penetrating into the truth of a person's character in a very short time. I was even more confounded by his statement that Gurdjieff had been "sent in." Whatever, I asked, did he mean? Were people sometimes returned from the dead for a particular mission?

Ashish replied by alluding briefly to the Buddhist doctrine of the bodhisattva. These were the great beings who are said to have attained to all that can be attained through earthly experience, but who reject the quiet rest of nirvana and take incarnation again in order to help their fellow human beings. Ashish spoke in glowing terms of Gurdjieff, comparing him with beings such as the Buddha and Jesus. Ashish asked one of his pupils to fetch him a particular book on Gurdjieff. It arrived; entitled *The Gurdjieff Work*, it listed in the back many of the Gurdjieff groups and umbrella organizations around the world.

"Find one of these groups," Ashish instructed me. "Work with them. It is what Gurdjieff called 'the Fourth Way.'"

I found his eclecticism remarkable. It was not that Ashish held a particular brief for Gurdjieff. He seemed to have a comprehensive understanding of just about every spiritual teacher who had ever lived, with differences between individual spiritual traditions seeming to be of little importance to him. I was certain that, for quite a different seeker, he could have just as knowledgeably brought forth quite a different name.

I mentioned this to him. "Truth," replied Ashish, "is what is important. Look for the truth and look inward to find it. You will never find it outside yourself hunting for a guru or following an external spiritual tradition. These things can only serve as guideposts for you in your own search. No one can do that search for you. Each of us must tread that path for himself. Remember that the path is inward, always inward."

I asked him how I should begin my search, irrespective of whether my "guru" was Gurdjieff or not.

"Your dreams are important," he told me. "Begin to pay attention to them. Your dreams will tell you things about yourself that you have buried too deeply to uncover directly. It's another way to 'know thyself,' that famous injunction of the Delphic oracle about which Gurdjieff speaks."

I enjoyed my two days at the ashram. We were 7,000 feet above sea level. The air on those richly green slopes was cool and thin, filled with the sounds of silence. The small two-story Hindu temple, with its gray concrete dome, was the ashram's center and had been so since the founding of Mirtola in 1930. In its inner sanctum, small figurines of Krishna and his consort Radha, representing the male and female aspects of the deity, stood side by side on a marble altar with fresh flowers lying at their feet. At the evening service, this inner shrine was lit up like a glowing cave, while the din of gongs, bells and a kettledrum reverberated through the ashram.

The sides of the temple had been extended to make space for cubicles, these cubicles providing the residents with the simplest of accommodations. Three huge stone slabs, hunkered down in a corner of the garden, served as seats in moments of relaxation. A small separate building, called the library, stood in as a guest house, and, a short distance away, there stood the rose-covered cabin that had served as the residence of Moti Rani.

Mirtola was far larger than this simple temple-ashram compound suggested. It comprised 60 acres in all, with fully a quarter of them given over to terraced hillside farming while the rest were kept wooded. The improvement of the ashram's land had been undertaken by a young Australian disciple, Dev Ashish—he is now, in 2001, Mirtola's head—who raised high-yielding dairy cattle by cross-breeding with local stock, thereby transforming the farm into a demonstration of what could be done with degraded land by improved management. I learned that Ashish, an engineer by training, was better known among Indians for his efforts to improve the ecology than for his spiritual status. He had written articles on land reform and was actively involved with the Indian government in implementing those reforms. It would not be till my next visit to Mirtola, seven months later, that I would find out very much about this, or even become fully aware of the extent of the ashram's land and its accomplishments; and so I will leave further discussion of that until a later chapter.

I was soon to discover, though, that this tiny Mirtola ashram had a remarkably rich history. Madhava Ashish had come to India because of World War Two. He had been born Alexander Phipps, in Edinburgh, Scotland, in 1920. His father had been a lieutenant colonel of artillery and at one time aide-de-camp to Lord Kitchener in the Sudan. His mother had been the daughter of a Ceylon tea planter and the granddaughter of a Scottish Laird. Phipps had gone to the College of Aeronautical Engineering, in Chelsea, England. This had equipped him to work when war broke out first on the repair of Wellington bombers in England, and then, from 1942 onward, on the overhaul of Rolls Royce engines for Spitfires on a military base near Calcutta in India.

In 1944, the young Phipps, by now much taken by Indian culture and especially its spiritual aspect, took advantage of some leave time to visit Madras State (Tamil Nadu) and, at Tiruvannamalai, the ashram of the renowned guru Ramana Maharshi. The experience of Ramana's presence had a transformative effect on him. At the end of the War, Phipps embarked on a spiritual search, ending up "almost by accident" at the little town of Almora in the rustic setting of the Kumaon Hills. Here he met Sri Krishna Prem, then Mirtola's guru, and traveled to the ashram a week later to visit with Krishna Prem at length. The visit became a lifelong stay. Phipps soon took the holy orders of a Vaishnav monk and, now known as Madhava Ashish, became a disciple of Sri Krishna Prem.

This was the life he had been meant to live. In 1957, when a disciple commented on Madhava Ashish's glowing presence, Krishna Prem replied: "Yes, what took me twenty years, Ashish has done in ten." Life at Mirtola was not without its austerities.

16

Ashramites bathed in cold water summer and winter, and at 7,000 feet winter meant snow. Neither meat nor fish were allowed; meditation was the staple. Here, the Scots Madhava Ashish flourished. Gradually, he took over many of the ashram's functions, performing the temple *puja*, developing the farm, and introducing basic amenities like latrines and water storage tanks. At Krishna Prem's death in 1965, Madhava Ashish assumed the role of guru to the new disciples. He began to write. Soon, he had expanded and rewritten an unpublished work of Sri Krishna Prem which would become *Man, the Measure of All Things*. In due course, he completed *Man, Son of Man*. The completion of these works marked the end of an initial phase in Madhava Ashish's life. From the early 1970's on, he began to become more and more involved in public affairs. He traveled more, and began to write on subjects other than the strictly spiritual; in particular, he wrote on the ecology. It wasn't long after this new interest had begun that I first met Madhava Ashish at Mirtola.

If World War Two had successfully brought Ashish, née Phipps, to India, World War One had come within an ace of killing Krishna Prem. Like Ashish, Sri Krishna Prem had been a Briton. Born Ronald Nixon, in Cheltenham, England, in 1898, the future guru of Mirtola had been a brilliant student of philosophy and literature at Cambridge. Developing a fascination for eastern religion and India, he had sought and obtained upon graduation a teaching post as lecturer in English at the University of Lucknow.

Nixon had not gone straight from public school to Cambridge. World War One had intervened, and he had been a fighter pilot over France and Germany in 1917. This had led to a narrow escape from death which the young Englishman, telling the story afterward, would never hesitate to call a miracle.

"One day," he would tell his friends, "as I was reconnoitering, I was about to steer to the right, where half-a-dozen fighter planes whirred and zoomed, thinking that they were ours—that is, R.A.F. planes. Just then some mighty force caught hold of my wrist and made me veer right round to the left. I was quite bewildered, the more so as the force was too incredible to be doubted. In a few

17

minutes I returned to our base and was told that I had done well to come back so promptly as a number of enemy planes had just come into action. It was then I realized, with a shock of thankful delight, that I had just had a miraculous escape. I am as certain as certain can be that the miracle had been wrought by a power beyond our ken."

The brilliant and personable young Nixon, hugely successful as a lecturer at the University of Lucknow, had fallen in love with India, her people, her philosophy and her way of life. The founder and vice-chancellor of the university, Dr. Gyanendra Nath Chakravarti, observing Nixon's growing predilection for all things Indian and the young lecturer's growing uneasiness with his fellow Englishmen, had invited Nixon to stay with him and his family in the adjoining guesthouse. Very soon, Nixon had become almost an adopted son to the Chakravartis.

Ronald Nixon had become involved with a Hindu family of great spiritual distinction. Dr. G. N. Chakravarti practiced what Ashish would characterize in later years as "Theosophicalized Hinduism." Throughout his life, the vice-chancellor, wherever he was staying, rose at three in the morning and meditated until six. He had met Madame Blavatsky, joined the Theosophical Society, and become Secretary General of the Indian branch. Dr. Chakravarti had been born in 1875; his wife, a Bengali woman named Monica Devi, born in 1882, was every bit his equal, if not more. A *salon* hostess and fashion leader in her early years, this finely bred aristocrat of a woman possessed a passionate, explosive temperament; it was, avowed the vice-chancellor, the equal of Madame Blavatsky's. The dark, big-eyed Mrs. Chakravarti had had four children and adopted forty more. Her powerful maternal streak extended to once suckling a litter of abandoned puppies. Through Dr. Chakravarti, Monica met and traveled with world-renowned spiritual figures, including Blavatsky's successor, Annie Besant—but beneath the glittering surface, a spiritual pursuit all her own was catching fire within the vice-chancellor's wife. Traveling in Europe with her husband, Monica was mobbed by a crowd at St. Peter's in Rome; she was wearing a blue saree embroidered with silver stars, and they had mistaken her for the Virgin Mary. At the Paris Exhibition of 1902, dressed in all her finery, she was mistaken for the Queen of Madagascar. Queen Victoria, seeing Monica from a distance at Windsor Castle, summoned her to the palace.

This once-so-worldly woman was fast becoming a visionary and a mystic. During the several years that he lived with the Chakravartis, so was Ronald Nixon. Monica began to have personal experiences of Krishna and of other gods and goddesses. In 1925, she had an overwhelming experience of the unitive vision. She sought her husband's permission to become a wandering mendicant monk. As his wife's guru, Dr. Chakravarti invested Monica with the robes of the Vaishnava order of Vairagis. She shaved her head and took the name Sri Yashoda Mai. Nixon had become increasingly enraptured of the deep spirituality of Dr. Chakravarti's wife. At his request, he became her disciple; Sri Yashoda Mai in turn inducted the young Englishman into the Vaishnava order, giving him the name of Sri Krishna Prem.

Few scenes can be more typical of the rich cultural fibers that make up India—and yet more startling—than that of this couple, the young English disciple and his female guru old enough to be his mother, both shaven-headed, both penniless and begging from door to door as is required by the Vaishnava order, setting off as they now did for the foothills of the Himalayas. Their goal was to found a temple to Krishna; Monica's health had begun to fail and, unable to tolerate the heat of the Indian plains, she had no choice but to pursue her spiritual mission in the friendlier climate of the Indian hill country. Eventually, the two settled on the site near Almora that would become the Mirtola ashram. By 1930 they had built and consecrated, to Sri Krishna and his consort Radha, the gray-domed temple that is still the center of Mirtola.

Yashoda Mai's health began to fail so badly that she came to spend much of her time in bed. Such was Krishna Prem's devotion that he spent the nights curled up on a mat on the floor at the foot of the bed, ready to help her whenever she needed help. This was the path the brilliant young English intellectual had chosen, to attain to the unitive vision: utterly selfless devotion to the guru.

Sri Yashoda Mai died in 1944; she had lived a dozen years longer than the doctors had predicted. Now her youngest daughter, the rotund, joyful, irreverent Moti Rani, took orders and became the disciple of Krishna Prem. Moti died in 1951, at age 35; it was in the same rose-covered cabin in which she had lived that I stayed during my first visit to Mirtola.

It was into this rich and intense if tightly focused atmosphere that Alexander Phipps, soon to be Madhava Ashish, first came in 1946. Within a week, he had seen in Krishna Prem a power which he could hardly have named at the time, but which he would one day recognize as that guru's establishment in the unitive vision. Ashish would write many years later, in his introduction to Sri Krishna Prem's *Initiation into Yoga*, that at the end of that first week he had suddenly seen—having gotten beyond Krishna Prem's outer, intellectual, armor—"the man behind. It was the sort of man I had never seen before: simple, in the sense of uncomplicated, clean, soft and sunlike. I was torn between embarrassment at my intrusion, and desire to feast my soul on such rare beauty. For the next few days I felt like the country bumpkin of legend who stumbled into fairyland."

Here Ashish would stay until his death in 1997. It was into this atmosphere, pregnant with the power of the unitive vision, that I, an American businessman who had no business being there at all, would, by the grace of whatever unknown force, have, in 1978, the great good fortune to stumble.

Blavatsky, *Secret Doctrine*, 1.
Roy, 54.
Prem, *Initiation into Yoga*, 14.

2

The Self
and a Saints' Gallery

Ashish had not only suggested that I become involved with the teachings of G.I.Gurdjieff. He had also recommended that I systematically examine my dreams. About dreams themselves, he had very specific, non-western ideas. They were bound up with his concept of the Self.

The Self? In that first letter Ashish had sent me, and which I had stuffed in my pocket before boarding the plane to India, he had recommended that I read a book, the foreword of which he had written himself, called *Initiation into Yoga: An Introduction to the Spiritual Life*. I had picked up a copy of this slim, 128-page volume written by Ashish's guru, Krishna Prem, while I was in India, en route to meeting Ashish at Mirtola. This book proved to be my first introduction to the Self—what Krishna Prem also called "the Light." I learned that the true guru was synonymous with this Self. Prem wrote eloquently of "the pure Consciousness itself dwelling in the heart of every living being and particularly that Light...[which] dwells in all beings and speaks (that is why some traditions have termed it the Logos, the Word) in our hearts with the voice of conscience; though only too often we confuse its voice with various other voices that speak with louder accents." In all of us, said Krishna Prem, there dwelt, beyond the flux of daily thought and endeavor, this Light, this Self—the higher Self.

The concept of the higher Self was bound up with the notion of the unitive vision. Krishna Prem's little book would be my first contact, coming by way of the Mirtola ashram, with the concept of the unitive vision. More immediately, the book gave me a working notion of the concept of the Self. This was certainly necessary because, not long after I returned to the U.S., Ashish would begin to guide me, through our correspondence, in the analysis of my dreams.

Ashish's ideas about dream analysis are expressed in a manuscript, *An Open Window: Dreams and the Inner Reality*, which he gave me a year after I first visited the ashram. At the time of his death almost 20 years later, it had been completed but not yet been published. In that manuscript, as in everything he said, Ashish took a wholly non-western, non-Freudian, non-Jungian approach to the study of dreams. He believed our dreams are essentially messages from our higher Self, our Inner Light; I later understood that he meant they were, in a sense, dispatches from the heart of the unitive vision. But often we had trouble picking up these messages, because our capability to receive them was controlled by our willingness and ability to be open to the prompting of that Inner Light. Still, we should be in no doubt that, in our dreams every night, that higher Self sought to make its presence known, through whatever openings, whatever chinks in our protective non-believer's armor, it could find. The Self, of which our personality was only a facet, gave us direction through our dreams, urging us on to growth, to maturity, and to wholeness.

Ashish's distance from modern psychology can, I think, be measured by the fact that contemporary therapy scarcely even posits the existence of a God. Carl Jung's notion of the collective unconscious—a sort of repository of all human experience, to which the dreamer is given access through the experience of archetypal images—comes closest to suggesting the existence of a kind of objective reality encompassing all of us and greater than us all. But even Jung never admitted, at least publicly, to the independent existence of a Self that transcends the individual self of each human being (though Jung may have believed more than he let on).

For Ashish, there was never any question of the reality of the Self. His overarching belief was that there is at work in all of us an intelligence greater and wiser than our ordinary waking state. When we examined our dreams from this perspective, we would begin to perceive this intelligence guiding us in our dreams through the use of symbolic messages.

A.   Your inquiry about dreams is difficult to answer for the reason that I know of no book which handles dreams as a guide to the inner life. Every analyst seems to have his own views on the meaning of dreams, but they all appear to agree that social adaptation is the be-all and end-all of psychology.

Even C.G. Jung, with his archetypal dreams and collective unconscious, stops short of publicly admitting the independent reality of the Self. He slurs the point by admitting that it is real as a human experience, but avoids admitting that it is real in itself. However, *Man and His Symbols*, written by Jung and a number of his followers, is the only book I know of which I care to recommend (since much of its value lies in the illustrations, one wants to get a good edition).

Apart from this, any reading of psychology and related dream interpretation is valuable insofar as it throws light on the workings of the mind. But one has always to read with caution. There is a clear, though not always recognized, distinction between accepting many of the thoughts of Freud, Jung, etc., and becoming a Freudian, Jungian, etc. One needs every bit of help one can get in learning the language of dreams. But it is difficult to learn the language without having a lot of psychological theories foisted on one, most theories being based on the assumption that the psyche's concern is with the current standards of normality. [Dec. 28, 1978]

My dreams, as I have described them to Ashish, are for the most part too personal in nature to be of much interest to the reader. I'll touch on them here only insofar as they shed light on the general subjects of parapsychology or spirituality. There was one such dream, which struck Ashish and myself as being precognitive in nature. It was not the sort of dream that, up until then, I thought that anybody ever had, let alone myself. I dreamt I was visiting the great ruins of Egyptian antiquity at Abu Simbel—a trip which I would actually make, though I didn't know it at the time, about a year later.

Ashish believed that my dream not only represented a flight through time, but that it might also have been an out-of-body experience, i.e., I hadn't only traveled to Abu Simbel temporally, but I had gone there in my "astral body" as well. Ashish's concept of the Self included the notion of several interpenetrating "bodies" within each one of us besides the physical, including the astral body in which we could engage in "out-of-the-body" journeys. One aspect of my "dream therapy" with him would consist of my becoming accustomed to, and gradually accepting (if possible), such notions as that of the astral body.

But Ashish's main emphasis consisted in this, that we should always regard the stuff of dreams as symbolic, encoded in a symbolism emanating from the higher Self. Ashish suggested that my dream of Abu Simbel had primarily to do with my growing preoccupation with my "spiritual quest" (later, I would dream a number of times of visits to vast underground caverns, and Ashish would interpret these dreams in the same way).

Dream therapy was only one facet of my "apprenticeship" on the spiritual path. There was also my growing immersion in the teachings of Gurdjieff. Sometimes, the two clashed. Before I discuss these two at length, I will tie up some loose ends remaining from my ongoing discussion with Ashish, based on my encounter with Sathya Sai Baba, of the nature and importance of this latter guru's feats, and of the nature of "gurudom" in general.

I'd continued to be alternately intrigued and dismayed by this Sathya Sai Baba whom so many adored and so many regarded as a charlatan, so much so that I decided to return to India in May, 1979, and, with another group of Sai Baba devotees and inquirers from Florida, visit the guru for a second time. I hoped that I'd also be able to see Ashish again. I wrote to Ashish in March, telling him of my plans and asking him if such a sensationalistic performer as Sathya Sai Baba could possibly—however successful his manifestations—have an intimate relationship with the Self. Though I hardly had the words or the understanding at the time, this was the first of many questions that I would ask Ashish about "being established in the unitive vision."

A.   Your question about Sai Baba: Almost any man can experience the unitive vision, irrespective of his education and intellectual capacity. In other words, the capacity to have the experience is, to a large degree, independent of the capacity to understand it and to appreciate its full implications. There have not been many people who combined both capacities.

Any expressed understanding of the experience is an interpretation—words expressing the ineffable. Interpretation by any one man is necessarily limited both by the existent state of knowledge at that time and by the particular seer's familiarity with that knowledge. It is also limited by his knowledge of the formulations of his own spiritual tradition and by the extent of his knowledge of other traditions.

I personally accept Sai Baba's status as a man of spiritual attainment. So far as I am concerned, his status "shows through" his words; it is not in his words as such.

As to his statement that he is "God," it is true that in his essential nature he stands united with the divine unity. So do we all. As he himself says, "I know it. You don't." But when he says, "I know it," in what sense does he know it? When standing in the unity, he "knows." But when attempting to describe it, he is limited by the vehicle of expression as we all are: his mind, his stock of concepts, his capacity for subtle understanding, his life experience. In other words, if he is God, he is God in a limited vehicle. Yet it is the same vehicle that gives him his powers.

The value of the phenomena [he manifests] lies in their demonstration that the world is not limited to the framework of contemporary materialistic science—not limited to sensory perception. But one can discover this without having it mixed with religious teaching. The phenomena and the teaching are related only to the extent that if such phenomena cannot occur, then God is an impossibility. To know this is a net gain for anyone, anywhere, at any cultural level.

To me it appears that you, for instance, would find yourself in great difficulties were you to try to submit yourself to a man in whose utterances you could see so many contradictions.

It is always of value to experience the presence of a man of attainment. In this, the "feeling response" is truly of greater significance than the response to the literal truth or falsity of anything he says. He is true, even if his statements may be only relatively true. If one feels that he is true in himself, then anything he says must be taken seriously, if not necessarily literally. One must not allow one's mind to be overwhelmed either by phenomena or by real status, into uncritical acceptance—except in areas where one knows that one does not know. One must trust one's perception of truth, even though one knows that one's formulations of truth may require modification.

Since you are going to be in India, I would suggest that you take the opportunity to visit Nisarga Datta, who lives in Bombay and can be called on without prior arrangement. Kersy, whom you met here, lives in Bombay and would be glad to introduce you. The old man of 85 is of equal or greater attainment as Sai Baba, but his approach is entirely different, being similar to that of Ramana Maharshi. He has a bright and active mind and enjoys answering questions. Like anyone, he has his limitations, because he had little education and knows little of systems of thought outside his own tradition. I think that to see the "same" attainment in a different form would be of value to you in helping you to discriminate between the spirit as such and the forms in which it manifests. [March 23, 1979]

As it turned out, I did manage to get back to Mirtola, in May, 1979; I'll speak about my second visit to Ashish's ashram shortly. My itinerary arranged itself in such a way that I ended up visiting Ashish first, then proceeding south to visit Nisarga Datta at Mumbai. Then I continued on to visit Sathya Sai Baba a second time, this time at Bangalore.

Meeting Nisarga Datta gave me the opportunity to learn at first hand about this famous Indian guru. Nisarga Datta lived a simple life in a poor section of Mumbai. He had gone off into the Indian countryside to follow a guru after raising his family and starting a small tobacco business selling Indian cigarettes known as *bidi's*. When he returned to Mumbai, he was a changed man, and people recognized this. Colloquially, he became known to some seekers as the *bidi* guru. Many people came to ask him questions and to hear his views on the spiritual life. A small loft was built above the tobacco shop (then being run by his family), and it was there that he held forth in daily sessions. A multilingual Pole named Maurice Frydman became his translator for these sessions.

Frydman eventually set down in book form a series of questions people asked and Nisarga Datta's answers to those questions. The book was entitled *I Am That*, and it was through this book especially that Nisarga Datta became known to western seekers. Still, the number of westerners coming to see him when I did was modest. On the occasion of my visit, there were about ten Americans or Europeans present along with a like number of Indians.

I visited Nisarga Datta once more in 1981, shortly before his death. His message to me then, as it was in 1979, and as it was repeated over and over again by him to visitors and recounted in *I Am That*, is that he is the divinity. So are we all, he says, but he knows it and we don't. It is a message similar to that given by Sathya Sai Baba. At the time, my conception of the divinity— based on teaching received in my childhood, although even then I trusted not a word of it—was that God was an ineffable being separate and apart from me. It was rather like the popular characterization of George Burns in the motion picture series *Oh God*, as a separate Mr. God who has "descended" onto this planet.

A conception closer to the truth, as Nisarga Datta expressed it—as all the other gurus express it, and as I have now come to understand it—is that each of us and all things animate and inanimate are an inseparable part of that oneness which is the divinity.

The more aware of ourselves we become, the more fully do we know we are God. It is in this context that Nisarga Datta and Sathya Sai Baba and all the other gurus and genuine spiritual teachers mean such a statement. But, in 1978 and 1979, when I first heard this view of the divinity expressed, I laughed at it. It is only with the study and experience that the years have brought that I have begun to understand what these gurus were getting at.

After this visit to meet Nisarga Datta, I went on to Bangalore, where Sathya Sai Baba was then in residence at his estate. I joined up with the group from Florida and went with them to visit Sai Baba for a second time.

Once again, I witnessed his demonstration of the production of phenomena. During my stay in Bangalore, in an attempt to come up with an unbiased evaluation of what we had observed, a friend and myself gathered information about Sathya Sai Baba from sources which were not devoted to him. Within a week we were able to ferret out a considerable body of criticism challenging the claims of Sathya Sai Baba's avatarship and the genuineness of his "miracles." As a part of our investigations we talked at some length with a former vice-chancellor of Bangalore University who, in 1976, had headed a committee to look into the alleged "miracles" claimed by various Indian gurus, including Sathya Sai Baba. This academic complained to us of a lack of cooperation; Sathya Sai Baba, he said, had refused to be tested.

All this raised a lot of doubts for me. By the end of a week during which I visited Sathya Sai Baba every day, the man as I now saw him seemed like a good and spiritually developed person, but not a man to whom I could supplicate. He was certainly a special person; but I, at least, did not hold him in the Mr. God-like esteem in which he is held by many of his devotees. Still, I believed he meant well, and I recognized that he played an important spiritual role for millions of people. In truth, he had played an important role for me by drawing me to India; this had set up the occasion leading to my first meeting with Madhava Ashish and the relationship that followed. I suppose I would eventually have gotten to India without having been driven by my curiosity to witness the production of phenomena at Sathya Sai Baba's command. But of this I cannot be certain.

In late July, back in the U. S., I wrote to Ashish asking him among other things what he thought of this negative information my friend and I had gathered about Sathya Sai Baba.

A. I sympathize with Sai Baba in his refusal to be tested. If I could do the same things, I would also refuse. The attitude of the tester and the attitude of the man who is using his powers to attract people to the spirit are so different that there can be no agreement. The tester always aims at a material explanation, of which fraud is the easiest, while a man like Sai Baba thinks in terms of powers of consciousness. Obviously, a reconciliation is possible, but the world of psychical research still seems far from it.

There is no reputable body of psychical research in India. In Europe and the States over the past 100 years, a great deal of specialized knowledge has been amassed, yet even there amateurs often set themselves up as judges over the producers of phenomena. None of the committee who set themselves up to test Sai Baba had any claim either to experience or to specialized knowledge. There were acceptable grounds for suspecting political motivation. The affair occurred during Mrs. Gandhi's emergency. Sai Baba spoke openly against her excesses. Mrs. Gandhi spitefully refused him use of a central park in Delhi for his visit (yes, in India even such petty matters are decided by the prime minister). And Sai Baba could control five million votes. Under such circumstances, no one in his senses would permit a test. No matter how genuine the phenomena, the report would "prove" that they were fraudulent.

The committee "tested" a small boy who, ostensibly with Sai Baba's blessings, was also producing *vibuthi*. The investigators jumped him and found ash in the folds of his clothes around stomach and abdomen. To start with: Trained investigators never jump their subjects—the results are always negative and prove nothing. Then, in a pre-puberty boy spontaneously producing phenomena, materializations around navel, breasts, armpits and crotch are to be expected. That the materializations stopped after the investigation is proof only that the affects of jumping the subject are negative.

It has to be considered that this boy's supposed phenomena could have begun as a spin-off effect from Sai Baba, in precisely the same way that numerous people, mostly children, started producing phenomena similar to Uri Geller's in Britain after seeing his TV programs. Also, phenomena with genuine beginnings can, in India, be later falsified by parents greedy for the fame (and money) they bring. I mention all this only to show how many problems beset so-called investigations.

One more point comes to mind. Associated with this inquiry was a Ceylonese professor, author of a book on the subject, who does claim to be a professional investigator. In this book, he describes his investigation of poltergeist phenomena—objects being thrown about a room. He correctly spotted the person responsible for the phenomena.

From my personal experience of several such cases, I can say that there was no physical connection between the woman and the objects moved; but, on the level at which she was conscious of having moved them, it felt to her exactly as if she had moved them physically. A person with consciously developed powers might say, "Of course it feels the same. Whenever I move an object, I do it with my subtle-physical arm. Sometimes I do it directly, sometimes the subtle-physical arm makes the physical arm do it. The subtle arm has a longer reach." [July 6, 1979]

By the time of this exchange with Ashish, I was well and good embarked on my adventures with the teachings of G. I. Gurdjieff.

They had begun in my hotel room in London, England, where, on my way back to the U.S. from India after my first visit with Ashish, I had stayed up two nights running to read *In Search of the Miraculous* by Peter D. Ouspensky. Ashish had recommended I read this book. Ouspensky is arguably Gurdjieff's most influential student. A Russia-born philosopher and writer, he had been intensely involved with the first series of Gurdjieff's classes, those taking place in Moscow, St. Petersburg and Essentuki in the Caucasus from 1915 to 1918. This was a difficult time, when even the hugely resourceful Gurdjieff was beginning to be balked by the appalling conditions of the Russian Revolution. By 1918, Ouspensky had begun to break off relations with the ever fascinating but always unpredictable Gurdjieff.

The reasons for Ouspensky's break with Gurdjieff—one which was for some time inconclusive—are still hotly debated among Gurdjieffians. It's not my purpose to discuss that break here, nor to discuss Ouspensky's *In Search of the Miraculous*, which is a lively and detailed account of the numerous stratagems, including "Sacred Dancing," which Gurdjieff employed to awaken his students from the state he called "sleep" to a whole new way of being and thinking that he christened the Fourth Way. Certainly, Ouspensky's book awakened me to a passionate interest in Gurdjieff.

G.I. Gurdjieff was to write three books himself, the best-known of which is *Meetings with Remarkable Men*, first published in French in 1960, eleven years after Gurdjieff's death, and then published in English in 1963. It so happened that, the first year I became involved in the Gurdjieffian "Work"—in 1979—the British filmmaker Peter Brook (*Lord of the Flies*, 1963; *The Mahabharata*, 1990) made a movie based on *Meetings with Remarkable Men*. I sat through this film a number of times with great delight. Brook is himself a student of Gurdjieff's teachings, and I later learned that, in making *Meetings with Remarkable Men*, he tried to use Gurdjieff's exact words, managing to do so for the greater part of the film. This dialogue straight from Gurdjieff lends a certain solemnity to the film, which a number of more conventional critics have found irritating, but which many Gurdjieff group members find accords Gurdjieff the respect that he deserves.

I was mesmerized by this movie and its unfolding sequence of stark, exotic vignettes. Gurdjieff was born in Alexandropol (now Gyumri), close to the present-day western border of Armenia, sometime between 1866 and 1877. Brook's film was shot in Afghanistan, and as it opens we are greeted with a scene of a small, rocky valley whose floor is streaming with Transcaspian peoples come to witness a most unusual, periodically-performed music competition. Some of the musicians have extremely ancient instruments. All of them compete to produce a sound that will evoke a response from the rocky slopes—an echo, perhaps, or a boulder coming tumbling down. Finally, it is the unique ululation of a single human voice that draws an answering echo from the surrounding peaks. The contest has been won, and an opening note of supernormal feats accomplished by ancient, almost-forgotten techniques—feats typical of Gurdjieff himself—has been sounded in the movie.

The boy Gurdjieff has been present at the competition. He goes home, and we observe his peculiar relationship with his father. The father unexpectedly places a live snake in his son's hands. He imparts strange wisdom to him. Is there life after death? young Gurdjieff asks. Yes, replies the father, for some people: those who have through a lifetime of exceptional acts allowed to crystallize within themselves a kind of substance which will survive the body's death.

The boy is drawn to all that is occult in the village. A dead man rises, zombie-like, from the grave; a demon must be responsible, so a village elder slits the "dead" man's throat. A *Yezidi* boy is placed in an "enchanted" circle drawn on the ground and cannot tear himself away. The simplest of herbal potions cure violent, deadly maladies.

The central theme of the movie, as in Gurdjieff's book, is the future mystic's growing, burning, insatiable desire to track down the secret Brotherhood of the Sarmoung, a group of Masters said to possess powerful esoteric knowledge passed down through the ages. It is in attempting to find this group that the young Gurdjieff encounters the "remarkable men" of the title. He makes several unsuccessful efforts. Then we find him, along with a fellow seeker, blindfolded and mounted on horseback, guided by four Kara-Kirghiz tribesmen, travelling across the rocky plains of Turkestan on a two-week journey to the secret monastery of the Sarmoung Brotherhood. Once installed in the monastery, Gurdjieff watches sacred dances that have been preserved for at least 5,000 years, and which may encode in their movements the motions of the heavenly spheres and much other arcane knowledge. When properly executed, these dances evoke corresponding motions in the dancer's soul. We are led to believe these are the same Sacred Dances that Gurdjieff will introduce into his classes some years later when he returns to Moscow (the movie includes eleven minutes of these "Sacred Dances" performed by members of the contemporary Gurdjieff group in Paris, in costume for their middle eastern roles). Brook's film concludes with the youthful Gurdjieff, still at the monastery of the Sarmoung Brotherhood, sadly bidding farewell to his dearest friend who is departing for a monastery in Tibet.

There is far more in Gurdjieff's equally captivating autobiographical book. We read about his father, one of a vanishing breed of bards ("*ashokhs*") who improvise epic songs and recite from memory ancient epics going back as far as the Babylonian *Gilgamesh* (which Gurdjieff says his father knew by heart); we can understand how it was that the young boy's fascination with things ancient and mysterious first caught fire.

Brook has shown us snakes slipped into the young boy's hands; Gurdjieff writes that "my father took measures on every suitable occasion so that there should be formed in me, instead of data engendering impulses such as fastidiousness, repulsion, squeamishness, fear, timidity and so on, the data for an attitude of indifference to everything that usually evokes these impulses." Along with slipping small animals to him, Gurdjieff's father "forced me to get up early in the morning, when a child's sleep is particularly sweet, and go to the fountain and splash myself all over with cold spring water, and afterwards to run about naked..."

Gurdjieff implies that this harsh regime helped him to become extremely tough, resilient and resourceful. It seems to have formed the basis for some of the techniques he would later use to "shock" his pupils out of "sleep" and onto the path to the Fourth Way. Gurdjieff tells us yet more. Caught up in a ridiculous adolescent prank, he finds himself lying in the middle of an artillery range while soldiers, unaware he's there, fire shells any one of which

33

could kill him. He writes: "...At the beginning I was completely stupefied, but soon the intensity of feeling which flooded through me, and the force of logical confrontation of my thoughts increased to such an extent that, at each moment, I thought and experienced more than during an entire twelvemonth.... Simultaneously, there arose in me for the first time the 'whole sensation of myself.'" The reader involved in Gurdjieffian group Work, reading this passage, wonders if he or she is not present at the birth of Gurdjieff's concept of the modality of "self-remembering."

The book takes us only to the point where Gurdjieff is continuing his travels in the Middle and Far East, still drawing from his adventures and explorations lessons which he will put to good account when he becomes a teacher. Ouspensky and others students recount that Gurdjieff eventually returned to Russia, where he began the classes Ouspensky describes so compellingly in *In Search of the Miraculous*. The horrors of the Russian Revolution soon forced Gurdjieff and his students to flee from Russia via Constantinople, finally settling in France, in 1922, at the Prieuré des Basses Loges, at Avon near Fontainebleau. Here, Gurdjieff established the residential school through which he would promulgate the greater part of his teachings. A serious automobile accident in 1924 led him to eventually close the school. Gurdjieff turned to setting forth his teachings in writing. He gave his three books the series name of *All and Everything*, with the first and second volumes essentially completed by 1934. Preceding *Meetings with Remarkable Men* was Gurdjieff's bizarre, baroque and gigantic space-travel allegory, *An Objectively Impartial Criticism of the Life of Man, or Beelzebub's Tales to His Grandson*, considered to be his *magnum opus*. The first draft of this book was completed in 1928, but the mystic/teacher continued to revise *Beelzebub* until his death in 1949. Gurdjieff's third book, *Life Is Real Only Then, When "I Am,"* circulated privately among his pupils during his lifetime and was published posthumously. From 1934 until 1949, he lived in Paris and continued to receive and teach pupils.

Such was the man whose life played the decisive role in the creation of the teachings which, at the suggestion of Ashish, I was beginning to absorb in Gurdjieff group Work classes. Of those classes, and my reaction to them, and Ashish's reactions to my reactions, I'll have more to say in the next two chapters.

All the time, I continued to be intensely involved with the Mirtola ashram and Sri Madhava Ashish. I'd visited Ashish a second time in May, 1979, just before going to meet Nisarga Datta and observe Sathya Sai Baba for a second time. During this second visit to Mirtola, I continued to learn much about the ashram, its history, and the living conditions there.

Daily life at Mirtola was simple indeed by western standards. There were no telephones. There was no television. Ashish asked the ashram devotees—there were usually no more than half-a-dozen residents at one time—to do eight hours of manual work a day. He considered five hours of sleep a night to be sufficient. There was no hot water in summer, and just enough to take the edge off the cold in winter. Ashish considered this more than appropriate. He advised no more than one blanket at night throughout the year. "If you get cold, sit over the fire," was his comment. He recommended at least two hours of meditation a day. "If you can't meditate, at least sit still," was his further comment.

Part of the reason for the plainness of the ashram's amenities, and the plainness of regime that that necessarily entailed, was geographic: Mirtola was in a remote area. When Ashish had first come there, in the 1940's, there had not been even a road, only an eighteen-mile-long footpath stretching from Almora to Mirtola. By the 1970's, conditions could have been made more comfortable, but Ashish preferred to maintain the earlier simplicity and a kind of physical rigorousness. This was in part a method of enhancing the self-awareness he wanted to instill in the ashram inhabitants, and which he encouraged me to experience as best as I could in my urban environment while working with a group of people in accordance with the Gurdjieff teachings.

During his first decades at the ashram, Ashish had carefully observed the increasing poverty of the local villagers, the degradation of the land, and its continuing deforestation. A tragedy of the area is over-cropping by domestic animals, making it impossible for younger plants to replace older trees when they are felled, leading to huge erosion. Ashish had written letters about this to the Lucknow government, along with publishing articles. This led to his being invited to join the Planning Commission's committees on hill development. Because so much Indian land has, through passage by inheritance, been subdivided into uneconomically small plots, the ashram property was relatively large by Indian standards. Ashish was able to enclose the ashram land on the mountain so that wild animals such as tigers and leopards were kept out. Its size allowed experimentation with ecologically advanced farming, and permitted conservation methods suitable to the surrounding hills, for soil, trees and water. The ashram grew wheat, barley, sweetcorn and some fruit. Bovine cows were kept from which milk, butter and ghee were derived for consumption by the ashram dwellers, the excess being sold as a cash crop to the local villages. This, along with visitors' contributions to the temple, provided some measure of financial security to the ashram.

There was another, quite different aspect to Ashish's writings. It would be some time before I would learn about it. But at just about the time I was beginning to visit Mirtola annually, Ashish was embarked upon writing articles for India's leading intellectual journal, *Seminar*, published in New Delhi.

Seminar was managed by a husband-and-wife team, Raj and Romesh Thapar. Romesh, its founder and editor/publisher, was India's best-known ex-communist. His reputation as a former radical attracted much intellectual firepower to the publication. He had seen some of Ashish's writings on ecology and, finding them impressive, had invited the Mirtola monk to write on this and other themes for *Seminar*. Ashish began to contribute articles, some on "spiritual" topics. He and Romesh and Raj Thapar became good friends.

Through the pages of *Seminar* Ashish began to enter into the greatest of India's national debates, a debate that was raging fiercely at the time, which raged all through the twentieth century, and which rages fiercely to this day. The substance of that debate can be summed up in two questions: Does India have a soul different from, and spiritually superior to, those of other nations? And, if it does, is it beginning to lose that soul?

I was not surprised to learn that Ashish was passionately concerned with these questions. A profound feeling that India was spiritually superior had been, after all, what first brought Ronald Nixon to India. The same conviction had, I think, prompted both Krishna Prem (née Ronald Nixon) and Madhava Ashish (née Alexander Phipps) to remain in this country. It was a belief that had placed both of them on the path to becoming gurus. In *Yogi Sri Krishnaprem*, Dilip Kumar Roy has recorded one of Prem's typical, lyrical outbursts on the subject of the uniqueness and superiority of the Indian soul (this was in the 1940s). "Often, while meditating, I find myself praying to Krishna that He may never let India's immemorial soul be swamped by the rational, robustious, God-deriding, scientific agnosticism of the blatant West, blaring over a thousand loudspeakers: 'Religion is the opium of the mind.' May He always shower His blessing on India, whose very dust heaves with latent godliness, in whose tiniest crannies mystic faith flowers like green grass-blades through chinks in rocks—India, whose people have only to anoint wayside stones with vermilion to endow them with sanctity."

Ashish was to write in the same vein in an article for *Seminar* for January, 1985, "The Moral Stream":

"....India stands out in the world as a land where the transcendental significance of human life is still recognized, where the man of spiritual attainment is still honored, and the path of spiritual inquiry is still accepted as a valid life aim and occupation. Unlike in countries of the developed world, here the immaterial roots of consciousness and being are not so deeply buried that they need heavy excavation to rediscover them. The reflection can be discovered at the back of every Indian's mind, even in the minds of our seemingly uprooted intelligentsia who have outwardly aligned themselves with the Western life style and all that it stands for."

It was good to know that Ashish, once trained as an engineer, was still be so powerfully involved in the issues of the time. Both his involvement with *Seminar*, and his involvement with Romesh and Raj Thapar, would grow. I'll have more to say about that later. Now, it's time to say more about my own involvement with the teachings of Gurdjieff, and Ashish's thoughts on Gurdjieff and that involvement.

Prem, *Initiation into Yoga*, 35-36.
Gurdjieff, *Meetings*, 45.
Ibid., 204-205.
Roy, 94-95.
Ashish, *Relating to Reality*, 338.

3
_____

Esoteric Dreams and Awakenings

*D*ear Sy:
You may find the dream readings seemingly a bit negative. Don't let it upset you. You see, I find that when dreams yield signs of negative tendencies, it shows that the dreamer is approaching awareness of his negative motivations.

Thus Ashish's words to me, in a letter dated October 18, 1982. I wasn't finding this esoteric dream study easy—nor, for that matter, was I finding any of my spiritual adventuring easy. But I had at least, by this point, gotten together a number of rules of thumb for the interpretation of dreams according to the world-view of Ashish (though I was hardly managing to put into perspective my early experiences with the Gurdjieff group work—see below and following chapters—nor all that I was hearing from Ashish about the Self and the unitive vision). I'll finish quoting Ashish's words to me, then set down for the reader those seven rules of thumb for the esoteric study of dreams.

A.   And this means that it's becoming possible for him to view the distortions of his conditioned nature with some degree of dispassion. That's a rather important point, because your dreams won't show you what you can't accept and so even if some of the things are hurtful, it means that something in you, as it were, is ready to accept the hurt, ready to accept the criticism, and to look on the criticism with more objectivity, as something which is not totally identified with you. The pain comes because of the identification, but there's enough of a sort of freeing from the identification to be able to make it acceptable on afterthought.

Well, I call this sort of thing progress, which is just as important as the sort of experiences you've been having. It's as if there's a sort of, well, it shows that the awareness has moved up a bit, so that the inner thing becomes more real and the outer thing becomes a little less important. It's a sort of shift in the center of gravity. [Oct. 18, 1982]

I thought that a little progress was a lot of progress. I *had*, after all, managed to formulate the following rules of thumb, using to some extent Ashish's words:

1. Although on occasion dreams can tell us about others, we need to look at them as if they apply only to us. In fact, almost all our dreams do apply only to us. Even if a dream appears to involve another person, we should mainly take the dream as showing us something about ourselves. The other person in the dream is usually a symbol for a characteristic that we need to see in ourselves.
2. The Self (which we are but don't know it), is giving us direction through our dreams and is urging us to growth, maturity and wholeness.
3. We should take dreams as giving us useful criticism about ourselves, about things in us that need looking at and changing. Yes, dreams can appear to be complimentary, but when they are, they are not necessarily of therapeutic value. The good stuff takes care of itself so we need not bother with congratulating ourselves when our dreams seem to compliment us. We need to see the bad qualities in us that our dreams are trying to show us.
4. We need to be ready to look at the lowest and most disgusting parts of ourselves as shown to us by our dreams. Since the Self

(the unchanging real), with which we seek unification, includes everything in the universe and beyond, nothing can be excluded from it. We must look at everything with which we as personalities (our lesser self) identify, for example, all manner of anger, rage, sexual problems, fear, greed and the whole long list of other personality identifications. We can take as a guide to these identifications whatever features there are in us that capture our attention. We need to let go of all these features of our personality.

5. The purpose of releasing repressed material in us through dream interpretation is not just to help make our lives better here, although it is certainly valuable for that. These things are blocks to our entering into higher states of consciousness that are the characteristic of unification with the Self.

6. If we take as a hypothesis that our dreams are guided by an intelligence greater and wiser than our ordinary waking state, the intelligence of the Self, we need to honor that intelligence by acting on its guidance. We should not take dreams as ordering us to do something, but if advice is given us through our interpretations, we need to see what the advice is and then act on that advice in an intelligent manner.

7. Everyone dreams. If we claim that we do not dream, it is a question of not making sufficient efforts to remember and record our dreams.

Ashish would have a great deal more to say to me about dreaming. In late 1980, I found myself "lucid dreaming"—having dreams in which I was conscious that I was dreaming. Gurdjieff used "sleep" as an analogy for the lowest form of consciousness, but lucid dreaming seemed to me to attest to quite the opposite regarding this lowest state of consciousness. I asked Ashish if it were useful to try to "awaken" while the body was asleep, that is, remain conscious while one was dreaming—and even attempt to control that dreaming. And, if it were useful, how did you do it?

A. Sleep: One of the recommended exercises is to attempt to carry waking consciousness into the sleep state. There are various ways and the first is to hold the intention throughout the day and while falling asleep.

It may take many weeks or months of effort. It first happened to me unintentionally, when I was engrossed in a problem that kept my mind occupied almost every waking moment for some three months.

G's relaxation exercises can lead to the same state—body asleep, mind awake. Any real meditation has the same result. Few people recognize this fact, because sleep is a dirty word for meditators.

Don Juan [the teacher of Carlos Castaneda in his books on sorcery] works the other way around, not by carrying waking consciousness through the barrier, but by planning to wake up and stay awake in the dream state—effectively the state of astral projection. [Nov. 2, 1980]

A few months later, Ashish would give me techniques for carrying wakefulness into sleeping.

A. Do a lot of physical work during the course of a day. Then, being exhausted, instead of lying down to go to sleep, quietly remain sitting up. This may allow the body to actually go to sleep while you are in the sitting position, whereas the conscious mind, functioning through the brain, remains awake. These [hypnagogic and hypnopompic] states, the first being that which immediately precedes sleep and the second being that which immediately precedes complete awakening from sleep, are states in which it is possible to experience what G calls "the real world," the objectively conscious state. In the moments of pre-awakening, one cannot stop the physical body from awakening, but one can maintain the state of self-awareness so that one is free from identification, and then go further. [March 6, 1981]

I had, as I have already said, joined a Gurdjieff group then meeting in Dania, near Fort Lauderdale, in South Florida.

The group was one of perhaps thirty groups affiliated with the Gurdjieff Foundation of the U.S.A., headquartered in New York

City. That group, in turn, was affiliated with the Gurdjieff Institute in Paris, headed by Jeanne de Salzmann. Madame de Salzmann, which was how she was referred to in the Gurdjieff groups, was then, in 1978, 89 years old, and had been a student of Gurdjieff himself from 1919 until G.'s death in 1949. The Paris groups were probably the most influential of the Gurdjieff umbrella organizations. Madame de Salzmann died in 1990, at which time her son, Michel, took over the leadership of the Paris Gurdjieff Institute. Michel died in 2001 at the age of 75. At the time of writing, the new leadership of this umbrella organization has yet to be decided. I will have more to say about Madame de Salzmann later. Meanwhile, before I relate what happens in the Gurdjieff groups and what happened to me, I'll set forth a few of the basic concepts, first formulated by Gurdjieff himself, that lie behind the innovative dynamics of these Gurdjieff groups.

In Gurdjieffian theory, there are posited four possible states of human consciousness, of which most people know about and experience only the lowest two. These two are sleep at night and our ordinary waking state in which we work, play, make love, make war, and all the rest. Sometimes, this latter state is called "waking sleep"—a kind of sleep in which almost all human beings are kept enthralled without suspecting that they are asleep. Consequently, most people have no idea that there actually are two higher states of consciousness.

The highest state of human consciousness as described by Gurdjieff is that which he called objective consciousness, but which has been given other names in other traditions. Ashish placed it in the same category as standing in the unity or the unitive vision. It is the state of peak or extraordinary experience, enlightenment or illumination, often described as a oneness with everything, but the actual description of which can only be expressed imperfectly. According to Gurdjieff, this fourth state of consciousness is a state which the un-awakened person cannot intentionally experience, although sometimes it comes for brief moments by itself.

In the Gurdjieff group, the emphasis is always on coming back to a sensation of the physical body to stop thoughts. When I was well into my Gurdjieff group, Ashish warned me that, using this technique, one had to take care not to remain with the sensation.

A.   As for meditational advice, I have never found it useful to substitute awareness of sensation for awareness of thought. I have done it but found I had, as it were, built a new prison in attempting to escape from the old one. However, since one has to be able to stop thought, any means, fair or foul, can be tried. Every man has to find the way that suits his temperament. [August 9, 1981]

Still, I have never failed to find coming back to a sensation to stop thoughts a crucially important exercise. It is the third state of human consciousness that is the key to the practical work, because it is a state into which a person can enter intentionally through practice and special exercises. Gurdjieff called this third state self-consciousness, or self-awareness, or sometimes self-remembering. The central characteristic of this state is the division of attention so that the experience of the observer or witness in us is included in our attention. Some people like to express this effort as an expanding of the attention to include more in it, to include the experience of oneself. This state gives a kind of detachment from the worldly identifications that keep us "asleep" in the esoteric sense.

It is from the continued existence in this third state that the fourth state of human consciousness can be intentionally accessed. Thus, almost all practical work lies in working with divided (or expanded) attention to experience self-awareness, the chief characteristic of the third state of consciousness. From within that state there are, again, special exercises, through which a person can prepare his or herself for the experience of objective consciousness.

In *In Search of the Miraculous*, Ouspensky details the traditional historical "ways," as Gurdjieff called them, of entering into these higher states of consciousness. The First Way is the way of the fakir, characterized by a prodigious use of the will to acquire extraordinary control over the body. The fakir may develop this control, but by and large, writes Ouspensky, "his other functions—emotional, intellectual, and so forth—remain undeveloped." For example, Gurdjieff tells Ouspensky of a fakir who day and night for 20 years "had been standing on the tips of his fingers and toes. He was no longer able to straighten himself. His pupils carried him from one place to another, took him to the river and washed him like some inanimate object." The way of the fakir is the physical way, the way of using one's physicality as a tool to detach from identifications with the small "self" and develop the inner will needed to enter into higher states of being. The Second Way, Gurdjieff calls the way of the monk. It is the emotional, religious way, characterized by ardent prayer, passionate longing, devotion and deep faith. The end result of pursuing this way can be a very unbalanced person, though, what Gurdjieff called a "stupid saint." "Subjecting all his other emotions to one emotion, that is, to faith, he develops unity in himself, will over the emotions," writes Ouspensky, but "...his physical body and his thinking capacities may remain undeveloped." The Third Way is the way of the yogi, the development of intellect and insight. The way of the yogi may include vast exercises in intellectual endurance, just as the way of the fakir includes vast exercises in physical endurance. Ouspensky writes, recording Gurdjieff's thoughts: "...he has the advantage of understanding his position, of knowing what he lacks, what he must do, and in what direction he must go."

Gurdjieff called man a "three-brained being." This refers to man's tripartite nature: physical, emotional and mental. Indeed, Gurdjieff spoke of man as having three brains or centers, each focused on one of these natures. Recent advances in science give some evidence of an "emotional brain" or seat of the emotions centered where Gurdjieff indicated, in the solar plexus. The intellectual brain is located in the head, and the physical brain (which Gurdjieff called the "moving-instinctive center") was, he speculated, centered in the spinal column.

Gurdjieff insisted that contemporary human beings are unbalanced as to the use of these three brains or centers, each of us favoring one or another. He believed that the beings of older and particularly less urban civilizations were more balanced. The Fourth Way of spiritual development, which Gurdjieff represented, aimed at balancing these three brains and the work that they produced into a single harmonious whole, the balancing of which inhibits identifications, promotes detachment, and facilitates entering into the higher states of conscious, "self-consciousness" and "objective consciousness."

Most important for me was that the Fourth Way, unlike the three traditional ways, was according to Gurdjieff a way in life. One could work on the Fourth Way without going into the seclusion of the monastic life. For me, this held out the hope that I could attain to the unitive vision in the midst of urban life, as Ashish had done under his teacher, Sri Krishna Prem, in the monastic confines of Mirtola.

Such was the modest task I had set myself in joining up with the south Florida, Gurdjieff group!

But, could I *really* do it without leaving the everyday world behind? Some six months into the "G. Work," I asked Ashish whether the pursuit of the Fourth Way was really compatible with being in the world—would it "eventually require a man to get out of worldly life altogether and go off to a monastery?"

A.   Monastic life: a necessity? In the literal sense, no. The total self-dedication which it symbolizes, yes. But in practice many people need an imposed discipline to help change their life-orientation. Perhaps the only real discipline is the discipline of love. [July 6, 1979]

I was also wondering if I had come across the Gurdjieffian teachings purely by chance, and I asked Ashish about this.

A.   In no significant sense have you "come across these teachings by chance." What made you respond to them when they came? You might not have noticed the event. Or your response could have been to join the Theosophical Society and "learn Theosophy by heart." In either of these cases your practical attitude to "gross materiality" need not have changed at all. But you have quickly come to see that you have to do something yourself. That being the case, you won't find it easy to stop, however frightening the prospect. Eventually you will have to give your willing consent and, in some sense, confirm your conscious self-dedication to the search—through whatever avenue suits your make-up. (This is an important part of what ceremonial initiation is about—placing an outward and visible seal on an inner commitment.) You can try running away, but the "terror" lies in there being no escape. If you come, your personal selfhood is threatened by the all-consuming unity of being. If you refuse the call, you condemn yourself to insignificance, a series of lives that dim out in meaningless repetitiousness. There's no heaven at the end of the road for people who have refused the call after it has reached the point of becoming a consciously appreciated choice. It's like reaching the age of majority: Thereafter the law holds [one] responsible for one's acts. [July 6, 1979]

I continued to be in close touch with Ashish, since running parallel to my participation twice a week and more in the South Florida Gurdjieff group were my annual visits (upon occasion, I got there twice in a year) to Ashish and the Mirtola ashram. The rural way of life at the ashram was new to a city boy like myself, and all the newer in that life at an ashram is intended as a spiritual apprenticeship in itself. Usually, I was never able to stay longer than a week. But these stays—charged as they were by the presence of Ashish, by the spectacular beauty of the fields leading up to the foothills of the Himalayas, by the long talks at night, and by the special purity of the rustic and reverent life there—seemed far, far longer than a week, and every detail of those visits remains to this day vividly etched in my memory.

Since Mirtola was a farm, a great deal of manual work was required. The residents were assigned various daily jobs such as milking the cows, churning butter, tending the vegetable garden, working in the terraced hillside grain fields and so on. Other assigned tasks included work in the kitchen, maintaining the temple and conducting a typical thrice-daily traditional Hindu temple ceremony. Ashish, as "task master," had stringent requirements as to how things were to be done, especially in the temple and the kitchen. Residents caught getting things wrong would be berated. Dev (who would later take over the ashram) did the same regarding the dairy and in the fields. For example, the concrete kitchen floor served as the dining table. If a resident, or a regular visitor like myself, was inattentive and walked across that floor—in effect walking across the table—that person would get a scolding.

The day began each morning at dawn with someone, usually Dev, blowing into a ram's horn as a wake up call. In the next two hours, in some cases before that, people meditated separately, and whoever was assigned to the kitchen prepared meals for Ashish and the few residents and visitors. Sometimes, Ashish himself would prepare the meals and clean up, demonstrating that no one was above these mundane tasks (mainly because of limited space in the kitchen, some of the residents took meals in their houses). Breakfast was usually fruit followed by *rotis* (a traditional Indian puff pancake), bread, butter, jam, and coffee or tea.

Before breakfast as well as at the noon and evening meal, there was a temple ceremony which involved banging and clanging a lot of percussion instruments like drums, cymbals, gongs, bells. Visitors as well as residents were invited to participate in the banging and clanging. These ceremonies are really very much like a kind of Gurdjieff stop exercise, intended to remind people to be aware of themselves and of the centrality of the temple figures, those figures being a reminder of the centeredness they are seeking in themselves. This ceremony, and breakfast, were from about 7:00 to 8:30.

Afterward, residents did their chores, and visitors performed their ablutions and in general could do as they liked. Toilet facilities consisted of outhouses. Showering was an affair that required people to heat up a bucket of their own hot water by gathering wood for a fire in a special water heating tank, filling the bucket, then taking it to a shower room and ladling it out over their bodies. Visitors not meeting with Ashish might visit with some of the other residents, take long walks, or participate as they wished in some of the daily chores.

From 10:00 to 12:00, and also in the late afternoon from 3:00 to 5:00, Ashish would see visitors privately, usually over coffee or tea in his room, dealing with their questions, problems, and spiritual search. Many people came to him for advice about family and other worldly matters. Others, like myself, were looking for spiritual knowledge. Meals and meetings were all sitting-on-the-floor affairs, whether in the kitchen, in Ashish's room, or in any of the residents' houses. On days when there were no visitors, Ashish would see the residents privately.

Noon brought another, similar temple ceremony, followed by lunch, the main meal of the day. Lunch was invariably rice based (as much as you wanted) topped with *dal* (a lentil soup) and usually a cooked vegetable. Desert was yogurt, usually sweetened. Meals were almost always the same, Ashish's theory being that we didn't want to become identified with wanting this or that particular kind of food. Thus food was seen as sustenance, not as something to become identified with. Its preparation, however, demanded severe and strict procedures, not only for cleanliness—which is a problem in India—but also as a task in attention for those responsible for the meals and for the cleanup afterward. Visitors generally participated in the cleanup and in some cases in the meal preparation. The time from after lunch till about 3:00 was another quiet time, when people could meditate or do as they pleased.

Sunset brought yet another, similar temple ceremony—a sort of putting of the gods to sleep—followed by a simple meal with Ashish in his room for the visitors. This meal usually consisted of just bread and cheese, or bread and jam with, sometimes, a potato.

In the evenings, whoever wanted to would assemble with Ashish in a building called the library, where, with everyone sitting casually on the floor, usually with their backs against the wall, anyone could hold forth on any subject that he or she wanted. Sometimes the subjects were mundane, but for the most part they involved spiritual questions, particularly when visitors were there and Ashish would try to answer them. The questions tended to orient themselves around the visitors' interests and particular searches. In my case, for example, there were inevitably questions about the Gurdjieff Work or about theosophical ideas. Sometimes some of the participants would challenge Ashish on some matter or other, but he usually had the last word—at least on spiritual matters. He was seen by the residents and by most visitors as a being of a higher level, someone who could answer speculative questions apparently from his own inner vision, like those having to do with a person's chain of lives. Often, especially during the winter months when there were no visitors, Ashish and the residents would collectively read from a book such as Gurdjieff's *Views from the Real World* or the *Bhagavad Gita* and discuss it. Evening discussions usually ended about 10:00-10:30. Afterward, people would go to their rooms to sleep, to meditate, or to do whatever.

All the days of the week were the same at Mirtola; that is, Sunday was treated like just another day, though certain tasks such as thoroughly washing the kitchen floor were carried out mainly on Sunday. However, a certain number of holidays were celebrated, and on those days there was some variance in the schedule with usually a temple ceremony. These holidays included the birthdays of all the Masters recognized there: Buddha, Djwhal Khul, Gurdjieff, Jesus Christ, Koot Houmi, Krishna, Maurya and others I've forgotten, along with the birthdays of the Mirtola gurus, Sri Yashoda Mai and Sri Krishna Prem—and now, I suppose, Madhava Ashish.

Days at Mirtola were like real life if subtly adapted to Ashish's teachings. My Gurdjieff classes back in the U.S., though, seemed a little other-worldly at times, since they were intended to wrench real life into a more ideal shape. In the next chapter, the reader will find out what I mean.

Ouspensky, *Miraculous*, 44-47.

4

The Unimportance of Being Seymour

In any Gurdjieff Work group—my own was no exception—you are considered to be a weak-willed creature. An important aspect of group work is that the group serves as a kind of "will," standing in for the will that each one of us supposes we have, but which, when we are put to the test, most of us discover that we don't have at all. In a Gurdjieff Work group, our individual will is exposed to the hard light of observation and verification.

The kind of individual will that is regularly put to the test of observation and verification in a Gurdjieff group is the will to intentionally try to be more conscious, more established in the "essence," less established in the personality. At each weekly meeting of my Work group, we agreed on a task that, during the coming week, we would all try to work on in our everyday lives, and which we would then discuss at the next meeting. The concept of a "group will" came into it in this way, that without the group's demanding that we attempt such a task and then demanding that we discuss it at the next meeting, most of us would simply be too lazy to really carry out this type of self-observation which is absolutely essential to the Gurdjieffian Work.

To better facilitate the discussion of inner psychological work, Gurdjieff groups generally range in size from five to twelve people.

Groups with larger numbers are generally subdivided into these smaller groups. There is also, of course, the group leader. (As people who have led Gurdjieff groups can attest to, more is demanded of the leader in that he or she is required to be more conscious of self more of the time. In this sense, the leader actually gets more from the group's work than do the participants, although everyone benefits from the group.) At the meeting following the assigned task, the participants relate their experiences to the leader, doing so not only to elicit the leader's response but also to elicit discussion from the entire group, to the extent that the leader permits it. Commonly, the experience one participant relates will be recognized by the other participants as paralleling the one they themselves had during the week. This helps the participants to verify the efficacy of the exercise that has been carried out. Verification is an essential part of Gurdjieff's teachings, since he believed that everything had to be verified, that blind faith was quite insufficient.

In my initial group, as in successive groups, most of these tasks were tasks of self-observation—in particular, observation of our identification with our negative states. The theory was that the act of self-observation helped in itself to free us from identification with what was being observed. A typical task, for example, might entail observing one's own irritation, anger, or rage, using, typically, a modality that Gurdjieff called "internal considering." I might observe my worrying about what people think of me, or my being hurt over not being given the recognition that I consider that I deserve. I might observe my reactions when I go to the supermarket, fill up my cart, go to the checkout counter, and then am forced to wait while the woman in front of me starts chatting with the cashier about her babies and the two even show each other photographs. I might think: 'How dare they interfere with my precious time! I'm an important, paying customer of this supermarket chain, and this cashier, in not checking me out promptly, isn't giving me my proper valuation.' The task of self-observation of 'internal considering' which I now need to carry out consists of my self-observing what is going on within me, taking note of the extent to which I am identified with my irritation and self-righteousness. I would have to see that what was going on at the checkout counter was merely an affront to my personality, which sees itself as real and important, though it is neither. Another example—the obverse—might be for me to observe the worries I have when I appear before an audience of any sort, worries that might run the gamut of: Am I dressed right? Do I sound right? Will they think what I have to say is stupid? To the extent that I can self-observe myself in the act of having these worries, I can gain control over them and in that sense become free of them. This act of self-observation is, in other traditions, sometimes called "self-witnessing."

There was also in my group—as there is to a greater or lesser extent in all groups—an array of tasks which belonged more to what is called the "stop" category. The group might agree, for example, that at each meal during the coming week we would not simply plunge into our eating. Instead, before starting to eat, we would stop and sense our hands holding the cups and utensils; we would stop and sense ourselves taking the first bite; we would stop and observe our mastication. We would do all this using the tool of attention, one which can be employed to expand our self-consciousness in such a way that we find ourselves including in our consciousness much more than is ordinarily included within that awareness. And, most important of all, we would intentionally include in our attention the experience of ourselves. (I have mentioned above only the simplest level of "stop" exercises. These could be far more stressful and traumatic, and potentially effective, as I describe in Chapter Seven, "Soul Farmer of the Everglades.")

At the group discussion of the task, people would relate what they had observed during the week, and their observations would be discussed. Very often, what a person would observe was that he or she had simply forgotten to perform the task at all.

There are hundreds of tasks of this sort, which were devised not only by Gurdjieff himself but by the many practitioners of the Work throughout the years. There is a sense in which these tasks, in being tools for practicing the Fourth Way, mimic more traditional practices such as those traditionally carried out in monasteries, i.e., saying grace. Even the practice of families' saying grace around the dinner table is, however mechanically executed, really a sort of Gurdjieffian "stop" exercise carried out to help us become more conscious of ourselves.

E arly on in my Gurdjieff group Work, I found I sometimes had difficulty in reining in a certain attitude of superiority in order to do what was required of me and what I was told to do. Other times, I positively enjoyed it. Sometimes, I was astonished to see myself working at these exercises. Other times, I was appalled. I'm quite sure I've never had what is called a lust for power; but, as head of a large business with hundreds and later thousands of employees, I had had a fair degree of power itself and the responsibility, either directly or through subordinates, of telling people what to do. But now, *I* was being told what to do—and by a "group will," yet!

Usually, I was able to swallow this. Sometimes, I was fascinated by it. But, as swallowable as I found it, or as fascinating, I early on had severe misgivings, which I did not hesitate to communicate to Ashish: "The Gurdjieff group in which I participate is run very formally, and there is clearly a hierarchy within the organization. The idea of such a hierarchy smacks of church politics. I don't care for it, just as I do not care for the policy of making inquirers about the Gurdjieff group call back a second time. They are never answered on their first telephone call. Nor do I care for the policy of not disclosing the group's telephone number."

I was very genuine in my complaint. This policy of the Gurdjieff groups made me genuinely uneasy. This was among the first of a series of considered complaints that I would level at my Gurdjieff groups through the years, and about which I would keep Ashish minutely informed.

Of course, what I only dimly perceived at the beginning—and what Ashish saw with the utmost clarity from the start—was that this complaining was only the complaining of my ego, which felt itself to be mortally threatened by these Gurdjieffian practices.

But I was not factually wrong. My Gurdjieff Work group really was structured as I have described it above. I had the impression that one's level of placement in the hierarchy was governed at least in theory by the level of "being" one was considered to be at. In practice, however, I noticed that people were placed in leadership positions often having to do with how many years they had been in the Work. Those presumably at the highest level of being were thought to be able from time to time to commune or enter into telepathic contact with the spirit of Gurdjieff, whether or not they were actually aware of this. For the one energy individualized as Gurdjieff was considered to be, though in a discarnate state, at the call of those among his disciples who merited his attention. This latter, I complained about to Ashish.

A.   Since we have not got the data to assess the claim that the instructions for wider group activities come from G himself, and do not even know whether there is anyone in the groups who has the capacity to communicate with him, one has to judge it on its own merits. What we were told about the Gurdjieff group practice of always making a first time caller call again later is consistent with the general rule that candidates should come to this work because they really want it, not out of mere curiosity. But since this is a standard group practice, refusal to list your group's phone number does not seem inconsistent. O.K. I support your view. But what does it matter to you whether more people are attracted?

You seem to be looking for inadequacies in the leaders of the organization which will support your wish to reject the group work. And don't belittle the group because the work is "preliminary." The group work is teaching you how to handle your negative thoughts/emotions by producing situations which will make you aware of them. First become aware that you have them, then learn to manage them. If you do not, you will not get much further either with the work or with your relationships. [March 21, 1980]

Two months later, I was complaining to Ashish that "learning about the ideas is very much different from actually trying to get past all the negative emotions I come up against in the effort to be self-conscious."

A. The trouble you complain of is not really surprising at all. Things have been going fairly easily for you. Excitement, picking up on ideas, teachings coming easily, and then bang, up against it you come. The next step is breaking new ground. And then as soon as you start breaking new ground, you realize how rough it is.

Perhaps what makes it all seem so rough is that there is nothing in this work from which the ordinary ego gets any satisfaction. It comes as a steady grind one gets on with. This is why Krishna Prem used to say to people, that if there is anything else you think you can do, go and do it. Don't do this thing. It's because so long as you think you can get any satisfaction from anything else in the sense that any other ordinary activity in life feels or promises you fulfillment, then you must go and do it and learn the hard way that it won't. There has to be the sense that we've got no other way. Perhaps you'll be feeling that, "Look, I do accept that, but what I want is a quick method to be sure that I'm on the right track." Yet, the way you can be sure you are on the right track is by getting on with the job. [June 6, 1980]

Ashish was right; I think in those early days I was looking for some magic key or other, some Open Sesame of the Soul from Ashish that would make everything all right. In that same letter, I had asked him just what it was you did to get from the Gurdjieffian third state of "self-remembering" or "self-consciousness" to the Gurdjieffian fourth state of "objective consciousness." I asked him this as if I thought you could do it in one single bound.

A. Follow your awareness in. Stop this chattering mind. It may chatter in what seems to you to be a very interesting and important way, raising all sorts of questions and doubts, but it's still chatter. It's got to be stopped, stopped dead. Only then can you hope to find what is behind it, what you are in yourself. And only when you understand what you are in yourself, can you begin really to make sense of life. Until you can make sense of it for yourself, you have to accept what other people suggest it may be.

Surely you know what it's like in ordinary life to be doing a job which seems full of interest and excitement when you begin it, and then gradually it just becomes a daily routine. The things that happen repeat themselves and they lose their freshness. Eventually, you got down to realizing that this is just something you get on with every day. It's not that life loses all its interest.

Perhaps it is because this thing does attack the ego directly that you find your ego opposing what you are doing, sort of throwing up these doubts, saying that, well, perhaps there isn't anything, perhaps I'm being a fool, perhaps this is all there is. Perhaps I am just looking for a new form of excitement, that life's become a bit dull.

Well, you have to sit down and think this out and see what it is. But even if there are these elements in your approach, if they have brought you to something real, no matter how inadequate some of your ideas may have been, fair enough then, you've found the path. Travel it. Don't let yourself be pulled away from it. [June 6, 1980]

Along with my gripe about the rigidly hierarchical structure of the Gurdjieff group, I had I think a better-grounded gripe. This was that my group would not permit psychological discussion, e.g., the analysis of dreams. I could not help but think that this was important, seeing as Ashish himself, at the same time as he had decisively put me on the path to Gurdjieff, had also launched me on a program of dream analysis with himself as analyst, trying to train me to do that analysis myself. However valid my objections were, I can see now, though, looking back at it, that I was also introducing this subject of the importance of dreams into the group in order to get some control over the group—or to keep the group from getting too much control over me. In other words, my ego was introducing the subject. I am sure other people were introducing their issues into the group for the same dual reasons. It may be that, having formerly been a hard-driving businessman, I kept my own issues going with unusual persistence. At the same time, I thought I was merely trying to help. I wrote to Ashish about this: "...The current leader of the Gurdjieff group in which I participate is a really fine man. He does not like it, however, when I introduce anything about you or my visits to Mirtola into the group discussions."

In reply, Ashish focussed solely on my rebellious ego (later, as the reader will see, he waded more deeply into the problem of Gurdjieffianism and dreams).

A.   In fact, you are free to get hints, information and teaching anywhere you wish. If you can read any books you like, you can meet anyone you like. In this context, the deeper question of personal commitment has less to do with the intellectual quality of the teaching than it has with the character/personality/being of the teacher. Theoretically, your commitment is to the spirit itself (whatever name you like to give it). The problem is that you cannot commit yourself to something that is as yet a rather vague concept/feeling. Attempts to get by without commitment to one particular place/person usually stem from reluctance to give up or surrender one's egotistic self-evaluation.

Whenever this talk comes up, people fear they are expected to turn themselves into mush, whereas what has to be surrendered is not manhood, but "my aim to add to my personal achievements." What has to be found is beyond personality. This is difficult to do without the support of assurance from someone who is deeply respected and, preferably, loved.

Once you can get your aim clear, problems about how to live, what to do, how to reconcile the outer life with the inner, etc., begin to get straightened out. This is why I try to get people to clarify their inner aim first. On the other hand, current G groups appear to knock people around and shake up or demolish their socially conditioned assumptions about themselves and to the false values they have adopted, while giving exercises that should bring the individual essence into real existence (as opposed to its being potentially existent). What I notice, however, is that even when it achieves its purpose, there is nothing explicit to lead people to look further. While G himself was there, it was presumably different. He was there.

However, the demolition of false standards and self-pride is necessary. This is why you have to submit yourself voluntarily to the group work in Florida. Who else is going to take you to bits in public and let you see yourself? Like an army volunteer who hopes to become an officer, you have to agree to being buggered about on the parade ground. If you rebel because you think yourself superior to the drill sergeant, you will never get to being an officer. [Aug. 9, 1981]

My ego had other ways of rebelling—ways which were not in themselves bad, which were in fact highly rewarding, but which, despite appearances, had little to do with my actual journeying down the spiritual path. I had taken in a big way to the reading of books on esotericism. From 1980 to1982 (and often later), I ate up books not only on Gurdjieff, Theosophy, and the mystics and mystical systems of the Far East, but also on alchemy, the Cabala, the hermeticists, and so forth, two of my favorites being *The Candle of Vision* by A. E. (George Russell) and *The Occult Way* by P. G. Bowen.

Ashish smiled upon all this with a benign indulgence. He had read all the books himself. He was sure that I was enjoying them and getting a lot out of them. He was equally sure that all my reading would advance me not one whit down the path to the unitive vision. "Will it be worth my while to study alchemy and the Cabala as part of the inner inquiry?" I asked him earnestly in 1980.

A.   If you like. But don't confuse the study of symbolic systems of thought with the immediacy of actual work. The most you will get from the study is a widening of the range of symbols available to the psyche for its use in your dreams, and, perhaps, occasional insights into what it is you are trying to do. [March 21, 1980]

This turned out to be true. References to the likes of Hermes Trismegistus and the Cabalist Isaac Luria began to appear in my dreams, and helped me learn more about myself. But, as Ashish never tired of reminding me, the path to the greater Self, and to Gurdjieff's objective consciousness, lay not in libraries, but inward.

A. The "knowledge" you seek is of a quite different order from the sort of knowledge that enables you to read this letter. It belongs to the order of knowledge that you are. You are because you are. You know it. It is a fact of self-experience. It is self-demonstrable, but cannot be demonstrated to anyone else. I can tell you that this "knowledge of self" is independent of sensory stimuli, or of brain activity, or of thoughts and images. I can tell you that it can eventually be found as identical with the "knowledge of self" in all being. But my telling you turns it into information. You can grasp the information and understand it. You can get a feeling appreciation of it. But it is knowledge at second-hand.

You cannot assess your own progress towards a goal whose proximity is beyond your power of judgment. However much information you may have about it, you do not know it until you find it. Seymour Ginsburg will never find it. Seymour Ginsburg is a tissue of sensations and memories. You are real. But the essential you, the individualized essence which, as a first step, must be identified, is not Seymour B. Ginsburg.

So what does Seymour do? Seymour must let go of Seymour and go beyond himself. How? By trust in another, through the self-transcendence of love, or through a feeling of self-disgust or despair which makes him feel that he would rather disappear in annihilation than continue in meaningless existence. Seymour can reason himself into a sublime state of intellectual abstraction, or he can jolly himself into a state of ecstatic euphoria, but he will never find the thing so long as he continues to believe in the importance of being Seymour. [March 6, 1981]

Ashish would always turn from my gripes and preoccupations to the main subject at hand: what was going on in my soul in general. About the existence of this latter, I was continuing to have the gravest of doubts. In early 1982, I advanced to Ashish the singularly unoriginal hypothesis (but one that I had held all my life) that a belief in a "higher life" was based merely on the fear of death. He replied:

A.   You are not being very honest with your "doubts." How can you be, when you work with your intellect to protect yourself from the challenge of the inner truth? Honesty is a value, belonging to the domain of the feelings. The intellect is a lawyer who argues in favor of the person who pays him.

What sort of proof or demonstration can anyone give you? When you saw Sai Baba producing *vibhuti*, you wondered if it was real. If you saw someone cured of a disease by "magic," you could argue it away as autosuggestion (which is itself as big a mystery as magic), or by saying that the diagnosis had been wrong, as it often is. If you were given an "experience," you could call it hypnosis (another mystery). No one is going to show you anything so long as you need convincing, because there is nothing for which you cannot find a seemingly "logical" rebuttal. Experiences are given as confirmation, not as persuasive proof.

Let us posit there is nothing beyond this life. In the face of tradition and of affirmations by people you have met face-to-face, you cannot be certain of that, either.

You are left with doubt. How will you tackle it? If you were content with your life, you could brush it aside and wait to see what happens when you die—the one certain event. But you were not, and are not, content. You started searching, questioning and casting around for information. Is it honest to say that all the people your search led you to are driven merely by fear of death? If so, you are driven by the same fear, subsequent to your wife's death. But you are not sure of that, either.

Supposing you are right. Let the motive be fear of death. "Some wise man, seeking deathlessness, with in-turned gaze beheld the Lord of all that is and is to be" (*Upanishads*). If there were only people who said, "I believe," you could reply, "I don't." But when you meet a man who says, "I know," all you can reply is, "I don't know," which leaves the matter open, particularly because positive evidence (I saw A killing B) weighs more heavily than negative evidence (I did not see A killing B). But, if you then pursue the matter with, "How do you know? What is your evidence?" then it is illogical to demand that your criteria of what constitutes evidence be satisfied, when your criteria are restricted to the evidence of the sense organs and, by definition, the data of the spiritual experience are non-sensual. If it is an article in your faith that there can be no experience other than through the sense organs (one has to bend over backwards to square this with dreams), then by what right do you denigrate another man's faith (as you name it) in non-sensual experience?

You are concerned with sensible phenomena, thinking to "see God as one sees a cow" (Eckhardt); the other man is concerned with who or what sees. "Even the man who has the vision of the Universal Mind must ask 'who sees'" (Nisarga Datta). It seems to me that any inquiry into the nature of being must include inquiry into the nature of consciousness. The only consciousness known to a man at first hand is his own. Turning consciousness back upon itself and being aware of being aware is the crux of this inquiry. Where do doubts about God, etc., come into this?

The sticking point in this is that one cannot know the source of awareness while the mind is running with fantasies of greatness, fantasies of achievement, fantasies of sex, fantasies that there is nothing in the universe outside of what the senses can be aware of. To misquote Descartes: "I fantasize. Therefore I am." To get beyond thought, one has to be able in some measure to stop thought, one has to be willing to admit to oneself that one has no control over one's mind in matters of negative emotions, etc. And since one knows a great deal more about what goes on in one's mind than anyone else, one should have a worse opinion of oneself than others have of one.

So-called intellectual doubts seem to me to come from emotional reluctance to apply the intellectual discipline with sufficient rigor. Columbus's greatness lay in his determination to cross the

Atlantic when, apparently, there was no proof of the Atlantic's having another side. Similarly, we have to set sail without the support of proof and in the face of our associates' flat denials that there is anything to find.

What drives many people is not mere fear of death, but the sense of its being intolerable to be certain of dying and not to be certain of whether one is or is not after the event. Don't ask me to explain how it is that some people get there not from fear but from love. It is a fact that they do. But if there is nothing beyond death, then what is to be lost by dying in the attempt to find out? So one sees that those who hang back because of doubts find their doubts convenient; by harboring them, they avoid having to face these grim issues, and they can keep their comforts. [March 23, 1982]

In a letter of a month later, he concluded in the same vein:

A.   Your loyalty must be to the goal itself and nothing more nor less. The ancient wisdom is nothing if it is not present here, present as a living reality and not merely as a series of texts and mouthed words. It is nothing to you unless you find it in yourself. You have been shown the way to find it. Using a good mind on books may clarify ideas, broaden one's outlook, and make the whole thing more interesting. But you won't find what you are looking for in books. Dances, postures, movements and other exercises may provide opportunities for identifying particular states of mind that will help you on your path, but you will not travel further by seeking out new exercises. All that you need is already in you. [April 14, 1982]

My doubts extended to my spiritual experiences: Was I having them, or not? Strange and suggestive sensations sometimes seized me; but, like Scrooge on seeing the ghost of Jacob Marley on Christmas Eve in Dickens's *A Christmas Carol*, I wondered if these visitations were merely indigestion from the soup I'd eaten for dinner. Other times, I was convinced that something quite ineffable was happening to me, though it turned to be the result of my having had one too many Scotches. In sum, I was easily confused in these matters, and, after having had, while sitting in a synagogue, an experience that seemed truly suggestive of the unitive vision, I wrote to Ashish for guidance: "I feel I need a better understanding of just what it is of a transcendental nature that we are trying for," I declared. "I have seen some things. For example, there was an experience sitting in a synagogue a month ago to attend a relative's Bar Mitzvah ceremony, when I had an overwhelmingly vivid experience of the unity of all being. There was another similar experience one morning when I was sitting, meditating. I have written these up separately, but cannot really recapture the experience on paper."

A. Now, as for the things you've seen, first of all this question of the sort of transcendental nature of what you've seen: I think you ought to rely on the feeling that comes with it, the feeling of its validity. You see, the trouble is, Sy, that one is so habitually centered in the life here that when you first begin to see things of a different order, they seem strange and one doubts their reality. The mind throws up all the doubts about, is it fantasy, is it sort of hallucination? Because it is strange, because it is outside the ordinary range of one's experience, that doesn't affect their validity as such. It's only that one is sort of hesitating. But you know, the other side of the coin is, of course, "Oh, I've had something—come on let's sort of have it again."

The man in the G group is quite right in telling you not to try to repeat an experience or a vision. But of course, when he says, "don't hold on to it," it doesn't mean that you don't remember or record it and later try to understand it. The state in which visions come can be tried for if you remember, as it were, the way in which you got in, the feeling situation you were in on the way toward seeing. This means that that sort of trying is a quite different sort of trying than trying for worldly achievements. It's a subtle feeling, trying, an invocation. But I admit that people so frequently try in the wrong way that the advice not to try is pretty well as good as the advice, to try.

Now you see, what we can call the "synagogue vision" is clearly something given to you. And a thing that is given cannot be tried for again. It was possible to be given at that moment because of the state of mind brought about by the religious atmosphere. There was your acceptance of the situation. You weren't putting up a sort of barrier and saying, "God is bunk," and the fact was that you were charged. Now this could be the taste you wanted but it has to be understood. You mustn't take it to yourself. There's no mystical universe inside Sy Ginsburg. Just for the moment, Sy wasn't there. Sy Ginsburg is sort of like a toy doll with a label on it giving its name. The awareness that animates Sy isn't the doll, it isn't the personality.

That morning meditation to which you referred, light and the sort of transparent walls with people in and passing through them, that sounds to me like awareness operating on a subtle level, on sort of the etheric level where walls are not solid. That's not exactly transcendental. It's the sort of thing that helps you to get accustomed to the fact that this physical world is not as grossly physical and unchangeable and constrictive as it may have seemed to be at the beginning.

If you learn what mystical vision can be like, you still can't and mustn't keep a sort of duality between the utterly transcendent perception on the one hand and this sort of gross material world on the other. It needs to be seen that the world's grossness is a thing in consciousness, not in its unchanging grossness.

One of the things that might help you in this respect in the question of understanding what's going on, what it is that you're aiming for, would be to try going back over some of the stuff you have already read about cosmogony, the mystical philosophies. Things which you only could understand at the level you were then, when you move, grow, then when you read it again, you find that you are understanding more. Or even things you thought you understood, you realize that you didn't and now they have more meaning for you. And of course, always read with the humility to accept that the next time you read it, you may find that you were again being wrong.

But how else can you do it? The understanding, the capacity to understand depends upon the development of something in you which is not your intellect as such. With your intellect you can learn to take and cerebrate and so on about it, but the understanding is always a combination of knowledge and feeling. And it's the feeling that gives it a sense of, "Yes, well now I understand, now I really know what it means."

It's a subtle business and I don't know that any purpose is served by talking too much about it. Then one runs into the problem of thinking one knows when, in fact, one has merely got an intellectual grasp of it all.

Well, I think that's quite enough about you. I hope all is still going well. As you can imagine, we're pretty busy here with all these people planning to build. You know most of them and it's quite a challenge for me and the change in life style that it means. I mean more people to be concerned with. But it doesn't, in fact, mean you know, that I don't have any time to myself or for people because when people come here to live, they're here. They aren't sort of like people who come just for a visit, sitting on my doorstep sort of, "When will he see me," the when will he see me kind of thing. It's a much more leisurely business even though they're having to work pretty hard. [Oct. 18, 1982]

In September—the month before—I had written to Ashish that I was canceling my October trip to Mirtola, giving as my reasons that "I really have nothing new to bring with me in terms of material. I thought it would be best to postpone the next visit to Mirtola to a time when I have at least made some further progress along this path, and then to seek the kind of support and advice from you that needs a visit rather than a letter."

Ashish was quick to reply, in the same letter as I have quoted from above:

A.   I do have to give you a word of warning here and particularly because its linked with the reasons you've given for not coming. Don't try to assess your own progress. Not only is a man incompetent to assess his own progress in this field, but the very fact that you are doing it sort of comes from ego insecurity, the need for reassurance that one is getting on.

And that means, as it were, that the progress is being taken to the "I." The "I" is trying to reassure itself. And yet it's that very "I" which has to be pushed out of the way. So, the more you try to assess, the more you block the progress you're trying to assess—progress in my terms, not in your terms. You're accustomed to thinking of progress in terms of the sort of, well, achievement orientation. I know it's difficult, but this is where trust is needed. [Oct. 18, 1982]

This by no means quashed my tendency to want to self-diagnose my own progress. At times, a certain impatience—some might say a certain hostility—entered my thoughts about the Gurdjieff Work. I wondered if, not just me, but anybody at all, could ever profit from following this particular path. That next year, these feelings prompted me to write Ashish that "I have by now had so many admissions from people in Gurdjieff group work that they have not attained anything even after many years of the Work, that I begin again to doubt its spiritual value. Ultimately, I am left with only my own experience. These give some extraordinary moments, but my doubts continue."

A.   Do you imagine that your ordinary self-identity is going to "know" the mysteries of being? It is not. In the sense that Gurdjieff said, "Not everyone has a soul," and the interpretation that he meant, "If you don't know you have a soul, then you have not got one," you have not yet got a soul. You believe that you have. One may say you are certain that you have. But you have not yet identified it. Until you have found it and are living in its presence, you do not know its qualities. It is far greater than you—you in your limited state of ego-integration. Until you have found it, it is other than you—not you. Even when you find it, you will find that its powers are not "yours." They are, as it were, available to you.

People who try to identify with it, without honoring it as greater than themselves, merely build a new ego-integration at that level. They become some sort of hasnamusses [hasnamuss: a term Gurdjieff used to describe destructive individuals in whom "for some reason or other, data have not been crystallized for the Divine impulse of 'Objective-Conscience.'"]. Therefore, stop thinking of finding the self or soul as part of yourself. Treat it as something great which you honor. Understand that even if you find it, there are always higher levels beyond it which you must honour as greater than the self.

What is greater than you, cannot be less than you. If you set store by your personal individuality, then what you seek must be more truly personal, more intelligent, more knowledgeable, more worthy of respect. You, as you are, are nothing in comparison to that which is above you, from which not just you, but the whole of being has come. Don't think of it only as an unrealized potential that has no existence until you make it real. It exists prior to you. Your potential is only to bring it into waking awareness.

If you approach it as a person, it will respond as a person, for it is the Person, the living root of the individualized human persons. What person? The forms in which the Person shows himself.

If I say Krishna, you think of a mythological blue boy with a flute. If I say Gopalda [Sri Krishna Prem], you think of a tall Englishman with a Cambridge degree. If I say the Master M, you think of Blavatsky and Theosophical fantasies. G?—what do you think of?

The trouble is in your mind. If you hold an imaginary conversation with me, you may be able to guess at the sorts of things I would say, because you know me and have had many conversations. Can you guess at what G would say? Can you distinguish in your mind between what you would like any of us to say, and what we would actually say? Can you put a question to one of us in your mind, and let your mind receive a reply, without distorting it to fit what you want or to flatter yourself?

If you can put a question to the ultimate being, you will not be able to judge the reply, because, as yet, you have no standard of comparison. You are not yet ready to say: "This is the expression of the ultimate truth." But you might be able to say: "This has the ring of truth, as I have heard truth from G. And it rings the same as I have heard from X.Y.Z."

Apart from ultimate truth, there are the questions of daily life in relation to the truth. "How should I act in this particular situation?"

Answers can also come to this sort of question. It is not that one wants to become a stupid slob who can't decide a thing for himself, nor is that being asked for. One wants to learn how to act according to the truth, and not merely from personal habit and egotistical desire. So one begins by asking. As one learns, one needs to ask less. One grows up in a new mode. One goes back to school to re-learn how to live. One does not ask, "What will bring me the greatest profit?" but, "How should a real man behave under these circumstances?" [Dec. 6, 1983]

But the farther I advanced along my spiritual journey—the more fascinated and even excited I became—the more powerful my periodic doubts seemed to become. By 1984, I was contemplating leaving my Gurdjieff group, where I had by now from time to time assisted in the teaching; I would soon be talking with a friend about setting up my own Gurdjieff group, this time in a rural setting (see Chapter Seven). I was besieged by doubts about all this. I communicated those doubts to Ashish. He replied:

A.   Your not wanting to move out into the countryside fits in with your doubt about your faith, as you call it. One is up against a sort of double bind here because if you don't get past your doubts you tend to get stuck with nothing sort of solid to take hold of. You see, you can't really say that you can't do anything until you know what it is, even though you say you know what it isn't. What matters is you know that there is something. That's what you have to hang onto. You have to say that "there is something there and in order to get the confirmation of it then I've got to push within myself rather than simply relying on support from other people's faith and belief."

Well, I know all that comes in its own time but it's something you've got to work on. Now you see, it's really only when you get the certainty, feeling, whatever you like to call it, that there is something, that you begin to be able to distinguish between merely the thing as expressed by a certain religious teaching or by many religious teachings (if you think of the many then it's a question of saying, "yes, but which one am I going to follow"), to a thing that says, "look, all these religious teachings have been pointing in the same direction and it is real." It's quite true, as you say, that they all stem from the same source of truth. However, in most religions as such, the teachings have been very much distorted in the interests of the priesthoods.

And you can't counter with saying, "all these years in the Work and I have not acquired the ordinary religious faith." Because it isn't the ordinary religious faith that you are looking for. The ordinary religious faith says that, "yes, it is the Buddha, or the Christ, or this or the other thing."

But it's known that there is something. What it is I don't know. Some people call it this, some people call it that. You've been fortunate in coming across a number of teachings which cut across the ordinary religious stuff. But you're still tending to see these things as if they were religions rather than pointers to something which is beyond any of these specific religions. So then it is that you sit down and say, "Look, I've got to get past this ordinary out-turned personality, the ordinary waking person, to see that there is something beyond this. What is it like? What's its significance?" The only faith you need is the certainty that if you do find anything, that what you find is what everybody has been talking about. You'll see that what you thought about it, how you understood what people said, is probably quite different. But there's no doubt about the recognition.

So this brings up all this sort of thing about meditation exercises, breathing exercises. These things only come up as problems when you're still confused as to whether you are joining a specific group, i.e., the Gurdjieff group. It's O.K for some people, but, Sy, one can't tie oneself down to this. One's got to say that "Look, I'll use any method, anything. I'll try it. People say things are danger-ous, well if they say they're dangerous, I'll be careful about them, but I'm not going to let them frighten me off." [Sept. 23, 1984]

Ashish had published, in *The American Theosophist* for Janu-ary, 1979, an article entitled, "The Value of Uncertainty." During my April, 1981 visit to Mirtola, he had drawn my attention to it. I read and re-read it avidly. I am still reading it. I recommend it to the reader. It comprises the next chapter of this book.

5

The Value of Uncertainty

By Sri Madhava Ashish

We journey into the unknown through a trackless jungle. If we are truthful to ourselves, we must admit that we do not know what it is that we seek; we do not even know that there is anything to be found. If we already knew it, there would be no search: we would have only to recall it to mind.

All that we have heard about God, the Spirit, Atman, the Void, derives at its best from other people's experience; and we have not yet shared that experience. It may be their knowledge, but it is not ours; and that is why we are still seekers and not finders. The experience they claim is so foreign to what we call 'normal' waking experience that we cannot share it, even by comparison with familiar events. We cannot even be sure that we understand their words in the senses that they use them.

We hear of a path, even of many paths that lead to the same goal. Yet no one who has blazed a trail through the jungle of his mind has thereby left a trail in ours. We cannot follow in his footsteps. No one but ourselves has ever trodden or can ever tread our private jungles.

Beyond the jungle, they say, there lies a mystery. But the mists that shroud it are not dispersed for us when they melt before another seeker's gaze.

The mystery comes to the very edge of the jungle and entices us with promises of joy, knowledge, power and fulfillment. We see its reflections in the mysteries of birth and death, the joys of love, temporal power, the satisfactions of appetites, and the mysteries of the material universe. Yet the very solidity of the mirrors makes us doubt our perception of the reflected mystery.

In the face of these inherent uncertainties, what is it that drives us to seek? It is not just the voices of those who affirm the reality of the goal, for there are as many, perhaps more, voices that deny it. Nor is it just the tendency of the human mind to evade the immediacy of real life by pursuing abstractions: religion may sometimes be an opiate, but no real search for the ground of being can be construed as an escape from reality.

There is also something in us that drives us to question and to seek the answers to our questions. There is something in us that responds to the answers given by those who have found, and responds to their affirmation of an experienceable ultimate reality. It is as though that 'something' does already know what we seek. It responds, as the string of a violin vibrates when the note to which it is tuned is sounded by another instrument.

This subtle resonance stirs us on a level as deep and as difficult to isolate as the homing instinct of our animal natures. Often, we seek to satisfy the longings it inspires with outer substitutes that seem to harmonize with its urgings. We may join a church or a religious society, take up the practice of yoga, communicate with the dead, become followers of the fashionable guru, or just content ourselves with reading books and trying to be good. And if, as so many people do, we become bigots in support of our chosen sect, it is because the inner resonance is so small in relation to the doubts that invade us that we dare not let go of the one bit of the harmony we have recognized.

We seem, in fact, to be caught between the rationalizations of the surface mind and the urgings of something so deep as to be almost unrecognizable as part of ourselves. And since we are normally aware of things only when they find their way into the surface mind, the terms in which we become aware of this urge depend on how our surface minds interpret it. The divergencies of these interpretations run through the whole gamut of possible human attitudes.

If we are fortunate, we may be able in one lifetime to leave these outer reflections of the inner call—reflections distorted in the troubled waters of life—and pass to a clearer formulation of what it is we feel ourselves called to seek. But we are still apt to accept the ready-made formulations of religious and philosophical systems. The inner resonances now sound more clearly, and we find ourselves responding to the words, phrases, and concepts. Feeling wells up within us, triggered by names and ideas that seem infused with the being and power of what they represent. And here lies a trap for the unwary, for we are apt to take the concept for the reality and subtly assume that our pleasurable feeling is experience of what we seek.

A time comes when we need to question the terms of our search, terms drawn from the religious or philosophical systems with which we are familiar and which arouse what we feel to be the right sorts of resonances in our beings. These terms are all very well so far as they go, because they have the validity that inheres in anything that has withstood the test of time. For countless generations they have expressed man's faith in an ultimate knowledge, and they were used by men who achieved that knowledge. We may even argue that we need no other terms. Adequately or inadequately these terms express our aim, and we humbly seek only to approach the mystery which others, greater than ourselves, have unveiled.

Yet a niggling doubt remains. Despite the promptings of the soul and faith in whatever teachings are received, we know that in this search there can be no substitute for personal experience. We are not looking merely for an adequate philosophy which will put the problems of life into a rational perspective and so make them more bearable. We are not looking for someone to tell us the secrets of existence—as if such secrets could be told. We seek the answer that only we can know, just as only we can eat our own meals.

We know, or ought to know, that when the experience comes it will probably be so unlike anything we have ever imagined that we shall have to struggle to find terms to describe it. If we then use the familiar terms, it will be for the sake of being understood by others, and not because those terms are necessarily the best.

Such reflections on what is likely to be our state when we achieve our goal should make us cautious of using terms to describe it in a manner that suggests our already knowing what we are seeking. We may have feelings, such as I have called the promptings of the soul. We may have had experiences of the psychic sort which enlarge the horizons of our world and, at least, allow us to expect that there may be something more beyond. But we cannot know what it is we are looking for. We can know it only by experiencing it. And to experience it we have to seek. But seek for what? We may justifiably say that we seek certainty, or that we seek to discover our place in the cosmic whole. Perhaps it would be more truthful to say that we seek to discover whether we have any place and whether there is any cosmic order to have a place in. The philosopher's prayer, "Oh God—if there be a God—Save my soul—if I have a soul," is perhaps not so stupid as it sounds.

This is the point at which we must come to terms with our own uncertainties. Instead of quelling them with affirmations of faith, we must learn to live with them. Indeed, instead of uncertainty being a hindrance, it is now seen as the spur which drives us to effort, for we cannot any longer tolerate substitutes for personal experience.

It is perhaps here that the seeker appreciates that all the talk about there being many paths to the one goal expresses only a half truth, for all paths end where the individual turns away from teaching, discussion, and obedient performance of set practices to face the trackless unknown of his inner being. To say that he follows in the footsteps of his predecessors is but metaphor; all he has is their assurance that they found their way through. Occasionally he may find recognisable similarities between his experience and that of another man, and the effect can be as encouraging as finding a tree blazed by another pioneer in unmapped forest. But the next sign he marks may have been left by a different pioneer on an apparently different route. None of these marks necessarily indicates that he is nearing his goal; they are indicative only in that others have been there. Like all pioneers, they may have had an aim, but they followed no path; and the route they followed may not have been the shortest, for each seeker takes the route dictated by his individual nature.

I am assuming that the seeker has already spent many questing years thinking, reading, discussing, and meeting teachers—possibly even meeting men whom he believes to have attained to the goal. And he may have submitted himself to one or more spiritual disciplines. All these have had their effect on him. He may feel himself a changed man, sure where he was previously uncertain, awake where he was previously asleep, more mature, controlled, and at peace with himself and the world. He has, in effect, gained sufficient experience to be sure that the results of the prescribed disciplines vindicate his having followed the urgings that motivated his search. But the disciplines do not by themselves bring him to the fulfillment of his search. They may define his nature, free his emotional potential, and clarify his ideas, but, without the fire of aspiration, the burning desire to plunge into the unknown territory of the spirit, nothing 'spiritual' will happen.

He may become a remarkably disciplined man or a remarkably integrated and free man. He may, indeed, be higher in the scale of human evolution than most. But, if he is honest with himself, he will admit that there is still a core of uncertainty in his being which waits to be filled with something, something he may have tasted, whose presence he yearns for, an indefinable something whose promise of ultimate fulfillment has supported him throughout his years of seeking.

It is this 'something' which he has habitually termed God, Spirit, the Void, the Goal of Life, etc., words that are but suggestive symbols which, by common agreement, represent what cannot be represented. If he is aware of this, then he knows that he is truly not seeking anything, and that to define his search in terms which, even if they are not descriptive, carry the associated value-attitudes of the systems that coined them, may result in vitiating his efforts.

These word associations also tend to attach themselves to the practices prescribed by the same schools that use the words. Thus the usefulness of mantra repetition may seem vitiated because the words of the formula are associated with Hindu, Muslim, Christian, or Buddhist theological or philosophical formulations. Meditation may be understood to mean only those particular mental exercises prescribed by a particular school and associated with particular mental and emotional attitudes. Such problems can be overcome when it is seen that, when many different schools prescribe variants of the same exercise, it is an indication that the exercise itself has recognized value, irrespective of the coloring attached to it in different localities.

The seeker thus finds that there are a number of exercises which common experience has found useful in the primary objective of withdrawing attention from out-turned sensing. They are well-tried tools, as common to the seeker as hammer and saw are to the carpenter. He may use them or not, as he pleases. And he may construct new tools, or variants of old ones, which are adapted to the peculiarities of his own nature.

He should also know that tools serve different purposes according to who is using them. No tool, no discipline, no practice is in itself sufficient to take a man to the term of the inner search, whether the seeker uses it himself or whether he surrenders himself to be worked on by his teacher. In one way or another, this is expressed in many traditions by the saying that the final attainment is given by divine grace. The operation of that 'grace' is in some way related to the seeker's ability to refuse substitute or partial experience for the whole.

Many genuine seekers harbor a belief that the numinous experience of the unity of being constitutes the spiritual attainment. In itself it does not. Such an experience may be given by a man of actual attainment, and may occasionally be obtained through meditational practices and even by drugs. To taste a strange fruit is not to possess it. It may ensure that he who tastes will be able both to recognize it again and to appreciate something of what its possessors speak of. But he may not like it, may or may not be prepared to give his whole being to the task of possessing it or, more properly, being possessed by it.

Full attainment implies not merely that a man has at some time known what it is to be submerged in the universal awareness nor that he can so submerge himself when he pleases, but that he has wholly integrated his perception of the universal within his individual nature. As one of the Sufis said: "Anyone can understand how the drop can blend with the ocean. But how the ocean can be contained within the drop is a very great mystery."

Perhaps that very word 'mystery,' the word which is at the root of the meaning of mysticism, is the crux of the matter. The seeker must know that what he seeks is a mystery. No matter how profound or glowing the words in which it is described, the thoughts and feelings they arouse in their hearer are pale nothings before the splendor of the revealed mystery. To give a name to that splendor is to pretend that we know it—almost that we need not seek it. Puzzlement, doubt, uncertainty, despair are the lot of the man who seeks to discover it, for he must hold steadily to the knowledge that he does not know and cannot know what that mystery is until it is revealed.

Against this uncertainty he pits the instinctive yearning of his being which, like a homing horse, finds its way when the rider thinks himself lost. Hope sustains him where reason fails. Love guides him when all else is dismayed.

6

The Reflected Glory of Objective Consciousness

The woman who was standing before me in the living room of the condo in Crans Montana, Switzerland, was slight of build, of average height, gray-haired, spry, and 90.

Her name was Jeanne de Salzmann, and you might have been forgiven for having trouble believing that her smallish unassuming person embodied the whole tumultuous history of the Gurdjieff movement.

Madame de Salzmann, as she was called, met Gurdjieff for the first time in Tbilisi, Georgia, Russia, in 1919, when he had come storming out of the Caucasus with his band of students and she was a performer and teacher of eurhythmics, the art of interpreting musical composition by a rhythmical, free-style movement of the body. Jeanne de Salzmann's husband, Alexander, was one of the great stage designers of his day, a visionary who rubbed shoulders with the likes of poet Rainer Maria Rilke and painter Wassily Kandinsky. It was through the de Salzmanns that the first public performance ever of Gurdjieff's Sacred Movements was staged, at the Tbilisi Opera House, in June of that year. Jeanne and Alexander soon became Gurdjieff's students, departing with him and his other students for Constantinople in May, 1920. Their travels took them on to Berlin and then to France, where in 1922

Gurdjieff set up the Institute for the Harmonious Development of Man at the Prieuré des Basses Loges near Fontainebleu (the institute had been given its name in Tbilisi). Madame de Salzmann studied with Gurdjieff for thirty years, and at his death in 1949 assumed primary responsibility for the Work, starting the Gurdjieff Institute in Paris. She maintained the overall direction of many Gurdjieff groups throughout the world, and had also overseen the publication of Gurdjieff's books and helped to preserve the form of his dance movements.

In standing before Jeanne de Salzmann, I wasn't only standing before a living page of history, still vibrant, still creating. I was also—or so the scuttlebutt in the Gurdjieff Work group had it—standing in the presence of someone who was established in objective consciousness. It was thought that Madame de Salzmann, by virtue of her three decades of association with the Master and her own work upon herself, had attained to the highest level of being, one in which her physical, emotional, and intellectual centers were in perfect equilibrium. People speculated that she was, in accordance with Gurdjieff's teaching, further connected to her higher emotional and higher intellectual centers, the *sine qua non* of objective consciousness.

I'm quite sure I didn't spend long enough with Madame de Salzmann to know if she were established in objective consciousness or not. Moreover, I'd been told that, if I didn't stand pretty close to that highest state myself, I couldn't hope to perceive it in somebody else! Gurdjieff taught that a person at a lower level of being could never assess the level of being of a person at a higher level. When filmmaker Peter Brook was about to meet Madame de Salzmann, a friend of his told him: "You will see; she is like a fan, which gradually opens until more and more is revealed." In his autobiographical *Threads of Time*, Brook alludes to the elusive refinement of Jeanne de Salzmann, writing that she had "achieved this freedom through a life devoted to the service of that unknown source of finer energy that can only become manifest when the human organism is completely open—open in body, feeling, and thought. When this condition is reached, the individuality does not vanish; it is illuminated in every aspect and can play its true role, which is to bend and adapt to every changing need."

All I can report about my own meeting with Madame de Salzmann is that she chatted pleasantly enough with me for a couple of hours and taught me an exercise, one used by Gurdjieff, having to do with sensing the flow of energies through the body. I came away from her condo certainly liking her—which I hadn't expected to, since it was my understanding that it was Madame de Salzmann who was responsible for the various restrictive practices around which the Gurdjieff groups are hedged (and which I've already mentioned), such as keeping the groups secret by not publishing their telephone numbers, never returning a first inquiry but waiting for a second call, and so on. Because I thought these practices emanated from Jeanne de Salzmann, I'd expected to find her secretive and guarded, even unfriendly. But I had found her, on the contrary, open and willing to talk.

Ironically, it was these elitist and exclusionary Gurdjieff group policies, promulgated by whomever, that had made it very hard for me to meet Jeanne de Salzmann in the first place. Neither my group leader in Florida nor her two lieutenants, all three of whom had been in Gurdjieff groups in New York before coming down to Florida, would give me an introduction to Jeanne de Salzmann, even though I had to be in New York on business at the same time that I knew she was going to be there. They told me it was because I hadn't been in the group long enough (this was in 1979); that such an introduction was premature.

There was an element of outright secrecy about these Gurdjieff groups that had bothered me from the outset. I'd written to Ashish that "it seems to me that there is too much secrecy amongst the groups I am involved with. This smacks of elitism that puffs people up with an imaginary specialness. Isn't this the opposite of what the Work is about?"

A.   The unknown part of the teaching is actually plastered up all over walls for everyone to see. But it remains "secret" because it cannot be truly understood until a man is ready to understand.

"Schools" treat it as secret and do not "explain" it to people who are not ready, for the reason that, wrongly handled, it can cause a man to crystallize on the wrong level. If he adds the crystallization of that teaching to the hard core of his egotism, his further progress is completely blocked.

This is why much stress is laid on steady, dedicated "work" doing what one has to do because one has to do it, and not for hope of gain. This helps to erode the ego integration.

This, too, is why many schools stress submission to the teacher. One cannot submit one's egotism to the demands of the spirit if one is incapable of submitting to another person. And this is why love is the guide to the path. [July 18, 1980]

I had managed to swallow that. But now this business of not being allowed to meet Jeanne de Salzmann seemed to me to smack of hierarchical church politics; the palace guard keeping the great woman separated from the masses. I refused to take no for an answer. I decided I would do an end run around the hierarchy. And I developed a means of doing so.

In 1979 I'd met the French-Swiss author/seeker Lizelle Reymond. She lived in Geneva, not far from where I maintained a condo in one of the city's suburbs. I had telephoned her and introduced myself after reading two of her books, *My Life with a Brahmin Family* and *To Live Within*. Lizelle and I became friends. She had spent five years at the ashram of Sri Anirvan in the Himalayan foothills, caring for the guru through several of his illnesses. Anirvan's ashram was just 20 miles from Mirtola, and Lizelle had visited Krishna Prem and Madhava Ashish a number of times. Mostly we talked about these two. To my surprise, it turned out that Lizelle was also a Gurdjieffian, but she preferred to follow the code of secrecy I've described above, wishing not to discuss the Gurdjieff Work but to keep our relationship based on the Mirtola connection.

Lizelle had become involved with the Gurdjieff Work in the following way: Sri Anirvan had been reading Ouspensky's *In Search of the Miraculous* just as she was preparing to leave the ashram, and had asked her to write back to him with some sense of what the Gurdjieff movement was doing. When she returned to Europe, Lizelle had gone directly to Paris to talk to Jeanne de Salzmann. Madame de Salzmann had liked Lizelle's background, and had asked her to set up a Gurdjieff Work group when she returned home to Geneva. This Lizelle did, and now she was the director of the Gurdjieff movement in Switzerland that at that time comprised about 100 members. My friendship with Lizelle led to my bringing her with me to Mirtola in the spring of 1981. She was in her eighties then, and, although a woman still formidably strong in spirit, not very anxious to travel alone.

I wrote to Ashish about meeting Lizelle Reymond.

A. Yes, I know her. One of the very few people I've seen who actually changed herself, almost unrecognizably. Acceptance of suffering! Work! In fact, one of the things that recommended Madame de Salzmann to me was her recognition of Lizelle's worth.

I met her guru a long time ago, in 1952. He was, then, a shy little man. But Madame de Salzmann met him later, 1970 or '72, whenever it was, even later than that maybe. She called it the highest point in her tour of Indian Mahatmas. Maybe. I haven't seen him since then. I haven't seen any of his writings since then. I feel whereas Lizelle has done something great with herself, she's never told me anything about Anirvan, her guru, that made me see anything there. But that may be my own blindness. [Dec. 22, 1979]

Lizelle had kept up her relationship with Jeanne de Salzmann—who, I had learned, also had a condo in Switzerland, at the ski resort of Crans Montana. Because my Gurdjieff group leaders refused to give me an introduction to Madame de Salzmann in New York, I telephoned Lizelle Reymond and asked her if she would give me an introduction to meet Madame de Salzmann in Switzerland when I expected to be there that summer. She replied that of course she would. So it was that, the next time I arrived in Geneva, I drove with Lizelle Reymond and my friend Jane, who had accompanied me to Switzerland and who was also active in the Florida

Gurdjieff group, around the northern shore of Lac Léman and up into the mountains to Crans Montana. Madame de Salzmann was waiting for us when we telephoned her apartment from the lobby. She came downstairs, introductions were made, and Lizelle left, I think to do some shopping.

As I said, I found the leader of the Gurdjieff Foundation and Institutes pleasant, relaxed and helpful. As for her being established in objective consciousness, I had no idea. Certainly, I felt no blasts of "soul energy" surging from her—though that may have been my own problem.

But, just a week later, I was to run into Jeanne de Salzmann one more time, quite accidentally, and that encounter—though it would hardly be my own encounter—would be almost electrifying.

Remember, this was the summer of 1979. The great spiritual teacher Jiddu Krishnamurti was still alive. As part of his annual teaching routine, Krishnamurti would address the public every July from under the canopy of a huge circus tent, at Saanen, near Gstaad in Switzerland. Usually he would attract crowds of about 2,000. The talks that summer were to go on for a week at the end of July.

It so happened that his annual talks were scheduled to take place the same week I was visiting with Jeanne de Salzmann.

I wanted to hear the celebrated seer speak, and Lizelle wanted to hear him too, though she'd heard him speak in Switzerland before. Krishnamurti was an exponent of the Advaita philosophy of esoteric Hinduism espoused by Lizelle's guru, Sri Anirvan, one that, in brief, posits oneness or wholeness, with everything in the universe being seen as part of one whole, and the advaitic practitioner regarding him/herself as that whole.

Krishnamurti was not, however, so easy to categorize. Ashish would write me in reply to a question about him that "Krishnamurti's teachings are characterized by an attempt to cut through these word identifications. I am not sure how successful he has been" [August 9, 1981]. In his talks, Krishnamurti was always urging people to live outside of time and space. To a hard-driving businessman like myself, such a concept was well-nigh ungraspable. My reasons for not being particularly interested in Krishnamurti can be summed up by reference to the title of his most famous talk (given in Holland in 1928), "Truth is a Pathless Land." As an American businessman, I couldn't stand the idea of "pathlessness"; as a spiritual seeker, I didn't do much better.

Jiddu Krishnamurti is also, of course, the Brahman boy who, in 1910 at the age of 14, was plucked from complete obscurity by the Theosophical Society and groomed to be the great teacher who would one day lead humanity in its evolution to the new root-race as described in Theosophical teachings. But, in 1929, speaking before Society leader Annie Besant and 3,000 members, he had renounced Theosophy, dissolved the new society (the Star in the East) which had been created especially for him, rejected all organized religion and even to a degree the notion that anyone can ever learn anything from anyone else, and set out on a life of teaching that would end up affecting the lives of tens of thousands of people.

(Some years later, Ashish would comment to me in a letter: "I had come across J. Krishnamurti's talks long before coming to Mirtola, and had never been able to make any sense of them: they said nothing to me. Against this background it was easy for me to adopt the view of J. K. I learned from Gopalda and Moti, for whom J. K.'s disbanding of the Star in the East was seen as a failure of J. K. to go through with his dedication to the Master's coming. This was exacerbated by the effect on Mrs. Besant, who was devastated. Then by what right did J. K. start teaching? It had never been suggested that he, J. K., would be the Teacher, but rather that the Teacher would take over the physical vehicle prepared by J. K. It was only after I read Mary Lutyens's *The Years of Awakening*, and found confirmation of events that I had both heard of and assumed must have happened, that I realized I had accepted a false view of the situation. This meant that I had to take responsibility for admitting that Moti, Gopalda and even Ma [Sri Yashoda Mai] had been biased in their view of events. If I had not by then been standing on my own feet, I might not have been able to do it. It would not have been a conscious concealment. An emotional inability to criticize my teachers would have blocked my perceptions. However, my faulty position would have shown up in obvious bigotry." [June 20, 1990])

At any rate, the three of us—Jane, Lizelle, and myself—piled into my car on a sunny July morning and took off on the three-hour drive to Saanen, high up in the mountains of German Switzerland. We arrived and made our way into the crowded circus tent. Krishnamurti had begun to speak.

The great man was sitting up tall and erect in a chair at the front of the tent. At 85, Krishnamurti was still dazzlingly handsome. His snow-white hair shone in the light that worked its way down from the top of the tent. Sitting in the front row, almost at his feet, was none other than Jeanne de Salzmann. She was listening to Krishnamurti raptly, like a schoolgirl.

My first reaction upon seeing this was that Jeanne de Salzmann didn't practice what she preached. Krishnamurti came from a very different tradition than hers. Gurdjieffians were not supposed to imbibe the words of other teachers. My group leaders did not like my ongoing relationship with Ashish at all, nor did they approve of my going around and meeting spiritual luminaries whether inside or outside the Gurdjieff Work. But here sat Jeanne de Salzmann, chief among the Gurdjieffians, listening in rapt attention to this world-famous proponent of Advaita.

Could such a person, who broke the rules of which she was the custodian, really be firmly established in objective consciousness?

Such was my first impression. I listened to Krishnamurti, finding him every bit as confusing in person as I had found him in his writings, especially as his voice seemed to waver in and out eerily. Soon, though, my first impression was followed by a second. It struck me that I was present at a kind of confrontation of spiritual titans—a confrontation that had little likelihood of happening again, since Krishnamurti was 85 at the time (he would die in 1986 at almost 91) and Jeanne de Salzmann was 90 (she would die in 1990 at age 101). It occurred to me that there might be no more rules in the domain of objective consciousness—or in the realm of the annihilated ego in which Krishnamurtu was said to dwell, with many believing of this latter that when he spoke his own personality abdicated, and Lord Krishna himself (or the Lord Maitreya, as some Theosophists would have it) spoke through him. This was a silent confrontation, with Jeanne de Salzmann, as if ceremonially voiding herself of her ego in his presence, sitting at Krishnamurti's feet, and Krishnamurti, though I'm quite sure he knew Jeanne de Salzmann, gazing beyond her as he spoke with that tremulous voice that was almost that of a channeled entity. It was, I would later think, a confrontation between their greater Selves, not them at all—or rather that, at such a high level of being, it was a merging of understanding into oneness, because there is only one greater Self, manifesting as it does through relatively separate individuals.

Writing to Ashish in 1981, shortly after Lizelle and I had visited him in Mirtola, I told him that Lizelle had "told me that she knows there are 'higher' beings in India than in the West. She specifically mentioned Sri Anirvan and you as examples. But, as a Westerner, she says that she has to get what she can in the West, hence her Gurdjieff group activities. Is she right?"

A.   Lizelle is right in her attitude toward east-west incompatibilities only insofar as she is concerned with the sort of teachings she has received from Anirvan. From his writings it appears that Anirvan thinks entirely within the framework of Hindu terminology, seldom distinguishing between the terms and what they represent. It should be clear that if terms represent reality, the reality is independent of the terms. Since terminology usually goes along with a way of thinking, people who first get a glimpse of the reality through a particular thought system and terminology often get into this confusion. They think that a different system with a different terminology is representing a different reality. One of the reasons for reading widely is that it helps to distinguish between the terms and what the terms refer to. Whereas words at first convey illumination, they may later become obstructions. [Aug. 9, 1981]

I do not believe that Ashish approved at all of my gallivanting around among the greats and near-greats of the Gurdjieff movement. I for my part was pleased with myself, and thought I was breaking out of the hidebound hierarchies of the Gurdjieff groups— and perhaps demonstrating that I was at a higher level of being than they thought, dammit!

But, though I doubt I was aware enough at the time to really pick up on what he was saying, Ashish was certain, I now feel, that what I was really trying to do was shine, so to speak, by the reflected light of objective consciousness. He was sure that all of this would advance me not one whit down the path to the unitive vision. For him, I was just another American businessman, running around and cornering as much of a share of the spiritual market as I could. He told me as much—though I was somehow able to persuade myself that he was not really talking about me at all. He first made these points in a letter written shortly after I told him about meeting Lizelle Reymond; he would reiterate them in later letters.:

A.   Now look, Sy! Going around meeting people, getting experience of the sorts of people there are, what they say, what they do, what their views are, that's one thing. But hunting for a teacher, hunting for some sort of external confirmation in the outside world, that is not desirable. The path is inward, inward into the heart of your own being, the center of your own being. Not something that you can see with the ordinary mind. Technically, it's still mind, all right, mind with a capital "M." But it's not the ordinary, thinking, rational mind. That is something, a screen, you have to get beyond. The questions that seem to be bugging you are whether there is a material basis for the inner work, and how you can square your interest in it with your integration as a successful businessman. Unfortunately, the businessman seems reluctant to let go of his success, so he distorts the facts to make his interest compatible with the success ethos—expansion of interests, intelligence, achievement, survival of the personality, and further success leading to identification with "our unibeing" [a Gurdjieffian synonym for the "Absolute"]. This replaces ego-annihilation, self-transcendence, Nirvana. Instead of aiming at bodhisattva-hood, he becomes a candidate for becoming a hasnamuss.

The problem of the material of the inner worlds reflects the question, "Is it all REAL?" The feeling, not the truth, is that if it is not material, it is imaginary. But what the devil does materiality count for without the consciousness to which it is objective? This very material dissolves before the inner vision. Consciousness holds it in being. Withdraw the consciousness, and it is literally nothing. Nothing now. [Dec. 22, 1979]

Well. Gradually, his words would work their way into my soul. But, even then, I felt that it was a real privilege to meet some of the people I was meeting through the Gurdjieff Work. In England, in 1983, I was put in touch with Pamela Travers, author of the *Mary Poppins* books. Ms. Travers, elderly by then, had been involved in the Gurdjieff Work groups for decades, and had even studied briefly in Paris with Gurdjieff. I met the author in her townhouse in the Chelsea district of London and participated in several evening sessions with her and the Gurdjieff group she led that met in the top-floor sitting room. I wasn't only name-dropping when I wrote Ashish that I thought such meetings were useful for me, that they showed me how the rest of the Gurdjieffian world worked, and that it was especially interesting to witness techniques in action that a single group had been using for many years.

A.   A connection with Pamela Travers is to me a recommendation. There has been so much talk of her visiting that I will write her, but there seem to be real physical difficulties. [July 24, 1983]

But, soon enough, I would no longer have the time to go gallivanting around reflecting the light of the Gurdjieffian objective consciousness, as the reader will discover in the next chapter.

Brook, *Threads of Time*, 108.

7

Soul Farmer of the Everglades

Was the world really going to wrack and ruin? Would we all blow ourselves off the face of the planet one day soon? What could one man do in the face of mankind's follies which seemed destined to obliterate us all? The only thing I could think of was getting out of the cities, heading for some rural setting. Certainly Florida, where I now spent more than half the year, offered a plenitude of opportunities. No matter where you were, you were only an hour or so by car from the Everglades.

For some time now I'd been talking about rural living, moving out to the country, trying to find a Gurdjieff Work group somewhere in a rural setting. It seemed to me that the urban world was on the brink of disaster, and I wanted to get out. Ashish and I had been talking about this since 1982 at least.

A.   I don't know what's going to happen in the future, Sy. I don't know that anybody knows for certain what is going to happen. These things are not fated in quite that sense of something which is utterly inevitable. It's inevitable that there is going to be change but in what mode it comes depends on the reactions of the men and women who are involved; well, all the men and women who are living because every single person is involved in this problem.

So, will it result in chaos, anarchy? Will people be able to reason it out and adjust things without descending into chaos? I don't know, perhaps one thing in one place, another in another. The present rather wretched state of affairs may continue for some time. We really can't say. But one has to be prepared.

There is the question of whether you've thought of working out this rural situation with the group and on behalf of the people in the group, a sort of joint affair. So that it wouldn't be a question of you moving out and leaving the group behind, but only that the whole group would be ready to possibly all move out, or move out at weekends or anything of that sort. I think it needs serious attention. [Oct. 18, 1982]

In 1984, this same subject of a possible move to the country came up again.

A. I hope you have not forgotten that the proposal to find a country place was not just with the view to follow an alternative or more balanced lifestyle, but was more significantly aimed at obtaining circumstances where life could be sustained in the event of any sort of breakdown in the socio-economic order.

I appreciate that your dreams on this subject could have sprung from your present anxieties. However, though I do not want to join the prophets of doom, I just do not see how current trends can lead to anything but breakdown. The world economy is so closely intermeshed that it no longer appears possible for the developed countries to stand aloof from (what appears to be) the certain collapse of third world economies due to overpopulation, because the developed world has been and is dependent on supplies from the third world.

Wherever one may be, in times of crisis the man with land can return to the primary economy of subsistence where labor is converted directly into food, fuel, etc., whereas the man who has only money may find himself with nothing. I don't like your dream [a night dream I'd had] of an approaching storm. It could presage not only an emotional storm. It could be more general.

As you rightly say, the inner work can be carried on in any location. This is for the simple reason that inquiry is into the nature of the Self and what lies beyond an individualized self. And that is something that is with one inescapably, wherever one is.

However, the fact remains that some physical conditions make it easier to keep the mind in check, than others, which is why, with rare but notable exceptions, there has been, throughout human history, a tendency for people seeking the inner goal to choose to live in quiet situations and/or to reduce their involvement in worldly affairs. In effect, this means reducing their desires. [Feb. 12, 1984]

To some extent my interest in a simpler, more rural, lifestyle had been engendered by my admiration for Ashish and my liking for the communal life I experienced during my stays at Mirtola. It was fascinating to see Ashish, with his excellent western education, perfectly satisfied to live in a remote mountain area with just two suits of clothes (two ochre robes, really), one of which he wore and the other of which hung on the clothesline (he had a few other bits and pieces of possessions, but really, the robes were it). In mid-1984, I'd even checked out some Gurdjieff groups located in more rural settings. I'd written to Ashish: "I am going to try once more to examine the practicality and advisability of living in a more rural situation in the United States. I have located some other groups both within and without the Gurdjieff teaching that exist in rural locations. But if I go off to the country and wind up disconnected completely from any group of people with an inner search, will I be able to sustain my own inner search?"

A.   So you really are planning to get out of the city. It does seem to me that the criterion should be a place you like for itself and that you can manage. Only if you were so fully dedicated to a teacher that you wanted to be as close to him as he permitted would it be right to put him before your liking for the place. As it is, the proximity of a sympathetic group could be a bonus, but I would doubt the advisability of making it a requirement. You don't want to find yourself disillusioned with whatever sort of group you find, and disliking your place on top of it.

Frankly, your first and biggest problem is going to be adapting yourself to an entirely strange way of life. There will be plenty of friction, new things to face, deprivation of accustomed social supports, and real feelings of inadequacy to keep you on your toes without having to take recourse to the fabricated "work situations" of a supposed school. In a sense, you will be graduating to the school of life.

Certainly, it would be fine to have a respected friend close by to whom you could turn for inspiration, reassurance, and stimulus in times of depression. That's more than a bonus. It's a blessing.

And you will probably make mistakes about the place itself. People who have never lived in the country may not think to inquire about dry season water supplies, where the drains run to, and where the sun goes to in the winter. And it's easy to be taken for a ride over an orchard. [I'd been thinking about growing citrus.]

Mohamed's followers asked him whether faith in God was sufficient, or should they also tie up their camels? He replied, "Trust in God and tie your camels." Put your inner aim first, but make sure that it is the inner aim and not a substitute. Insecurity makes for two pitfalls. One is to turn the place into another money spinning venture. The other is to seek security in turning it into a group house.

In general, don't go hunting teachers and groups. Find a place where you can grow yourself, and not just apples and potatoes.

Incidentally, since one is talking of this business about not wanting to live on a farm as such and sort of tie you down to the agricultural seasons and so on, does it necessarily imply that because you live in the country, that you run a farm or an orchard of this, that or the other thing? I know several people in America who live in the country, houses with presumably a few acres of land around them. They don't farm them. Obviously there is enough land there from what I hear to go a long way to supporting them in case things did degenerate into what you call the holocaust. It's a healthier, quieter life.

I know that you are sort of city born and bred and don't feel happy in the country. It's just that to me, the present day, modern city is an abomination. From my own viewpoint, I cannot see why anyone should want to live in the city if he doesn't have to do so on account of the sheer economics of a job or profession or something of that sort. But it does, of course, demand that you don't mind isolation. People say, "We are isolated, we don't know our neighbors and if we do, we don't like them," and all that sort of thing. That isn't the point. The point is that there's always the feeling that in case of trouble, in case of emergency, there are always people there. We share common interests with them. If thieves break into the flat, the other flat owners will come and help and that sort of thing. I'm not trying to push you into it. The only point I wanted to make is that living out of the city does not necessarily imply that you've got to have some sort of money making activity there. [July 14, 1984]

Then, in 1984, a couple of things happened to begin to gently nudge me toward putting at least some of my money where my mouth was.

The first was that I left the Gurdjieff Work group. More accurately, I was asked to leave. My conflicts with the leadership over whether or not esoteric dream study should be included in the curriculum had come to a head, and I had been the loser. It may have been that those conflicts were partly a stratagem of my ego to survive in the face of the power of the Gurdjieff Work. Be that as it may, at the end of 1984, I left the group—not quite definitively, for I returned once, very briefly, only to leave again.

I'd left the group once before, for a brief while, in 1983. Ashish had been glad when I'd returned:

A.   So, by leaving the group, you discovered it meant more to you than you had thought. I suppose it's as good a way as any to discover it. I am very glad you have gone back. [Jan. 15, 1983]

When I left in 1984, he struck a different note.

A.   All these western groups, with the possible exception of the Theosophists, appear to have taken on the same restrictive attitudes as the western churches. They tell you what you ought to believe. Although G frowned on "philosophizing," there is no sign in any of the literature that he required people to restrict their interests. His "philosophizing" appears to mean theorizing in the void, which is different from intelligent inquiry. He stressed the need to be aware of oneself, no matter what one was doing or thinking.

The degeneration of groups of "schools" after the withdrawal of the real Teacher is, unfortunately, more the rule than the exception. The most one can say is that there was still enough there to make your association with the Florida group of value. [Jan. 28, 1985]

The group's objection to what you call division of loyalty would be understandable in the context of their belief that "the system" is sufficient to itself. They don't see that one's loyalty must be to the goal—the spirit, the head, the absolute, whatever one calls it—but that the mind should be free to range.

Perhaps their view is justifiable in the Western context, where mental views have been stressed to the detriment of feeling and emotion. Loyalty is a feature of feeling/emotion; but in highly mental people one can get at it only through the mind. They do not, indeed cannot, expect you to be loyal because you love them or because you feel the presence in them of the spirit which is love. They substitute a sort of mental rule: you must be "loyal," in the same sense that you should not let your mind wander into other fields. It is similar to church discipline—you must think only in the way they tell you to think.

I prefer the Indian way in which discipline is imposed on behavior, leaving the mind free. Dedication is to the thing itself, or to the teacher in whom its presence is felt. However, once the person has made his self-dedication to a particular place, he must stick. Any wish to break away is correctly interpreted as an inability to deal with his egotism, his negativities, etc. His desire for the real is not strong enough to overcome his desires for comfort, security, fame, family affection, sexual experience, or lost freedom to do as he likes. What holds the man from breaking away is not just mental determination, but also such personal affection he feels for and is given by his teacher and his fellow disciples.

In India, your lecturing to Theosophists or anyone else would not be interpreted as disloyalty. If a teacher forbade you, it would be to make you face the ego-building effect of lecturing. It is easy to be trapped into thinking oneself a teacher in one's own right, just because one can talk well and get a good feedback from the audience. If one falls for it, one is stuck.

The present G groups and the Theosophists seem to represent two poles. The Theosophists are open, freethinking, and with some perception of the transcendental nature of the goal. The G groups offer a method of changing the nature but offer no reason why anyone should want to change, except out of a sense of the meaninglessness of life as it is. No resolution is made merely by mixing two poles. While G himself was there, he provided the "something extra." If Theosophy has degenerated into a new religion, so has the G work. Rare individuals may exist in both movements, but this does not prove anything. They also exist within Christianity or any other religion. [Nov. 25, 1984]

Now, groupless in Fort Lauderdale, I was in a position to do what I'd been threatening to do for some time: Go find a Gurdjieff group in a rural setting. I equivocated over this for awhile. Then another factor entered the picture. Though I'd left the Gurdjieff group, my friendship with Irving, the local group leader, had continued. In 1986, for reasons that again smacked of church politics, he, too, left the group—or rather, like me, was asked to leave by Peggy Flinsch, a very senior member of the Gurdjieff Foundation in New York.

His leaving brought us closer together. We talked. It occurred to us that we might set up a rural Gurdjieffian Work group together. Though I was facilitating a group studying Gurdjieff's teachings at the Theosophical Society at the time, I thought it might be useful if we had a piece of land on which physical work such as communal gardening could be carried out, as a means of enabling people to balance their intellect and emotions with their physicality in true Gurdjieffian fashion.

One reason I wanted to acquire a piece of land was, of course, personal: I was hankering after some version of the Mirtola experience. This hankering had led me to explore some of the parts of rural Florida where citrus groves and tomato farms are located. But after looking at a great many farms and groves, mostly in central and northern Florida, I found I just couldn't make the commitment to relocate to such a relatively isolated rural area.

Irving and I hit upon a compromise. We decided to buy a piece of land, one that could be dedicated to a Gurdjieffian communal school, in the western part of unincorporated Broward County on the northern outskirts of the Miami metropolitan area.

This turned out to be no light undertaking. We agreed to purchase five acres of land on which there already stood a substantial residence of about 3,000 square feet and a utility building that would make an excellent equipment and work room. This was expensive land, in the path of suburban development, but we each agreed to buy half, he buying the portion of the land on which the house was situated, I buying the portion on which the utility building stood. This would enable him to move from his existing apartment and live on the property. It was a step up for him and his wife in terms of gracious living. But his primary motivation was, I believed, that he like myself felt we needed the kind of group work that could best be undertaken on a sizable non-urban property.

I kept Ashish abreast of developments. "We are attempting to obtain the 'blessing' of the major Gurdjieff umbrella group, to which we previously belonged, for our new group," I wrote him.

A.   This is great news that the new group has started. If the official group gives its blessings, that will be fine, but you should not allow it to discourage you if blessings are withheld. [Dec. 13, 1986]

There was already one large dwelling and an additional utility building on the land, I told him, adding, "Do you have any advice on construction if we should decide to build another dwelling? For example, it is said that bedrooms should be oriented so that one sleeps with one's head to the north."

A.   Always sleep with your head toward the spirit. Where is that? Everywhere.

Given a choice, it is quite a good idea to have one's head towards north, because that is the astrological "circle of eternal apparition" (i.e., around the pole star) whereas the south is the region of death. Contrived symbolic buildings are usually flops. Design what you would like in relation to the sort of life you want to lead, to the amount of privacy you want, to convenience, and to climate. Forget status and fashion.

Security is an inescapable factor, but I would prefer a risk of robbery to living in a bank vault. The best security is not to have expensive things lying around. The sense of space is more a matter of design than of actual size.

What is one to do with esoteric design factors, when one wants low ceilings in a cold climate and high ones or open courtyards in a hot climate? Need one have air conditioning in an appropriately designed house?

Look around and take notice of the proportion of rooms you like and feel at ease in. Look at houses that attract you and find out who designed them. Learn to listen to your feelings.

Remember that whatever you build, you will be stuck with for many years, so you want something that you will be happy in. Don't set out to build a temple of objective art [a term used by Gurdjieff to describe art that has a definite emotional effect on each human being, that emotional effect being the same for everybody. See P. D. Ouspensky, *In Search of the Miraculous*, 295-297]. Build a dwelling where G would be comfortable.

Incidentally, half an acre of Florida land should produce enough to feed you, and more, if you were vegetarian, at rather less cost than it would take to buy food. [Dec. 13, 1986]

Our new Gurdjieff group developed rapidly. By early 1987, membership had grown to twenty-five. Because of the size of this piece of property, there weren't any problems with nearby neighbors. The unincorporated area was one in which there lived rather self-sufficient types who wanted a certain freedom to do what they wished on their property without running into zoning restrictions, noise ordinances and other compromises one makes when living in the city. Our needs were not those of shooting firearms, keeping big dogs, raising chickens or training horses. But we needed a place large enough to accommodate thirty or more people, not in a living situation, but where we could gather on a Sunday or a weekend or regularly in the evenings; and we needed a place to which those people, while living in the urban surroundings of the Miami area, could drive in an hour or less and engage in the physical work that Gurdjieff saw as so necessary for urban people.

Ashish didn't hesitate to express any misgivings he might have about my motivations. A year into the project, I was still working at drumming up membership. Apropos of one of my dreams, he commented:

A.   This dream expresses a warning (or a doubt) about your efforts to work up your group. If you don't "hang out your sign," no one will know you are there, so no one will come. But if you proselytize, you will waste your own time and get the wrong sort of people.

The great danger in drumming up a group is that you suppress your own doubts—the "proof" that you are right is found in the numbers of people you attract.

You will be safe only if you are determined to follow your path and handle your own doubts. [July 21, 1987]

In fact, running a semi-rural Gurdjieff Work group with a friend didn't do much to quell my periodic doubts about the Fourth Way and the whole esoteric shooting match. In mid-1987, I wrote to Ashish with just the gentlest touch of self-pity that "the grace about which you and Krishna Prem write in your articles (e.g., *The Value of Uncertainty*) has not been bestowed upon me. I find I am always backing into the Work teachings, not because I have demonstrable evidence for their transcendent reality, but because I see the obvious benefit that the teachings bestow on our group members in helping to make their lives here better."

A.   It seems you are going through a crisis of doubt. You are taking your doubts seriously at their own level, which is rather foolish because they cannot be answered within their own coordinates.

They can be met either by unreasoned faith or by the determination which springs from perception that there is only one possible way out of this intolerably meaningless and ephemeral world, and that this lies through the inquiry into the root of one's own awareness.

This inquiry/determination is supported (not proved) by the affirmations of numerous people, some highly intelligent and articulate, some less so, but all remarkable as human beings. They constitute a body of evidence for the inner reality which no sane man can afford to exclude from his world picture.

As it is, you sound as if you expect to be persuaded by a gift of grace before you make a gift of yourself, like a proprietor demanding earnest money before agreeing to a sale. It has to be the other way round: You have to pay with whatever you have available as a preliminary to the total ego-annihilation that will be demanded. The Lord pays cash; but his currency does not go to the credit of any worldly bank account.

As against all this, you seem to have shut your eyes to the fact that the dreams you have sent me this time are less representative of the usual psychological turmoil and more a matter of quiet advice, the framing of issues, and pointers to problems typical of a man in the Work. So go ahead! Shut your eyes. Refuse to see the evidence that these years have had their effect. Indulge in your belly-aching and "die like a dog" [an allusion to Gurdjieff's often repeated admonition that if we don't work on ourselves in life, we'll end up dying like some dumb animal]. [July 21, 1987]

I had a tendency to not really believe in the reality of the hidden levels of being that, through the teaching of certain exercises, we were attempting to evoke in our students. Ashish never failed to call me to account on this. One of these exercises was called "constructive imagination." It consisted of imagining a physical experience in order to help oneself perceive an actual physical experience that was going on without one's noticing it. The exercise was based on an exercise of Gurdjieff in which the pupil says, for example, "I am, I can, I wish," constructively imagining a vibration in the chest while he or she is doing so. The idea, according to Gurdjieff, was that a more highly developed being would actually experience the vibration. So, if you imagined the vibration, you could eventually bring an actual vibration into the experience because the vibration was there in the first place but going unnoticed. This would inevitably bring about the raising of your level of being to correspond with the actuality of experiencing the vibration.

I had written to Ashish about this exercise in these terms: "By saying repeatedly either inwardly and/or outwardly, things like 'I am, I can, I wish,' even if I really am not, cannot, nor wish not, a certain result can nevertheless be obtained. It has to do with the susceptibility of the machine [i.e., the 'asleep' human being] to be fooled by suggestion. In this way, one can bring the declaration of 'I am, I can, I wish' into a reality." Ashish responded:

A. Why do you have to give everything a negative twist? The machine is not "fooled by suggestion." I have taught you a method by which your limited awareness is extended to include an actually existing fact in sensible experience. Similarly, "I am, I can, I wish" affirms a fact of which you are not presently aware. The boot is on the other foot: Social conditioning has fooled you into limiting awareness. How can you overcome doubt if you think like this?" [July 21, 1987] Some years before, Ashish had said much the same thing: "If you chew your food too well, your digestion will not work properly. In dealing with these occult, subtle, matters, a degree of credulity is needed. In the subtle realm the power of the imagination is effective: imagine to yourself that you can feel the subtle breath, and, after a time, you will find that you are aware of an actual 'breath' that is not imaginary. But if you constantly chew over it, calling it 'just some imagination,' it never has a chance to grow into a convincing reality." [Jan. 11, 1981]. He had later added: "Feel (imagine) the 'thrill' of the energy being transmuted by and coursing through your body. Or, if you prefer the term, will it to move through and upward within your body. Real will is not intellectual effort. It's more like holding a concentrated feeling. Do it for aim, and you will be able to stop your ego from usurping your power for its own petty purposes." [May 12, 1981] And he said as well: "One begins by imagining things. This leads one to become more aware of the thing imagined. The thing is there, but one is not aware of it until one's attention has been drawn to it. Suppose someone to have lost something and asks you to help him hunt for it. He describes it. You hunt for it, having in mind the image you have built on his description. When you find it, you recognize it, even though your mental image, formed on the description, does not tally with the object you find. It is like it, though probably not the same. You show it for confirmation. In this case, the reply is that you are on the right track." [July 27, 1981]

I asked him how effective you could be as a teacher if you had trouble believing in some of these things; if you weren't (hopefully only temporarily) at a high enough level of being?

A.   A man who is firmly established in the Spirit can learn from anyone, even from his own disciples, without feeling himself in any way diminished by the ignorance he seeks to remove. But it is not so easy for the man who is not so centered. When the latter man finds that he can teach his teacher, he often takes pride in his superior knowledge. The truly superior man is humble, not because he is practicing that virtue, but because, by virtue of his being centered, he does not measure himself on the basis of any degree of worldly knowledge.

When someone is asked to perform a completely strange job in the Work, the hope is not only that he will gain courage and confidence, in the usual psychological way, but also that he will sense the influx of a new ability, a new power, *which is in no sense his own.* If he sees this, he will not add it to his list of worldly achievements, like a new medal pinned to his chest, but will feel the humility of a man who now knows that he (whatever constitutes his empirical self) is but an instrument for the manifestation of powers, possibly divine powers, but certainly not his own creation. This makes it easier for him to detach himself from his other achievements which his education and his cultural background encouraged him to believe his own. [Nov. 21, 1987]

We taught all the basics in our classes, such as the Gurdjieff meditation technique called "sitting" (which I describe to some extent in Chapter Thirteen). But, because we had larger facilities than do many Gurdjieff Work groups, we were sometimes able to do more things that many of them do. We developed a substantial vegetable garden, we did woodworking and related crafts projects, and we maintained the property. These outer activities, carried out in the true Gurdjieffian spirit, masked the inner work on self-awareness in which the participants were instructed to engage.

Some of what we did was just plain fun in the ordinary sense. In riding a tractor, I was playing farmer, and I particularly remember the enjoyment of riding around on a lawn tractor that we used primarily to mow the grass—or, more accurately, to cut down the ground cover of assorted scrub which was typical of this land just east of the Florida Everglades. Although we were close to Miami, there was still a ruralness about the area with the smells of the land, the sounds of the birds and insects, and the hot sun that beat down upon me.

As a group, we would typically spend Sundays on the property and on occasion whole weekends, dividing into teams for the external work. One team would weed the garden, another would tend seedlings, a third would trim bushes and trees, a fourth

103

might be building benches, a fifth would prepare lunch. These outward tasks were accompanied by an inner task typical of Gurdjieff Work. For example, the task for the day might be to do everything with the opposite hand, sensing the hand as it picked up an implement, or it might be to say "I am" every fifteen minutes during the day.

Gurdjieff has written of his early life, "I wished to create around myself conditions in which a man would be continuously reminded of the sense and aim of his existence by an unavoidable friction between his conscience and the automatic manifestations of his nature." Many Gurdjieff groups have get-togethers for a day, a weekend, or even longer, on a piece of property so that people can work together, rubbing up against one another to generate this same friction and hence observe their reactions to the friction. This is called "second line of work" within the tradition and means working with others, "first line of work" being one's self-observation of one's own psychological states along with studying the underlying concepts. There was a "third line of work" which was "working for the Work." A person who organized and was responsible for a group, for example, would be said to be engaged in third line of work. One well-known Gurdjieff adage is that if one engages in all three lines of work, then it is less easy for one to fall asleep.

I recall one instance of a "Work Day," which is what we called them, when we had a group of about twenty people in all working on our communal property gardening, woodworking and so on. Tasks were handed out, one of them being to pick up tools all day with the opposite hand; such devices, reminding us to wake up, would constantly prompt us to see that we were what amounted to asleep. We discussed our observations over lunch. On this particular Work Day, Irving secretly appointed one member to go around and "accidentally" soak people with a garden hose while he was ostensibly watering the vegetation. Observing one's reactions to something like getting squirted in this way is typical of the practical Gurdjieff work on oneself. It is not very different from the monk in some monasteries who is assigned to go around all day with a paddle and hit the other monks on the behind to help them to wake up.

From time to time, we engaged in the "stop" exercises made famous by Gurdjieff: When the word "stop" was shouted by myself or Irving, everyone would instantly cease all motion, freezing in mid-air just as if time had stopped. In *In Search of the Miraculous*, Ouspensky explains these "stop" exercises. Their invention arose from G's belief that we are all totally conditioned, going through life with only a very limited, very specific set of unchangeable, permanent physical motions and postures. Since our moving, emotional and intellectual centers are interlocked, you can't change one center without the other two changing as well. Something unexpected and powerful was needed to wrench you out of your habitual patterns of behavior. The "stop" exercises provided this insofar as they prevented you from following through on your actions in the normal, predetermined, conditioned way. Forced to stand still, you had to grope for new mechanisms to cope with this new state. However slightly, this would begin to change the dynamic of your moving, emotional and intellectual centers. We were urged to "self-remember" at the same time.

Ouspensky writes that he and fellow group members "very soon became convinced that the 'stop' exercise was not at all a joke. In the first place it required us to be constantly on the alert, constantly ready to interrupt what we were saying or doing, and secondly it sometimes required endurance and determination of quite a special kind. 'Stop' occurred at any moment of the day. Once during tea P., who was sitting opposite me, had raised to his lips a glass of hot tea, just poured out, and he was blowing on it. At this moment we heard 'Stop' from the next room. P's face, and his hand holding the glass, were just in front of my eyes. I saw him grow purple and I saw a little muscle near his eye quiver. But he held onto the glass. He said afterwards that his fingers only pained him during the first minute, the chief difficulty afterwards was with his arm, which was bent awkwardly at the elbow, that is, stopped halfway through a movement. But he had large blisters on his fingers and they were painful for a long time."

Ashish had always tried to keep me on the straight and narrow as far as taking these exercises in the proper spirit was concerned, speaking about the "sacred dances," for example, with a slight qualification. A few years before, I had written him that "our Gurdjieff group places great emphasis on sacred dance in general and the Gurdjieff movements in particular, but I question if the participants really understand the purpose." He had replied:

A.   Exercises for becoming aware of the body have value only to the extent that they lead to awareness of the awareness which is aware of the body. Merely to become aware of the body is not part of the work.

Exercises of any sort are means of achieving something which is not the exercise. Too much stress laid on the exercises leads to forgetting of what the exercise is for. On the other hand, once an exercise has had the effect it was designed to produce, there should be no need to go on with it.

The G exercises do not aim at body-awareness. They are intended to produce a state of awareness. But to win this state, it is usually necessary to continue with the exercises beyond the point where they seem to be rewarding. [Sept. 11, 1983]

Among Gurdjieff's best-known techniques were special music designed to evoke specific emotional responses in people and the sacred dances which have come to be known as the Gurdjieff Movements. Gurdjieff claimed that the sacred dances of antiquity—the vast majority of which have been lost—consisted of huge numbers of just those movements which he was trying to induce in his students so that their emotional and thinking centers, along with their physical centers, could be tugged up to a higher level of awareness. From his travels to the Far East and Middle East, Gurdjieff had brought back to the West one hundred or so of these sacred dances (the whirling dances of the Sufi dervishes provide an example with which the reader will be familiar). They involve a complicated series of movements performed by the dancer in which different rhythms are assigned, for example to the movements of the legs, of the arms, of the torso, and of the head. The result of attempting these movements is a breakdown of the dancer's intellectual ability to record and direct the different parts of the body to move in accordance with the differing rhythms. Consequently, the intellect becomes overloaded and gives up. However, as Gurdjieff taught, the body has its own mind which eventually takes over from the intellect. The dancer then experiences a detached awareness of his or her body performing the particular dance and handling the complicated rhythms in a way that is beyond the capability of the intellect.

When carried out by the proper people under the proper circumstances, the Gurdjieff Movements have great power. Gurdjieff took forty of his Prieuré des Basses Loges students to New York in 1924. There they put on displays consisting of both physical movements like the "stop" movement and fragments of the "sacred dances." Describing one of these New York displays of Gurdjieff's pupils, eyewitness William Seabrook wrote:

"At his command, they [the dancers] would race, spread out at breakneck speed from left to right across the stage, and at another low command from him freeze in full flight as if caught by a racetrack camera.

"....The troupe was deployed extreme back stage, facing the audience. At his command, they came racing full-tilt toward the footlights. We expected to see a wonderful exhibition of arrested motion. But instead, Gurdjieff calmly turned his back, and was lighting a cigarette. In the next split second, an aerial human avalanche was flying through the air, across the orchestra, down among empty chairs, on the floor, bodies pell-mell, piled on top of each other, arms and legs sticking out in weird postures—frozen there, fallen, in complete immobility and silence.

"Only after it had happened did Gurdjieff turn and look at them, as they lay there, still immobile. When they presently arose, by his permission, and it was evident that no arms, legs or necks had been broken—no one seemed to have suffered even so much as a scratch or bruise—there was a storm of applause, mingled with a little protest. It had almost been too much."

It was my own experience, from participating in movements classes over six years in the earlier Gurdjieff group and then in this new group, that I could at least on occasion attain a kind of "high" that might be described as a state transcendent of my ordinary state. In this sense, the movements give the participant a taste of something "higher"—something beyond his or her ordinary experience.

The movements are the central activity for some Gurdjieff groups composed of certain types of people. Other groups do not engage in them at all. Much of this depends on the competence of someone who has specially studied and been trained to engage in the movements and can then instruct a class of dancers.

Ours was not such a group, because neither Irving nor myself were particularly adept at instructing in the movements, nor did we have anyone in the group who had been properly trained and in whom the movements resonated. But we did receive more or less regular visits from practitioners of the movements in New York, who would lead us in these classes.

I recall one time when several people in our group were engaged in a movements class led by a visiting movements teacher from New York. Although some of the movements can be engaged in by one person alone, most require a group of people typically arranged in six files, with three to six people deep in each file, depending on how many participants there are. One is expected to engage in the movements/rhythms as an inner task, without consideration of what others in the class are doing. However, as a practical matter, people tend to want to observe the person in front of them and try to follow their motions instead of simply doing it internally. The result is that the six people at the front of each file tend to be the more accomplished movements practitioners, and the class leader will even put such people at the head of each file.

On this occasion, there were only three people in the class who were really good at the movements. So, when we took our places, the front row had only those three people in it; everyone else ran to be behind someone else so they could follow along, and consequently we were in only three files, each six deep instead of six files each three deep. In the Gurdjieff lexicon, this is called "internal considering" (I've previously mentioned this concept)—a kind of worrying about what other people will think of me if I make a mistake—and it is one of the important identifications that G asks us to observe in ourselves. It was entertaining as well as instructive to watch the eighteen of us fighting not to be in the front row. Finally, the class leader had to rearrange us.

It should not be supposed that during this time my ego was not always struggling to free itself from these gross infringements on its liberty, or that I was not, despite my greatest efforts, constantly fighting to keep myself looking inward and working toward what Gurdjieff called "objective consciousness" and Ashish the unitive vision. All along, in our correspondence, Ashish was fighting to keep me properly directed. A short time before Irving and I had started our semi-rural Gurdjieff group Work school—we called it the Gurdjieff Institute of Florida—Ashish had given me some advice which would always serve as a template for me of the wonderful things he was able to say whenever I seemed to be deviating badly from the path:

A. The main issue is clear. When in doubt, go to the source. The ordinary thinking mind can be used to clarify the question. But the question itself must be put to something which is higher than the ordinary mind. It is not what you think that matters, but what your inner being advises as being appropriate for you at this moment. And if you cannot get the thing clear, then withdraw from involvement in the groups and put the teaching into practice, namely meditate, cultivate awareness, hold back from unnecessary activities; don't let the mind run on recriminations and self-justification. This leaves you in what might seem to be an awkward predicament. As I see it, however, it brings you to an important crossroads. Do you continue hunting around for another group which will satisfy your need for supportive "belonging" and togetherness, while also satisfying your liking for occult, cosmic, and esoteric chat, or do you stop hunting for company and for an outer teaching, and instead turn within to seek for the things around which all talk revolves?

Perhaps my often-repeated statement may have more meaning for you in this context. "Seek for the thing where it is—within." Do not hunt for outer teachers and their teachings. If you seek it where it is, it will itself provide you opportunities for meeting its reflection in persons, books, and events. The inner search will also prepare you to recognize the true reflection and to distinguish it from the false or clouded reflection, even if the "recognition" is only a feeling that they make sense. Your outward adventures have not been wasted time. You have filled up with a lot of useful if unimportant information which is pertinent to the primary issue that there is "something more." The Florida group, with all its failings, has taught you something about awareness.

But you could multiply this sort of experience many times without necessarily drawing any closer to the thing itself. You would merely know more and more about it. More truly, you would know more and more of what others say about it. You would have no first-hand experience of it. You know enough to know that there is something referred to as the source of consciousness and being. You know that its experience is to be had by following an inquiry into the nature of your own consciousness or awareness. You know that you cannot objectify awareness itself, except to the extent that you are aware of being aware, so that you can never find yourself or what is beyond yourself except by tracing your own awareness to its source. Thinking about or discussing awareness is not the point. Awareness can be known only by itself. You either know it or you don't. Knowing about it is ignorance of it.

This change in direction, from seeking outwardly to seeking inwardly, may seem to promise only boredom and frustration. It deprives you of the cheap satisfaction of presenting yourself as someone who knows more about it than many—a trap for the person with a good mind and retentive memory. It forces you into responsibility for the sort of effort you make, and deprives you of group support for unconventional activity.... The way out of this impasse is to seek in the one direction where the truth lies, namely, in the dark silence of the heart. [Jan. 28, 1985]

I tended to fret badly about what we were doing. My intellect ate me up badly about whether our classes were too intellectual, whether we were emphasizing the physical at the expense of the emotional, whether we were emphasizing the emotional at the expense of the physical—my ruminations ran on endlessly. Periodically, Ashish put a brilliant stop to all this (after some time, I would revert to my ruminations, though perhaps less strongly, and I like to think that at least, each time I reverted, it took me a little longer to revert).

A.   Gopalda used to quote a joke about intellectuals thinking they shared a private box with god, watching the play of the world. So many people develop the mind at the cost of the feeling. If they are also quick-witted, they then find it easy to put off criticisms with quick answers which may quiet down their critics—but not convince them. The trouble is that they so easily convince themselves that there was no valid reason for criticism. And if someone then takes a heavy hammer to them, they run away, just because their feelings are not robust enough to take it. In effect, they have found an impregnable position. This syndrome constitutes a real danger for you. However, the fact that your dreams, this time, carry some fairly heavy criticism, implies that you ought to be ready to accept it.

All the "occult secrets" are either tools of service, or mere toys— useful to familiarize children on the path with the facts of the subtle universe. All that matters is that you concentrate on the inwardness of the work. I have said it before and will go on saying it: Seek the truth where it is, in your heart, at the root of your being. Anything and anyone outside this is, at best, a correspondence or reflection of what you seek within. If you forget this and, instead, engage in an external hunt for a teacher, you will invite deception, for the mirror of life cannot reflect brightly if the light is dim in your heart. Acting as a guide for an outer group is one way of occupying yourself while you work. It has the advantages that it keeps you occupied with things related to the true work, and that you can learn more of yourself by learning about others. But it

111

also has the danger that you may come to think of yourself as being more than you are in fact.

As to where you work, I agree there is little difference—"six of one and half-a-dozen of the other." However, for someone who has never known what it is to be without running water, electricity, shops, a doctor around the corner and all the other things taken for granted in the urban world, it is not easy to become aware of how much of the sense of personal security is locked into the system. When one is trying to transfer one's loyalty to the spirit from the affairs of the world, one does not want to deceive oneself. "Of course, I am totally dedicated to the spiritual quest—so long as there is a telephone to call the doctor." Agreed that the doctor is also part of the divine scheme of things. It is a question of whether one truly sees what one is dealing with, or whether one is adopting a philosophy of convenience. Is one in touch with reality, or is one living in a maze of illusions about the permanency of civilizations and their infrastructures? Can one accept the anxieties of insecurity and use them as a goad to the search for what is ultimately certain? [June 27, 1986]

The "Work" of the Gurdjieff Work groups is rarely one of dramatic events. It's a question of the accretion of many subtle changes over the weeks and months and years. It takes a lot of time to gain one's first purchase on the timeless realms! I will describe a weekend I attended in late 1987, the details of which I communicated to Ashish as follows, and the results of which were as strange and ambiguous as is so often the case in the world of spiritual endeavor. (In fact, you should in general beware of "dramatic" spiritual events which seem to spirit you into entirely new realms or transform you utterly in an instant. It's so easy to fool oneself!)

Here is what I told Ashish.

"We had what is called here a 'Work Weekend.' This consisted in a three-day weekend during which a number of the members of our group stayed out at the group property for a period of physical work. It is related to Gurdjieff's teaching to use the physical body as an instrument for gaining attention, for remembering one-self, and for the inevitable rubbing up against one another that occurs when people work side by side in a physical activity such as gardening or cooking.

"These are artificially created conditions that only mimic the actual conditions your pupils who live at Mirtola endure. They are, nevertheless, an integral part of practical work in urban Gurdjieff groups. In addition to a dozen members of our group, two men from the Gurdjieff Foundation in New York joined us. They had each been in the Gurdjieff work for more than thirty years. They came to participate in this weekend and to lead the group in doing the Gurdjieff Movements. One of the men is a proficient movements teacher.

"Among the activities of the weekend, they suggested a certain kind of working together exercise. I had participated once before in this activity, last spring, when they were also here. I asked them to give it a name, and they called it 'speaking in the present.' It is an activity that is participated in by some older members in the Gurdjieff groups. The occasion of these two fellows being here this past weekend provided an opportunity to engage in this kind of work again, because it requires more than two persons. I have had to assume that this is an exercise which was given by Gurdjieff orally to selected pupils. They, in turn, have attempted to pass it down to later comers such as these men and myself.

"It goes like this: Three (or more) of us sit in a closed room facing each other in a circle. There could be a few more people or possibly only three, but apparently two is insufficient. We sit on ordinary chairs, but sitting on the floor would also have served. We sit with our eyes closed, gradually including the experience of more and more of our physical presence in our attention, until there is a comprehensive global experience of oneself included in the attention. It takes perhaps twenty to thirty minutes to get quiet and collected in this way and to calm the turning thoughts from racing away with one's attention. This technique, as you know, is the standard Gurdjieff 'sitting' exercise that pupils are asked to engage in each morning.

"In this work between us, however, an additional effort is made. Eventually from this quietude one of us begins to speak. The idea is to permit the physical instrument at our command to speak whatever it wishes without the interference of the intellect formulating thoughts and while the attention remains expanded to include the entirety of one's presence. The further idea is to establish a kind of communication between us that does not exist in our ordinary states. It is a sharing of understanding, so to speak.

"I cannot recall all that I said nor most of what the others said during the two one-hour sessions that we undertook over the weekend, but much of the speaking was about energy. I recollect saying among other things the following: 'There is this inner thing that I am now experiencing, it is a kind of vibration that has a definite shape. It is almost like the shape of the human body only not quite. It has no arms or legs. It is rather elliptical in shape and stands vertically on its axis. It is very white, light, and bright, transversed by horizontal darker lines, and the whole thing is in motion, in a whirling motion sort of like a top. This is my essence. Is this my essence? This whole world is just a game, just an act.'

"Remarks of a similar nature were made by the other participants. For example, one of them said, 'There is this energy in me or I am in it.' In general, I had the feeling that the communication taking place between us, in these sessions, and in the state of presence in which we sat, was like a communication between our essential beings with the personalities having been made passive. There was also a palpable experience or 'feeling' of energy pervading the room.

"What do you make of all this?"

A.   "Speaking in the present": Firstly, what you specifically saw/ spoke of recalls HPB's put down to a woman who said, "Every time I close my eyes, I see a blue triangle." HPB replied, "So long as you see it, it is outside you." What you describe is what Theosophists and others (including Castaneda's Don Juan) call the etheric or astral body—the egg-shaped subtle form. I have never seen this, but it is such a common account that I assume it to represent something objectively perceptible—if it is not just a copied fantasy.

However, nothing that can be objectified corresponds to my perception of essence, for to me essence is the unobjectifiable awareness at the heart of all the many bodies—physical, etheric, astral, mental, etc. So, while you may have been truly aware of something real that is nearer to essence than is the physical body, you should beware of evaluating it too highly. In fact, one can do this sort of exercise by oneself, holding an internal conversation with the higher part of one's being and trying to see that it is a "higher" part, and not just a split-off part. Here, the ambiguity between what is a higher part of oneself, and what is an objectively distinct higher person, has to be accepted as unavoidable and, in some sense, unimportant.

Indeed, if I picture to myself that I am talking to a real person, I produce a greater sense of objectivity, and therefore of something I can look at critically, than if I feel I am merely having a conversation in fantasy with my higher being. But to do this by oneself demands great honesty, clarity, lack of self-deceit, and knowledge of what the "other person" is likely to say. No matter who or what that "other" may be, I am alone responsible for getting the conversation through and for deciding on its degree of genuineness.

Sharing this sort of thing with a group is no guarantee against the deceits of group hallucination. Nevertheless, it appears to offer more of a safeguard than the lone explorer has, because one of three is more likely to put on a check when he feels something going screwy, than when there is only one, or one of two.

Nothing ventured, nothing won. The dangers of self-deception are unfortunately obvious: e.g., have you all been fooled by reading about Don Juan's "luminous egg"; or is it that you have now personally confirmed the truth of Don Juan's and Leadbeater's perceptions? In these plastic regions, things tend to take on the forms one expects to see. Therefore, "Having learned thine own ignorance, flee from the Hall of Learning." But don't flee from the subtle avenues of knowledge. You can learn to handle these avenues only by trying and failing. Hold your knowledge lightly, keeping ready to change as further knowledge confirms or denies what you have found. As you go on, you will build up a store of ideas/facts that are reasonably certain—firm enough to support your next step. For the important thing to realize is that the certainty you seek is not certain knowledge about details of the subtle worlds, or even details of philosophy, but experiential certainty of your essential unity in Absolute Being. Given that certainty, you will never be shaken by such a discovery as that the luminous egg is not what you thought it was, or that "this whole world" is not what it seems, but is certainly not "just a game, just an act."

Perhaps I should mention one real danger in this sort of group Work. It might happen that a group member, unknown to him/herself, could be mediumistic. He might start bringing through fabulous stuff—exciting, true. People are swept off their feet. Next time it doesn't happen. But everyone, including the medium, wants it to happen. The medium obliges, or the medium may even see a chance of getting what he wants through a little bit of falsification—mediums are like that. And because the medium perhaps appears to be hobnobbing with Mr. G, even the group leader may think he has to bow to the medium. It can become a very tricky business. [Dec 28, 1987]

I was beginning to have misgivings about how things were going in the new group, and I was becoming critical of what we were doing. Ashish had earlier said to me that group work was preliminary work (Gurdjieffian work is usually capitalized as "Work." Where I use the word often—as here—I will revert to a small "w."). Perhaps looking for support, I asked him what he meant by "preliminary." His reply was not supportive.

A.   Preliminary work: Physical exercises, tables of hydrogens to be learned (and corresponding things in other disciplines) are presented in a way that makes them or seems to make them reflect the spirit and its harmonies. People in whom the spirit is urging them to seek begin by being attracted to this sort of thing. Even educated and well-read people will say: "I am attracted to the spiritual path. But what should I DO?" Tell them to identify their self-awareness, and they will go blank and run away. The exercises and disciplines are designed to develop their potential self-awareness and to wean them, slowly, from ego-orientation to a trans-egotistic orientation—i. e., they must begin to understand that what they seek is beyond themselves and calls for some sort of emotional dedication. This is what I call the preliminary work level.

At some point in the process, if the person sticks to it, the inner potential develops sufficiently for the aim to become clearer. Having been driven by an inarticulate feeling, a few people begin to get a bit of clarity on what it is all about. They begin to work in a different way, because they are not now just doing what they are told do to, but are beginning to understand/feel what it is they are seeking and why these exercises are effective. I would call this the beginning of real work. However, if people begin to harbor the idea that they are now superior beings, all the gains are lost. At this point one might qualify as a sort of junior instructor, helping with the group work. (Of course, there are lots of unqualified group instructors.)

So don't think that the G work as such is "preliminary." In any group there will be a preliminary stage. Some groups do not go beyond that, but G's teaching contains all that is really needed—provided that there is someone in the group able to understand it. You see the running of the group as important. Indeed it is. But you would not now say that without the group, G's teaching has no relevance to your life. Without the group, the beginner's involvement would be at best theoretical. You recognize that the group work has helped to bring you to the point where your "glimpses of truth" are a confirmation of your efforts. It is a recognizable change, even if it is not a sharply defined division. [July 7, 1989]

Some years before, Ashish had made some remarks of a highly pertinent nature about group work, which I will include at this point:

A.   The turning point in a man's life may come when he asks what the whole thing is about. Does "harder work" mean simply performing the exercises with greater intensity? Does it mean subjecting oneself to greater inter-personal friction? To what end? Is it merely to achieve greater freedom from automatism? Let one be entirely free. Then what? It is true that for most of the newcomers to the groups, conforming to the set exercises is important. It is usually only after those exercises have done their work that further questions can be asked. One difficulty in asking these questions is that they seem to deny the loyalty to the particular teaching (as understood). Loyalty may have powerfully held a man through the periods of despair and difficulty. How can he now be disloyal to something to which he feels he owes so much? If he sees that his loyalty is and must be to the essence of the teaching, and not to its form, then he can go ahead. In India there is a saying that the disciple's final attainment requires him to put his foot on his guru's head, as a stepping-stone—the ultimate insult. In Japanese Zen, "If you meet the Buddha on the path, kill him." The point being that a man has to get past misconceptions of the true nature of the teacher/teaching. [June 25, 1983]

It had happened again. I was always surprised when it happened. The reader, knowing me by now better than I knew myself then, will not be so surprised. The usual irreconcilable differences had surfaced between myself and the Gurdjieff leadership, in this case between myself and Irving, my friend with whom I'd founded in 1986 the Gurdjieff Institute of Florida.

By the spring of 1990, the relationship between Irving and myself had deteriorated badly on account of the usual (for me) defining issue of whether psychological therapy and counseling should be a part of the Gurdjieffian group Work. I believed that it should be, and relied for support on two statements in the Gurdjieff literature. One was a quote from Gurdjieff in Ouspensky's *In Search of the Miraculous*: "It is necessary to see and to study identifying to its very roots in oneself." The other was a quote from Gurdjieff in his published talks: "A man can develop his hidden capacities and powers only by cleaning his machine of the dirt that has clogged it in the course of his life."

For twelve years, Ashish had been telling me (in the context of the esoteric mode analysis of my own dreams) that it was necessary to see, and to clean one's psyche of, all the psychological garbage that one had accumulated in oneself since early childhood. How could you do this without talking psychology and employing psychology, even to the analysis of dreams?

I'd thought that my friend and co-leader in the Gurdjieff group was starting to appreciate this. I was very much mistaken. The more I advocated psychological probing, the more opposed to it Irving became. In the orthodox Gurdjieff lineage to which he belonged, you were simply supposed to observe the various negative emotions with which you had identified, and in those moments of observation come back to awareness of yourself through the physical sensation of the body. Other leaders of this same lineage (to which we had both belonged, and with which leaders we had both remained in contact) systematically bolstered his belief. But I'd become surer and surer that I was right.

On the one hand, Ashish did not take my quarrels with Irving or the Gurdjieff group leadership very seriously at all. I had written to him telling him that I thought I'd had, in one of my meditations, an intimation of the unitive vision, but wondering if, since I wasn't sure if that was what it was or not, I should simply dismiss the experience.

A.   Your meditation experiences constitute your data for "proof." Yet, despite the fact that you "experience" some sort of unity of being, of all things being "vibration" or "life energy," you still doubt, asking, "Is all this imagination?" It has not made you see this affair with Gurdjieff group leaders as being utterly trivial by comparison. You have learned what it is to be taken beyond yourself, yet you insist on identifying to the hilt with Sy Ginsburg's personality, its hurt feelings, its doubts, its self opinion. So where does your work lie? Surely it lies in accepting the truth of what you are shown, and in trying to transfer your identity from the

person of Sy to the essential being beyond Sy and beyond everyone and everything. What you have so far cannot, by definition,
be the ultimate experience, for that experience leaves no room for
doubt or dissatisfaction. It has not transformed you. But it cannot transform you until you are ready for transformation.

You have to train yourself to live as if all that you now know
about the unity of being were true in actual fact. Were it true to
you, your co-leader's behaviour would not touch you. You would
see Sy getting hurt only in those areas of life where he still asserts
his individuated separateness from the transcendental unity. Where
he acts as a separate entity, he must disturb the harmony both
within and without himself. The pain of the disturbance will act
to bring him back to his essence. [July 22, 1990]

On the other hand, when I gave Ashish by letter all the details
of my present disagreement with Irving, he responded with a mag-
isterial letter of his own setting forth clearly all the issues involved.

A.   The issue seems to be that you have aroused antagonism by
equating psychology with the work of Freud, Jung & Co. Let us
call this "modern psychology." Modern psychology in general
adopts the materialistic standpoint, especially in its psychiatric form,
and so denies the real existence of all that is represented by the
word soul. Ancient psychology is the science of the soul. In this
sense, Buddhism is known as the first psychological religion, because Buddha taught the causes of sorrow and their removal in
terms of states of mind and feeling. Thus, every teacher of the
inner work has been a psychologist. Our difficulty lies in the fact
that modern psychology has achieved remarkable insights into the
working of the subconscious mind-feeling complex and the effects
it has on the feelings and thoughts we are conscious of. All this is
of immense usefulness to anyone struggling to control his mind,
to deal with negative emotions, to distinguish between his essential
awareness and the sort of awareness that is present in what G calls
"sleep." But we cannot afford to use this knowledge without distinguishing it from the uses to which modern psychology puts it.

There are many fields in which this distinction has constantly to be made: interpretations of history, interpretations of archeological discoveries, interpretations of scientific discoveries, etc., etc. Established facts have to be distinguished from theories built on those facts. In our field we can treat as fact Freud's dictum that dreams are the royal road into the unconscious; but we do not therefore have to accept Freud's theories about ego and id, etc., or to accept the academic flavor that dulls so much of his work. Freud did not discover dreams; he gave some structure to the area of (un)consciousness from which dreams (and much of our compulsive behavior) take their rise. Dreams and visions have provided seekers with the data for their search since the beginning of time.

Our work is so difficult that we need every bit of help we can get. It really does not matter where or from whom we take help, provided that we have enough intelligence and a clear enough view of our goal to be able to take help that is consonant with our aim and to reject those components that are contrary to it.

It is obvious that danger lies in any inability to distinguish between the consonant and the contrary. The prestige of the modern psychologists is such that they are thought so profoundly wise that we must either believe them totally or not at all. On the other hand, we ourselves want to use their perceptions but to reject their conclusions.

In respect of modern psychology there are at least three classes of people we are concerned with:

Firstly, there are the pathological cases, people who are so disturbed that they are out of touch with reality and, at most, can be helped to lead "normal" lives.

Such people often feel attracted to the inner path, but it is dangerous to have anything to do with them. They should be advised to seek medical/psychological help.

Secondly, there are the people who may have considerable potential for the Work, but who are so tangled up with traumas, compulsions or emotional blocks of one sort or another that they cannot work with any sense of real purpose and joy. If we ourselves cannot provide the insights to help them, they may benefit from psychoanalysis, psychotherapy, etc. In this case we try to recommend a practitioner who is personally sympathetic to the Work. He will not aim to turn a confused patient into a well-adapted moron.

Thirdly, we have the reasonably well-adapted people who appear to be fit for the Work, but whom anyone can see to be tied up in the usual knots of parental "fixations," inhibited emotions, insecurities and all the rest of the desires and fears which make control of the mind so difficult a task that many of them despair. These are the ones who can benefit from psychological insight, but who should not be sent to professional practitioners. In order to qualify for practice, professionals have had to subscribe to the non-spiritual ethic of their particular schools, and this rubs off on their patients.

We have also to guard against the mistaken assumption that psychoanalysis can be equated with the Work. We want the analytic tools to help us in our work—specifically to help free us from the compulsions which, unless seen and dealt with, control our minds. But the Work itself is something quite different. Similarly, analysis helps us to still the mind, but a still mind is only a step towards transcending the mind. I must also add that there is no reason to suppose that psychological qualifications would be useful to a group leader. Just as wide reading of mysticism, mythology, religion, and other subjects is of value to anyone in this work, so is a familiarity with modern psychology. But one no more needs academic qualification in modern psychology to help people with their psychological problems vis-à-vis the inner Work, than one needs to be a priest or a professor to be inspired by mysticism and myth.

It also seems to be a fact that modern psychology suits the psyche of the modern man; and this is partly because it breaks through the old conventions in much the same way that modern life has broken from the old conventions. However, it is also plain that men have followed this path throughout the ages without the help of this particular set of insights we call modern psychology. Our point, therefore, is not that psychology is a sine qua non, but that it should not be rejected out of hand or its usefulness denied to people who could benefit from it.

For yourself, you must appreciate that you have been introduced to psychology as a useful adjunct to the Work. The people who are opposing you have been introduced to it as classical psychology, i.e., studying the development of intelligence in babies or the learning ability of rats, as psychiatry, i.e., treatment of mental states by drugs, shock therapy, etc., and as a lot of daft theories about the mind. They have read Sunday magazine articles, but not the original texts. You must either do a lot of work to introduce them to the non-professional aspects of modern psychology, or you must act as the sly man and use your tools without mentioning the word psychology. While it is very obvious to anyone who has open eyes that the whole of G's self-remembering, dealing with negative emotions and many other points are strictly psychological in the true sense, there are none so blind as those who refuse to see.

On the matter of dream interpretation, I checked in Nicoll's *Psychological Commentaries*, Volume I, where there are two talks. He gave the talks after meeting C. G. Jung, but he goes into a series of painful contortions in trying to present the case that there are some sorts of dream that can provide guidance from the higher aspects of our being. It is obvious that he feels he is saying something, which may be treated as heretical and will get him into trouble. Much of the rest of the books are excellent, if horribly verbose, but in places makes me wonder at the low level of intelligence and culture in an audience that requires such crudely simplistic explanations. However, if you are to get on with your co-leader, you need to make an effort to understand the condition of his mind. I can give an example of my own. [Here, Ashish describes the change in his feelings regarding Krishnamurti. I've quoted the passage in full in the chapter, "The Reflected Glory of Objective Consciousness."] It would not have been a conscious concealment. An emotional inability to criticize my teachers would have blocked my perceptions. However, my faulty position would have shown up in obvious bigotry.

With the hierarchical build up of the G Work groups, heresy is a real issue. If you two were true breakaways, you would have only your own mental hang-ups to deal with. But you both want some sort of official sanction so that you can be recognized as a true Gurdjieff group.

...It is clear that Irving's reactions have brought out some of your own negativity. While this lasts it throws doubt on the rightness of breaking away. From what you say it seems that he regards the G teaching as sufficient unto itself. Properly understood, so it is. But that is a dangerous line of argument, for it implies superior insight into what G meant by his teaching. If one really wants to upset Gurdjieff group leaders, and to insure that they will never agree to changes and introductions, such a claim of superior insight will do it. After all, many schools can lead their students to mystical experience without using the tools we want to use.

So my advice, albeit on inadequate grounds, is not to break away on account of your current anger and frustration. You must use the very methods you recommend to settle your mind. Get yourself clear about the distinction between the science of the soul and the pseudo science of the practitioners of a branch of social medicine which serves the interests of unregenerate society but not the interest of the Spirit. (O. K. in the last analysis all things are divine and all serve "His" purpose. But even "He" has priorities, and so draws distinctions.) Then talk to Irving again. If you admit that you were wrong in failing to distinguish adequately between the different forms of psychology, he might be ready to reconsider his own views.

It has to be emphasized that we need the tools, but not the men who fashioned these tools; they use them to help people who are so screwed up that they cannot even manage their daily lives; we intend to use them for liberating our minds from the compulsive forces which act on them. The two uses are as different as a school for retarded children and a post-graduate course in astrophysics.

I would also refer to a very early textbook on the study of insanity. The author suggests that the intention is not really to learn how to cure the insane, noble though that intention might

124

be. In the insane we see the exaggerations or caricatures of tendencies in the normal mind. Yet those tendencies may be so slight that we would not identify them if we had not seen their caricatures. The study of insanity therefore helps us to understand ourselves better. Since that book was written, prior to World War One, the emphasis of psychology has gone onto "curing" disturbed people. We are concerned with the higher sanity. [June 20, 1990]

The upshot of all this was that Irving and I would soon split, and in late 1990, with a few people, I would organize another less formal Gurdjieff group, using some of the traditional group techniques but also engaging in psychological probing for the purpose of "cleaning our machines." This included working one-on-one with others in the examination of dreams.

In the course of our correspondence, Ashish and I had been involved in an ongoing discussion of certain key aspects of my journey in search of objective consciousness or the unitive vision. In the coming chapters, I'll take these topics up separately. The first is Masters.

Gurdjieff, *Life Is Real Only Then, When "I Am,"* 135.
Ouspensky, *Miraculous*, 355-356.
Seabrook, 166.
Ouspensky, *Miraculous*, 150.
Gurdjieff, *Views from the Real World*, 50.

8

Masters Within and Without

Ronald Nixon, who would become Sri Krishna Prem, had stumbled upon Theosophy while a student at Cambridge, and been deeply influenced by its doctrines.

The reader will recall that Dr. Gyanendra Nath Chakravarti, at whose home Ronald Nixon stayed while he taught at the University of Lucknow, had been Secretary General of the Indian branch of the Theosophical Society, and that he and his wife Monica Devi—who would become Sri Yashoda Mai—had known Theosophical Society leader Annie Besant well and even traveled with her.

Thus was the Mirtola ashram, founded by Sri Yashoda Mai and Sri Krishna Prem in 1930, richly watered at its roots by the powerful influence of Theosophy.

Madhava Ashish, as well, had been fascinated by Theosophy while still a young and fledgling monk. He and Sri Krishna Prem had devoted much of their time to writing learned commentaries on that bewildering touchstone of theosophical learning, the *Stanzas of Dyzan* as interpreted by Madame Blavatsky in *The Secret Doctrine*. These commentaries make up *Man, the Measure of All Things* and *Man, Son of Man*—the very books that had brought me to Madhava Ashish in the first place. I've already remarked on the intense loyalty Madhava Ashish felt for those theosophical doctrines and teachings that had profoundly influenced him in his early years and set him on the path to becoming who he was. As I've earlier quoted, he told me in a letter that it had taken him some time to forgive Krishnamurti for his early apostasy vis-à-vis the Theosophical Society.

One of the central tenets of the Society was a belief in a hierarchy of discarnate "ascended" Masters, each of whom (as interpreted by later Theosophists) was somehow associated with one of the heavenly bodies of our Solar System. Given the importance of the early Society to Prem and Ashish, and the intense loyalty they felt toward it, it's perhaps not surprising that Ashish always took great care to pay homage to this hierarchy. As I've previously mentioned, holidays were celebrated at Mirtola for the birthdays of all the Masters recognized there, including Buddha, Djwhal Khul, Gurdjieff, Jesus Christ, Koot Houmi, Krishna, Maurya, the Mirtola gurus Sri Yashoda Mai and Sri Krishna Prem—and now, I suppose, Sri Madhava Ashish. There were others, but I've forgotten their names.

(Ashish displayed a similar intense loyalty toward Gurdjieff. In the pursuit of a guru after World War Two that had finally brought him to Mirtola, he had been greatly helped by the Englishwoman Ethel Merston, who years before had sat at the feet of Gurdjieff in France.)

While Ashish was devoted to the Theosophical Society's hierarchy of Masters, some of whom had been mortal, others not, he had, like Krishna Prem before him, voiced two reservations concerning this pantheon of great souls. The first was that we ought not to think that we could communicate regularly and easily with these now-discarnate entities. Ashish had written in *Man, Son of Man* that "all information coming from or through the subtle or 'astral' realms is liable to deformation or alteration, the cause of which is usually considered an objective property of those realms themselves." In theosophical mythology, a Tibetan named Djwhal Khul, or "D. K.," is believed to be responsible for the *Stanzas of Dzyan*. Ashish acknowledged that it was not impossible that the same Djwhal Khul, in spirit form, could be responsible for the writings channeled through the celebrated early twentieth-century medium/writer Alice Bailey. But he was quick to point out that, even if this were so "...I suspect that Bailey added a lot of her own ideas. This is inevitable and even desirable. The difficult question is how truly did she report from D. K., and how near or distant from the truth were her own speculations. You can ask the same questions about the *Man* books [*Man, the Measure of All Things* and *Man, Son of Man*]. This is why we [Prem and Ashish] wrote that the commentary has to stand on its own. Saying that inspiration and instruction was given by D. K. and others would add nothing to the validity of the work. We know to whom we owe it, but we are not going to make him answer for our misunderstandings and mistakes. By the same token, don't hold D. K. responsible for Alice Bailey's vaporings" [Jan. 7, 1992].

The second reservation Ashish expressed regarding "spiritual hierarchy Master worship" was that these beings finally were only reflections of our own being, and that the true Master to be sought and worshipped was that which dwelt in our own hearts.

Still, Ashish was always very sensitive to the historical concerns of the Theosophical Society. As he explained it to me: "The particular characteristic of the TS is its direct inspiration by the Masters or bodhisattvas. They fielded HPB and stood behind her all her life. G was one of them, which is why his teaching is in the same tradition....The burning question for the TS (and for the G groups) is whether anyone exists within or without the movement who is, and knows that he is, connected with the Masters, who is dedicated to and is travelling their path, who is dedicated to them personally, whose mind is free from bigotry, who has at least an intellectual grasp of the transcendental truths, who has the capacity to refer directly to the Masters for guidance and inspiration, and who is ready to accept the immense burden of responsibility. This may be a rather tall order, so tall that one suspects he/she would not be found without the Masters' intervention." [Dec. 12, 1988].

But, theosophical subtleties aside, I was fascinated, obsessed even, by this whole subject of Masters, Secret Masters who spoke to mankind, who controlled mankind, who were ready to tell us something about the Self! It was a tantalizing concept. I couldn't get it out of my mind. I remembered the images from Peter Brook's film of *Meetings with Remarkable Men*, of Gurdjieff, blindfolded, on horseback, with another seeker and guided by four Kara-Kirghez tribesmen, riding across the rocky deserts of Turkestan on his way to the secret monastery of the Brotherhood of the Sarmoung. Sri Krishna Prem himself, in *Initiation into Yoga: An Introduction to the Spiritual Life*, had written of the fascination of such quests: "All over the world and in all ages there has been a tradition of a wonderful hidden Knowledge and of a secret path that led to that Knowledge..." This was the path down which Gurdjieff had travelled. Arrived at the fortress-like monastery of the Sarmoung Brotherhood surrounded by its tall unbroken wall, G had watched sacred dances being performed—an ancient training for priestesses, he tells us in his book, and we know these were the same dances that Gurdjieff would one day introduce to his classes when he arrived back in the West...

But was he telling the truth? Or was he speaking allegorically? You had to think it was the latter when you reflected on Gurdjieff's mesmerizing description of the three apparatuses made of ebony inlaid with ivory and mother-of-pearl that stood against the wall of the room in which the dances took place. Each of these apparatuses consisted of a single column resting on a tripod from which seven arms projected. Each arm branched out into seven smaller arms of varying lengths. The segments of each arm were connected one inside the other by two hollow ivory balls, enabling them to move in any direction.

The balls contained inscriptions, and Gurdjieff writes that beside each apparatus stood "a little cupboard, filled with square plates of some metal, on which were also certain inscriptions...these plates were copies...[of]...the originals, made of pure gold...the plates and the apparatuses themselves were at least four thousand five hundred years old..." The inscriptions on the plates matched inscriptions on the balls. Each inscription contained a coded dance movement. When the balls were "set" according to a coded plate, the

129

dancers stood before the apparatus for hours as, "regulated in this way," it slowly and faithfully duplicated a posture which the dancers could "learn to sense and remember" as they watched.

Did such ancient esoteric knowledge really exist? It was a subject I couldn't drop; and, late in 1979, I asked Ashish outright: "Is there literally an inner circle of humanity, as spoken about in the Gurdjieff Work, or Masters as in theosophical terminology, who are beings of higher worlds clandestinely embodied on this planet?"

A.   Now look! Reading through your stuff, I find myself asking, what's the real question behind your interest in "beings of higher worlds clandestinely embodied on this planet?" Okay, I mean, for short, let's call them Masters.

What I suspect is that it may go something like this. If all the talk about the spiritual path is true, that there is a spiritual goal in which the individual consciously participates, without being lost in its transcendent unity, if all that is true, then someone must have attained it. If no one has attained it, then have we any confirmation of its truth? But if someone has attained it, then in some way he's still around. Now if I could find such a man, he would constitute a proof, a demonstration of the truth that would set all my doubts at rest. And in addition, I could then be quite sure I was getting true teaching straight from the horse's mouth. The truth!

And of course a master, wherever he is, does indeed constitute a confirmation of the truth. He is his own demonstration. But it's a demonstration only if I can perceive the truth he demonstrates. Only if I can perceive that truth, will my doubts be set at rest. If I don't cultivate my perception of the truth, then surely what a Master teaches is of no more value to me than what a charlatan says.

What are the criteria? Sai Baba's not a Master merely on account of his phenomena, even if he's one at all. What about teaching? Can we take a man's teaching as a criterion of his status? Well, how can one tell the truth of a teaching without putting it into practice? What about numenosity, the sort of charisma of a person, the numenosity of a vision, of an experience? Is that proof of validity? Maybe, but can I distinguish between the truly noumenous on the one hand or the euphoria induced by drugs, by hypnosis, by psychosis?

You see, one can go on doubting. I can churn doubts out by the thousand because it is the nature of the mind to churn out doubts. You see, certainty doesn't belong to the mind. Even what we call rational certainty. The certainty is a feeling. Feeling belongs to the heart. I don't just sort of mean young people getting emotional. I mean, the inner heart, the core of man's being.

The problem of having doubts is a problem that belongs to people who have good minds, good, reliable, clear, analytical minds. Like yours! Your mind has served you well in many areas. It's your tried and trusted friend, your developed faculty. Do you expect it to serve you in the same way in your search for inner certainty? But you see, as I've said before, certainty is not of the mind. The mind's a lawyer. It argues, actively argues in favor of the client who pays. Now if it is paid by you, Sy Ginsburg, then it will throw up doubts, rational doubts which will support Sy Ginsburg's claim to rights over his own being. But you see, when it's paid by the Self, when it acts in the service of the Self, it will assert the Self's rights over the being which Sy Ginsburg has usurped.

This is the whole game of finding the true person, the true identity, not the personality of this life only, but the identity with what has been there through the whole series of lives. The mind can't serve two masters. Either it serves Sy or it serves the Self. If you want it to serve the Self, the power has to be transferred. What will effect the transfer of power? Well, the simple answer is, your heart, your unexploited, unspoiled faculty.

In any case, the existence of Masters is only really of concern to you if you accept the Master's path, the path of compassion, the path of complete self-transcendence. So, if you see the point and are prepared to dedicate your life to that path, oddly, whether you understand it or not, then you do open yourself to the possibility of coming into contact with such persons. The whole question of recognizing Masters seems to be a mistake. What we need is contact with a man who gives us the teachings suited to our heart's demands, a man who can master our hearts. The recognition in this case is an individual act, taken on one's own responsibility without dependence on what amounts to the public claim, "This man is a Master," or this man is an avatar, therefore I am justified in following his teaching.

Of course there are Masters, Sy. There are lots of them.

Where? Wherever man's given his heart to them.

How to find them? Get past the glittering polish of your mind and make space for them in the inner darkness, that's dark only by comparison with the outer glare.

Where do you find them? At their wish.

Why? Why does any man love?

When will they appear physically to you? In dreams? In visions? That's up to them.

How will one recognize them? That, too, is up to them.

How will it benefit you? Well, if one thinks about one's own personal benefit, one won't get within shouting distance of anyone.

Give your heart to their path and maybe, maybe, if you deserve it, they will help you to become like them. [Dec. 22, 1979]

But the subject of Masters—of a secret society of Masters somehow in charge of mankind!—continued to fascinate me, to practically possess me. Perhaps I would scale down my longing to find out about the secret abode of mankind's Masters; perhaps I would give it another name; but some three years later I would still be hankering after a concrete Shangri La or Shambala, although by now I was euphemistically calling these places "esoteric centers."

I asked Ashish: "How should I understand the importance, if any, of being connected to the 'esoteric center' as expressed, for example, in *In Search of the Miraculous*? I have by this time been disabused of the notion that there is a hidden 'Shambala' in Tibet or elsewhere. But Ouspensky wrote of the teachings of the Work having been connected through Russian masons of the eighteenth century with several earlier authors; for instance, with Dr. Fludd. I'm confused by such statements in the literature of the Work.

On the surface at least, these statements posit a kind of esoteric center with a hierarchy of beings within beings."

A.   Do I have to say anything more about "esoteric centers"? Have I got to wrap it all up in Tibetan monasteries, Sufi monasteries, secret caverns and mysterious meetings, before you can accept those men as real? Enter the cavern of your heart and place a throne there for them to occupy with their glory. What other esoteric center is there? What is this academic nonsense about terminology and Dr. Fludd? What has it to do with the immediate presence of the spirit?

The path to the source of being lies through your own heart. You will gain nothing by tracing lines of tradition through the centuries. It is not tradition. It is present fact.

In your letter of June 5, you attached a copy of an Ouspensky diagram with reference to the esoteric center. What hit me in the eye as I turned to it was not the diagram, but the words at the head of the page (204): "No one can ascend onto a higher step until he places another man in his own place. What a man has received he must immediately give back; only then can he receive more. Otherwise from him will be taken even what he has already been given." [June 12, 1982]

I also asked, "In this Work, I keep coming across references to secret societies. Not only is there a secret or private group within the Theosophical Society—the Esoteric School—but there seem to be secret societies within many spiritual traditions such as the Masons and the builders of the Gothic cathedrals. I don't care for all the secrecy."

A.   The thing about secret societies connected with Gothic cathedrals seems to me as doubtful as secret monasteries in central Asia. Gurdjieff, Blavatsky...have played on people's susceptibilities in this respect. The purpose seems to be to arouse the sense of there being something wonderful and mysterious actually here in this world, as an introduction to the actual mystery which is considerably more subtle. It appears to me that there was a period in the history of human evolution—the evolution of the psyche—when the spiritual archetypes came to expression in form through fairly simple craftsmen. Their ability to produce correspondences to the inner harmony did not mean that they knew that harmony, any more than a poet has integrated what he expresses. Their capacity to act as vehicles for expression of the inner was not distorted, as it now so often is, by the later development of egotistic individualism. Some proportions, like those of the golden rectangle, were undoubtedly known and consciously included in architectural designs, but I take leave to doubt whether the proportions of the Gothic cathedrals were entirely planned. The guilds had their "secrets," but I doubt their being true "schools" in G's sense. [March 21, 1980]

Later that year, in commenting on my dreams, Ashish had told me that "the more you identify yourself with your true being, the more hope you may have of invoking the protection of the guardians of the truth." Just what did he mean by that? I asked.

A.   "Guardians of the truth": It is a plain fact that, in the event of the sort of world turmoil in which millions get killed, individuals whose lives are given to the teachers (Mahatmas, Masters, Saints or whatever) can often be saved by their intervention, while others tend to get killed or not on the basis of statistical averages. This means neither that everyone with an inner life is saved, nor that everyone saved has an inner life.

In particular, if one is genuinely identified with the Masters' family or community, then by the same token one is not identified with Jews, Christians, Moslems, Americans, Indians, or any other social, religious or ethnic group. Consequently, one is not automatically identified with them by others. No one needs to be seen as representing a particular target of attack. This makes it easier for the Masters to help.

However, it has to be well understood that the sort of giving or dedication spoken of is not in order to be saved from such situations. They are the ones who decide whether you are worth saving. For oneself, one asks only to be theirs, whether in this body or out of it. [Jan.15, 1983].

That silenced me for a time. Then, in mid-June of next year, I returned to the subject of Masters—it was stronger than I was—though I had a new angle this time. I wrote: "There is an idea in our Gurdjieff group, based on the literature, that one needs a direct connection with the 'inner circle of humanity' and that such a connection exists within the Gurdjieff Work only through Gurdjieff and, in turn, with the hierarchical leadership of the Gurdjieff lineage with which I have been connected. In the Theosophical Society there is a similar idea. It is said there by some people that one's connection with the Masters comes through the outer head of the Esoteric School of Theosophy. Does this idea make sense?"

I will not say Ashish lost his temper. But I sensed a certain abbreviation of his patience:

A. As for this matter of the inner connection being achieved through your Gurdjieff group hierarchical leadership than through Mr. Gurdjieff, to the center of all things, nonsense! It's complete bosh. These are things which get put out in the vested interests of the hierarchy, i.e., "to keep the power in my control." All right, perhaps they feel they've got to guard against people making claims to have a direct connection which bypasses the lot of them and makes them irrelevant, and then trying to mislead, break up the group, and take off their own followers. Well, that would be an abuse of the thing. If anyone said that, without very good reason, one would say that, "No, brother, you've got it wrong. You haven't really found your connection." A person who does find his own connection does not break away from another man who has a connection. It's ridiculous.

But you can't sort of boost your ego on the thing that "I've got a connection with someone, and now I'm going to find my own connection." It's only that if you have prepared yourself, are truly trying to let go of your damned ego and find what is within, then every man is capable of making his connection. Often enough, I know, this does work in a sense through somebody. We've used the silly analogy of joining a club where someone has to introduce you, to stand guardian for you, to guarantee that you are genuinely trying to do something. And also that there is someone there who will keep you in check and distinguish between things that actually come through from your fantasies and so protect you. But hierarchy? No! In some sense this is like asking you to believe that G himself can be sort of cut off from you if your group leader has a fit of spleen or something of that sort.

As I suggest, if one gives the group leader the benefit of the doubt, it can be a try-on. I mean, if you're threatened with this cutting off, will you simply say, "Well, I won't put up with it, I'll leave?" Or will you crawl and grovel or what? Will you say, "But the point is that this sort of thing were it so would be so irrational, that I can't accept it." In that sense it makes you strengthen your own determination to go on irrespective of the personality characteristics of the weaknesses of the particular person you're working under. [July 14, 1984]

I was still a very long way, in 1984, from letting go of my damned ego. The businessman in me wanted to boost that ego by finding a connection with the Masters, and this would go on for several more years. But Ashish seemed to have infinite patience, as will be seen in his responses to my questions about Masters that continued through 1989. I wondered to him in another letter: If you were guided by a discarnate Master, could that really work? Didn't you have to have a personal, in-the-flesh—even a loving—relationship with him? Like you had with a real, living Master—?

A.   I can't say it's impossible to get teaching from the Masters without feeling love for them, but I sense the absence of love makes it difficult to form the sort of relationship which is the best setting for the teaching. I know one cannot compel oneself to love; but one can certainly decide to approach with an attitude permitting respect to grow into affection, and affection to grow into love.

The essence of such an attitude lies in not wanting to get something for oneself, but wanting to pass beyond oneself, and so trying to surrender one's egotistic selfhood into the hands of something or someone one trusts—and trusts because one loves. [Jan. 24, 1989]

I asked: "If one reads the *Stanzas of Dzyan* and *Beelzebub's Tales* literally, it is implied that Masters have had prior experience on other places than earth, for example the planet Venus and the star system Sirius. How literally should I take such speculations?"

A. It may be a fact that some of the Masters derive their being from other worlds than this one. But too much attention given to this speculation can lead to the false view that they are so special as to have no relevance to the lives of ordinary mortals like us. In fact, so many of them have arisen from the ordinary mortals of this planet, and from so many different races and cultures on this planet, that they provide us with examples of what we should and can become here and now. [Jan. 24, 1989]

If this was not exactly an answer, it was a tantalizing hint—but no more so than what he would say some months later:

A. Any one of those beings (if it has any meaning to speak of these being more than one essential being) can look out through the eyes of any existing form that has eyes. There is a series of masks, shaped in the familiar forms of Gurdjieff, Jesus, the Buddha, Maurya, etc., so that idiots like us can recognize them, through which the one power can communicate with us. Yet there is a sense in which "The Great Russian Bodhisattva" whom we last knew as Gurdjieff, at a certain level, is distinguishable from other bodhisattvas. It is a mystery not worth unraveling from the level of ignorance. [Oct. 11, 1989]

By this time, I had been having experiences of channeling (see Chapter Thirteen); apparently, I had been listening to the words

137

of a channeled Master named Pastor. Or was the channeled entity I was listening to—if real at all—a being less than a master but greater than a disciple? I wanted to know about these hierarchies of the discarnate. I asked Ashish: "What or who is a guide? Pastor refers to himself as a guide as distinguished from a Master. How does a guide differ from a guru and/or a Master?"

A.   The Master is one with the spirit. He exemplifies the final attainment. He is what is as yet only a partially realized potential in your own being. You can "recognize" him only to the extent that you can feel the responses in your essence when like answers to like. G is a Master.

The sort of person who teaches in the world, and to whom people may refer as "guru," may be only someone who has got far enough ahead to be helpful to those who follow. Because he is learning, followers may find it easier to learn from him, for he is still in touch with the difficulties of life as they appear to someone in life. If this "guru" can recognize the Master, he may act as a go-between, carrying the Master's inspiration and messages to those who cannot yet communicate. Communication is important, not only for the directly personal teaching which may be given, but also because one has to learn to listen with the non-egotistic and subtle "spiritual" part of oneself. By doing it, that part develops.

If such a guru has not completed the work when he leaves the body, he may still act as a teacher, keeping in touch with his disciples and helping them even if they cannot see/hear him. A dedicated disciple after death may be encouraged to go on working by trying to help others, by conveying the Master's or guru's messages, until it is time for him to take birth again.

Remember G's saying that one has to put someone onto the step one is standing on before one can move up to the next. This is not to be taken too literally. The point is that dedication to all that inheres in the unity of being will result in a sort of altruism which leads one to help others—who are oneself. Helping others, even before one has that transcendental perception, helps to attune one to its truth.

Then, both in the world and out of it, there are a whole lot of people of varying degrees of true and false perception and motivation who, from a mixture of selfless and selfish motives, teach some sort of "spirituality." Examples are the hundreds of Californian gurus and more of the same sort everywhere in the world, and monks of every persuasion, plus numerous do-gooders, psychics and world reformers. A lot of the spirit guides are drawn from this rather soupy pool. And this is again complicated by jokers who find it amusing to intrude in séances, posing as great teachers. This is why one has to distrust psychic communications and, even when genuine stuff appears to be coming through, to scrutinize each communication for distortions. Any one phenomenon may give one certainty in the fact of such phenomena, and so be valuable. But the content has to be distinguished from the fact: a lying phenomenon is as real as a true phenomenon. One may need to see giraffes, rhinoceri and mambas before believing in their existence. But one ought not to risk being bitten by a mamba before believing it to have a fatally poisonous bite. [July 7, 1989]

Some time earlier, in the course of our ongoing discussion of Masters, I had become involved with yet another channeled entity, though this time my involvement was more scholarly than not. This was when I had left my Gurdjieff group, and then, missing the Gurdjieff-inspired, uniquely enhanced sense of community that is a part of such a group, I had gone back—but only briefly; shortly thereafter leaving once and for all to create with a friend a more rural Gurdjieff group in the wilds just north of Miami.

In the intervals between Gurdjieff groups, I had become practically infatuated with the writings of the rather well-known channeled entity Djwhal Khul, or D.K., who, in the early part of the twentieth century, spoke over a thirty-year period through a medium with Theosophical Society connections named Alice Bailey.

I mentioned Djwhal Khul earlier in this chapter. He was one of the Theosophical Society hierarchy of Masters whose birthday was celebrated every year at the Mirtola ashram, it being presumed by Theosophists that Djwhal Khul had really lived and was one

139

and the same with he who had written the actual *Stanzas of Dyzan* several millennia ago (I think they had to guess at the date of his birthday). It may have been because of this connection with Ashish and all that Mirtola stood for that, at that time, I began to study the Alice Bailey "teachings" with great care. I asked Ashish what he thought about what I was doing. His reply was unequivocal.

A.   In comparison to H.P.B. and her connection with the Masters, I find Alice Bailey coming a poor second. She appears to have had some sort of contact, but I find her stuff extraordinarily confused. H.P.B. was by no means perfect, but her dedication was utterly real. Alice Bailey seems to have taken too much to herself—hence the confusion.

There is a lure in all this cosmic esotericism which serves the purpose of catching fish. The fish that are truly hooked, get pulled out of the water—a painful process. The others follow the lure around, thinking they are learning all sorts of interesting things about the universe, yet missing the point, which is to get out. But there is no harm in sampling her stuff. [Dec. 27, 1984]

I had told Ashish: "I have been thinking of joining the 'Arcane School,' which is part of the organization that promotes the Alice Bailey teachings. This is conducted largely by correspondence, and, so far as I know, does not provide for the person-to-person contacts that I enjoy. I do get these contacts, however, from belonging to the local Theosophical Society. The Bailey teachings point to the necessity of man's effort to identify with 'the solar logos' within which 'we live and move and have our being,' and this, in my view, is in agreement with the theoretical part of what Gurdjieff taught. Bailey goes into matters like the star system Sirius and other galaxies. It is all very interesting, but I haven't seen indications in the Bailey material of instruction on the key practical work of increasing one's self-awareness. One theoretical question: Can one 'get out' of the universe or only the solar system?"

You would have thought that I was prepared to go just about anywhere in the universe but inward (it being my difficulties in turning inward to detach from the ego that had had much to do with my years of equivocation with the Gurdjieff groups, as I've earlier mentioned).

As usual, Ashish wasn't having any of it.

A.   In my arrogant opinion, the Bailey stuff is even more fuzzy than H.P.B.'s Theosophy from which it stems. H.P.B. used her occult mystery-mongering to attract people to the thing. Bailey seems to think that the occult stuff is the thing. In all fairness, however, Bailey seems to have had an independent connection with the Masters. But she also seems to have distorted what she got almost beyond recognition. One supposes it has served a purpose in encouraging people at least to think about related side issues. But your question about the universe and the solar system reminds me of the old lady who was "so relieved" to know that the solar system would last another billion years and not a mere million. How does the answer affect the urgency of what you have to do here and now?

One must not confuse that fizzing ball of gas in the sky with the source of the awareness that truly lightens all our lives. In all true symbolism there tends to be a confusion between symbol, as representing an immaterial and unrepresentable principle in consciousness, and the valid correspondence between an immaterial principle and its derivatives in objective form. The fizzing ball of gas is both symbol of and correspondential derivative of the inner "sun" or Universal Mind which lights our awareness, as the outer sun lights our senses and feeds earthly life. We all have something of the primitive in us. The primitive mind appears to lack the power of abstraction, and it therefore does not make this sort of differentiation between symbol and its immaterial content. This is what gives the glitter to statements of the sort that one can get beyond the solar system but not out of the universe. Translate this, and it means: One can get to the Universal Mind and beyond, but can never transcend the unity of being—a rather obvious fact.

The Universal Mind, the "Sun" of this universe, is what Plotinus describes as where "each star is itself and all the others." You may recall Nisarga Datta as saying that anyone who sees this still has to ask, "Who sees?" But Plotinus is not really talking of yet more fizzing balls of gas. In primitive thinking, "stars" both represent and "are" the souls of everything. Each soul is itself and all the others. In this context, the brightest star in the heavens, Sirius, is the greatest soul of all, the Master.

Such explanations seem to take all the sparkle out of symbols and "occultism." We like our primitive thinking which sees the star Sirius as "The Abode where the Immortals are." The dark cave of the heart seems dull by contrast. Seems dull. The truth is different.

The Buddha gave a teaching about a house full of children that caught fire. If one tells them about the fire, they will panic and get hurt. So one tells them there are lovely toys in the garden, and all the children troop out in pleasurable excitement to find the toys. When they are safely out, one tells them: "Look. The house is on fire."

G's talk of suns and hydrogens, Bailey's talk of the solar Logos, H.P.B.'s talk of the subtle worlds, is all about rather sophisticated toys. I am not sure about the others, but G knew what he was doing. Which reminds me that H.P.B. was privately reported as saying to an Indian who complained she was not telling the truth: "What does it matter to you if I bamboozle these fools to the greater glory of your Masters?" I would venture to say that G never explained unless someone saw through his deceit—which meant that the person was not so gullible as not to deserve an explanation.

There is a joke about a man who said to his companion: "They're all mad except thee and me. And thee's a bit." Ma [Yashoda Mai] used to say one has to be a bit mad to go this way. And I knew an old Bengali Guru whose greatest compliment was to call one *pagel* ("mad"). The point is that one cannot go this way and retain the conventional view of the world and of society. [Jan. 28, 1985]

The Arcane School had advocated a method of meditation very different from what I had learned in the Gurdjieff group;

Gurdjieffian "sitting" seemed better equipped for developing one's self-awareness. But, still hoping to hear something positive about the Arcane School, I asked Ashish about its type of meditation.

A.   Apart from being mixed, in the Bailey stuff you sent me, though talking about the higher Self, the stress is laid on the use of the inner power here, in this world. This is supposed to be in the service of "The Plan." But, what plan? Whose plan? Can people running a correspondence course discriminate between people seeking the truth and people seeking extensions to their egos?

As Jesus said, "Seek ye first the Kingdom of Heaven." First, discover what there is to be discovered. Find the true nature of the Self and its relationship to the unity. Only then can you know whether anything has to be done about this world, and, if so, what and how. Even then, before you are fit to put anyone else right, you must to some extent bring your own nature into line with whatever you understand of the essence. [Feb. 2, 1985]

That was the end of my infatuation with Alice Bailey, though, as the reader knows, Ashish and I would continue our discussion of Masters for several years to come.

I will jump ahead. In the last year of his life—he passed away on April 13, 1997—Ashish spoke with particular luminosity with regard to certain of the subjects about which we all had been talking for many years. It may be that, because he knew he was dying, he wished to sum up certain teachings he had given us, to recapitulate them, in the face of the death he knew was imminent, in a way that would even constitute hopefully an undying "last will and testament" of teachings from him.

This Ashish certainly did with respect to the "Masters." In mid-1996, in a letter to a friend of mine, he artfully summed up his thinking on the subject. The letter was long, and I will not give its full text here; that can be found in this book's Appendix. I will, though, quote two of the central paragraphs of that particularly compelling summation; with that, we will pass from the subject of Masters to that of Initiation.

A.   Then how does one recognize a Master? What is a Master, anyway? Someone who has fulfilled the evolutionary purpose and is Complete or Perfected. Fine words! What has he actually done? Raised his kundalini? I know dozens of people to whom that has happened and they are certainly not Masters. Seen God? What a vague definition! A vision of one's particular deity does not turn one into a Master, as I know very well from personal experience.

     Perhaps the nearest one can get to it is to say he has found the root of his individualized being, and has found how that individualized point of self-awareness relates to the universal awareness so that he stands in the unity. [April 22, 1996]

Ashish, *Man, Son of Man*, 8-9.
Gurdjieff, *Beelzebub's Tales*, 52.

9

The Uninitiated

The distinguished Lucknow University Vice-Chancellor Dr. Chakravarti—who was also a leading Theosophist and a friend of Annie Besant—held very definite opinions on the subject of initiation, and especially on the subject of initiation with regard to foreigners. These opinions he communicated to Krishna Prem, and Ashish, learning them from his guru, set them forth clearly in his foreword to Krishna Prem's *Initiation into Yoga: An Introduction to the Spiritual Life*, as follows:

"The old Indian concept of self-dedication and obedience to the guru invested initiation with great seriousness. Under the influence of Theosophy, Europeans began seeking oriental initiations, but they did not appreciate the single-pointed loyalty expected of initiates. When the novelty of one initiation wore off, they would take another elsewhere. For this reason, Dr. Chakravarti flatly refused initiation to several Europeans who applied to him. 'They don't stick,' he said, 'they expect to get something, put it in their pockets, and go back to Europe.'"

Was this why Ashish was always so reluctant to give me initiation, to formally make me his disciple and himself my guru—and, in fact, ended up never doing so? Did he think that I, an American who had formerly been intensely involved in business, and was still partly involved in business, simply "wouldn't stick?" That initiation was just an asset I wanted to acquire? That, at the slightest sign of difficulty, I would go elsewhere looking for a better deal? Ashish's reluctance made me doubt myself. Did he find my very eagerness suspect? Did he know something about me that I didn't know myself?

Our relationship certainly wasn't the traditional guru-disciple relationship. There had been no temple initiation ceremony. There had been no secret mantra. There had been no beads or sandals or other object to cement the traditional relationship between guru and disciple. I have to admit that I felt deprived. It seemed to me that Ashish must care less for me than for the dozens of others to whom he'd given formal initiation.

Looking back on it now, I know this wasn't so. But, over the years, I asked him many times why it was that he wouldn't formally initiate me as a disciple. His answer invariably was that I could not value that type of relationship; that I was too much the Westerner, too much the hardheaded businessman.

I broached the matter to him for the first time in a letter I sent in mid-June of 1979. I wanted him to tell me what "outward" initiation (which I understood he gave) was all about. I added that Gurdjieff said there was not, nor could there even be, such a thing as outward initiation.

A. See also *Views from the Real World*, "Glimpses of Truth" (in my edition, pp. 27 ff.). What Gurdjieff is really hitting at is the late Theosophical, Annie Besant/Leadbeater method, in which "initiations" were issued by post at intervals, i.e., the idea that an initiation confers a spiritual status upon a person. There have perhaps been systems in which initiations were ranked in confirmation of steps taken by initiates on their own efforts. But it is properly an introduction to the inner life.

Initiation is an outward seal on an essentially inner commitment. Many people feel it is easier to hold to that inner commitment if it is given an outward reference: "I can break my word to myself, but not the promise given to my teacher." And there is, inherent in this, the mutuality of commitment between teacher and disciple—a publicly admitted bond.

The psyche often treats initiation in this sense as a birth. Many people have brought me dreams of children—the child's age would make it born the year of their initiation—and it isn't always doing very well, needs more attention, etc. The self-commitment, whether backed by ceremony or not, is indeed a birth into a new life. [July 6, 1979]

And that was it. He offered no invitation, no further words about the possibility of my formally becoming a disciple. In a letter I wrote in mid-February, 1980, unable to hide my feelings any longer, I formally asked Ashish if he would be my teacher (or guru, if that were the appropriate word in his tradition). I added that I thought he'd been implying, in his last letter, an invitation that I make this request myself.

A.   My difficulty is this: It is our tradition, and a very sound one, that initiation should never be offered. The request must always come from the person of his own volition. Yet I gave you a broad hint.

The point is that the request must represent, as far as is ever possible, an uninfluenced decision. There must be no question of the person ever feeling that he has been persuaded or tricked into a commitment which is not supported by what he believes to be his fundamental wish. If there has been an element of persuasion, it will be easy for him, when under stress, to use the fact that it was not wholly his own decision as an excuse to evade his commitment. The mind behaves like a lawyer, hunting for an escape clause in a legal agreement. But the modern world, and the West in particular, has lost awareness of this. Many people expect to be persuaded and made much of. The teacher is supposed to recognize and to tell them of their spiritual worth, or he is supposed to persuade them because he wants to share his bliss with all men.

In fact, this path is so difficult that many people feel if you can do anything else, go and do it. Don't try to come this way unless nothing else holds any meaning for you. Sometimes, a challenge to one's ego can be overcome by love/respect for the teacher. But there are many occasions when preconceived notions of what the teacher should be as a man, blinds one to what he is as representing the teaching. So that only total commitment to the goal that transcends all one's personal ideas and values can get one past the crisis. For one cannot lay down conditions. One cannot make one's commitment conditional upon one's receiving the treatment one would like.

Compare this with its wider application in life, where life itself is the teacher. How many people can accept the seemingly cruel blows of life as coming from a benevolent power? They fight against it, trying to impose their individual wills upon the universe. They don't try to see what is. They tell "God" what, in their opinion, he ought to be.

So, while it is only fair to let you know that initiation is a possibility, I have also to assure you that I have no personal aim in attracting disciples. So far as I am concerned, I will give all the advice I can to anyone, irrespective of his being initiated.

Then why initiate at all?

One obvious reason is that more can be demanded of a man who is committed than of one who is not. And a man can draw up greater strength from the depths of his being when he feels himself to be committed than when he does not.

Perhaps the most important aspect of initiation is that it constitutes a public or "open" affirmation of dedication. For reasons I do not fully fathom, the psyche responds to an open or acted out affirmation in a way that it seldom does to a private resolution. This is why good intentions pave the way to hell. Giving one's word, clasping hands, signing one's name, impressing a thumb print, and the public fuss and ceremonial of marriages, are far from being mere legal requirements. They are all examples of what the human psyche demands as representing full intention to honor one's commitment.

In initiation here, before the guru and in the presence of the divinity, the person affirms the dedication of his life in the divinity's service. (I am using the word divinity as an abbreviation for the totality of what is sought, not as meaning gods and goddesses.) Its

148

aim is self-surrender to love. It is not a contractual agreement which can be broken, even though its implementation depends on one's individual capacity. [March 6, 1980]

I didn't want to see it (and wouldn't for some time), but he seemed to be telling me that my demand to be given initiation was a demand of my ego, that to accede to that demand would be, if anything, an obstacle to my growth.

I did not formally take up the matter with Ashish again for some years. However, on my visit to Mirtola in July, 1988, he gave me a small metal figurine of the Hindu elephant God Ganesha. I asked him if I should regard this gift as having some special significance, especially since he knew that I was not a follower of Hindu religious traditions. He replied, "I was just cleaning things out and I wanted you to have something of mine."

I thanked him, of course, but thought nothing more of it until some months later, after I had returned to the States. I was re-reading Ouspensky's *In Search of the Miraculous,* and came across Gurdjieff's statement about how people with astral bodies can communicate with each other. Regarding this, G. had said:

"People who have an 'astral body' can communicate with one another at a distance without having recourse to ordinary physical means. But for such communication to be possible they must establish some 'connection' between them. For this purpose when going to different places or different countries people sometimes take with them something belonging to another, especially things that have been in contact with his body and are permeated with his emanations, and so on."

This struck me as being the significance of Ashish's gift. When I realized it, I was thrilled. The figurine was not the string of beads that Ashish often gave to those he ceremonially initiated, but it was a special gift of one of his few possessions. I wondered if this were Ashish's way of giving me a type of initiation that he saw as suitable for my western psyche. However, the businessman in me, always skeptical of 'being had,' also wondered if I were making too much of the gift. Why couldn't it have been just a gift in the ordinary sense, and why shouldn't I take Ashish at his word when he said he was just cleaning things out?

But something in me still hankered after a kind of formal, outward initiation. A year or so later, I renewed my request to Ashish, pressing the matter by asking him if he would be more specific about the nature of this kind of initiation.

A.   Only when sufficient life experience has been gained for the soul to evolve can intelligent and intentional effort on the inner path be made. G's business about initiation—self-initiation—was to counter the common idea, spread by the later Theosophical Society, that some thing called "initiation" can be given, irrespective of the person's capacity to work. A few people may, indeed, do a great deal without specific guidance, but you must also recall G's emphasis on the need for a school with its imposed disciplines and its provision of imposed will.

The essential ingredient in the work is submission of the ego-integration to the higher being. Very few people are capable of this. People who try to work without submission to an embodied representation of the Self frequently succeed only in integrating around a hard core of superior egotism which can never even approach the borders of that state in which the individual is lost in the universal.

As for [the ceremonial] ritual, the psyche is infinitely more ancient than the newly evolved waking mind and its discriminative intellect, so it responds to symbols and to acts of dedication. You may make all sorts of mental plans, but their totality is less binding than a single signature—a symbolic act of agreement. Any ceremony associated with a ritual initiation is designed to impress the psyche. The dream life often confirms this.

Think of Freud and of the question: "If everything (according to Freud) symbolizes the phallus, then what does the phallus symbolize?" [March 30, 1989]

A.   With your sort of approach, I do not think a formal initiation would be useful. You are too skeptical and, like most "modern" men, you filter everything through the mind, seldom allowing the psyche to experience directly. You therefore have to push up your efforts until experience gives you "initiation" directly—i.e., you realize that your center lies beyond the mind and its doubts. [May 1, 1989]

But I remained unsatisfied. A couple of weeks later, I took up the matter with him again. Ostensibly, I was asking about "inward" initiation. But I was really asking about "outward" initiation—still hoping that Ashish would yield to my request of almost a decade before.

And indeed, he did yield—in a way. I'd asked him what further practical teachings might be useful in this matter of inward initiation: Aspiration? Longer meditation? Grace? Meditation on a particular chakra?

He replied:

A. About direct initiation:

1. Intensification of effort—Firstly, keep up the self-remembering exercises all the time. This demands that you sort out your priorities. Self-remembering does not go very well with anxiety about business affairs. If the aim is the spirit, then just how important is the business? This applies to many subjects. One acts while self-remembering, but when anxieties are attached to the actions, the self-remembering is destroyed.
2. Give your mind food for thought which stimulates your aim, or which is associated with it.
3. Increase the periods and frequencies of meditation.
4. Record dreams and visions and work on their meanings.
5. Try to get inner sanction for even simple daily actions. The point is that the whole of your life has to be integrated around the center, and not just the spiritual bit of it.
6. Open yourself to the psychic contents of events, from perceiving the flow of life in plants to noting synchronicities. See/feel the "magic" of the world.

7. There is a connection between self-remembering and meditation. Keeping yourself centered at all times makes it easier to get
into meditation at special times. Then, as you go deeper in meditation, you may find the need to modify your idea of what it is that
self-remembering is supposed to be remembering. Too many
people are stuck with a purely mental, aloof detachment.

8. Personally, I am not fond of chakras, etc. But it seems that
some people's thoughts are organized around them. I find it better
to grope directly for the roots of consciousness, rather than taking
a circuit via sensation. Similarly with "vibrations." What the guide
[Pastor; see Chapter Eleven] has to say about vibrations on the
tapes smacks of mystery-mongering to catch the people who feel
thrilled but don't understand what is being said.

   This sort of effort is directed to a transpersonal goal. If you are
dedicated to the way of the Masters (i.e., not to selfish liberation,
but to helping others), then the Masters personify the goal. So
your efforts take you directly towards them. They may help you
through any available channel, but your efforts are directed to the
source. The question is not whether you will stand in the unity; it
is, "What stands?" It is difficult for anyone, and particularly difficult for someone conditioned in the business ethos of the West, to
get the feel of what it is that can aspire and make effort non-egotis-
tically. [May 25, 1989]

I had been given the keys to inner self-initiation. And with that I
would have to remain content. All this caused me to ruminate
with renewed vigor on just who Sy was, and on how much the
American in me—the American businessman in me—was behind
(as it would be for anyone in my situation) my various needs and
requirements and wishes and longings in this long and earnest quest
of mine in search of the unitive vision.

   If I was to remain uninitiated, there were others in close proximity to Ashish, or far away with whom he kept in touch by correspondence, who were similarly uninitiated. But this did not keep
them from being excellent seekers in their own right, or indeed
people of real achievement in the world.

At the same time, there were many others whom Ashish had formally initiated. I don't know the exact number, and I know that some were people who visited him only infrequently. Others were regular visitors, and still others were invited to come and live at the ashram.

Starting in early 1980, Ashish had allowed six couples to live at Mirtola on a permanent basis. This was to be an experiment in communal living à la G.I. Gurdjieff, I believe. Ashish wanted to see if, through guiding them and employing the occasional Gurdjieffian exercise (and with the help of Dev and Dev's running of the farm), he could help some of these people move toward a higher level of being.

Three of the couples had to build their own houses. Another couple remodeled an existing structure, and still another moved into a structure built earlier by Dev. The sixth couple already had a house there, which they were living in on a part-time basis until the male partner, an army officer, could retire and move to Mirtola permanently. Dev was already living there; two other persons, a retired police officer named Mahesh Sexena and an elderly woman, had been living at Mirtola for some time, she in a small cottage, he in a kind of "monk's" room in the confines of the temple. Eventually, Mahesh would leave to become one of Krishnamurti's personal secretaries.

In 1981, then, there were sixteen residents at Mirtola (which may have been the maximum) including Ashish. During the many years of my visits, several other people took up residence, while others who had been living there left the ashram. I don't believe Ashish's experiment in group living worked out; but, certainly, these people learned a great deal, and were forever after marked by their experience in residence at Mirtola.

In addition to these full-time residents, there were usually visitors at Mirtola—except in the winter, when Ashish preferred to live a somewhat secluded life. It was during these winters that he was most fully engaged in his writing, and that writing included, as I've mentioned, articles on a wide variety of subjects, from ecology to spirituality, for Indian's leading intellectual journal, *Semi-*

nar, published by the husband and wife team who by now had become his close friends, Raj and Romesh Thapar.

In his collection of letters and essays, *Relating to Reality*, Ashish tells us a great deal about his relationship with this brilliant couple who were devoted to the service of India. As well as their friend, he had informally become their guru. *Seminar* was the leading forum of debate for the question that so much preoccupied the country, and which was also of concern to Madhava Ashish and Krishna Prem: Did India have a spiritual nature superior to that of other nations, which must be retained no matter what—and was she now in the process of losing that nature?

A turning point had come in the debate in 1984: the assassination of Prime Minister Indira Gandhi and the bloodbath that followed it in the form of what appeared to be the planned massacre of the Sikhs. Martial law had been imposed. For a brief period, the Thapars were not allowed to publish *Seminar*.

It was in this period that, for the first time, Indian intellectuals began to know real despair. Perhaps India would not, was not to, fulfil its historical destiny as the torchbearer of spirituality to the world. Ashish took as deep an interest in this changed debate as anyone else. In letters to him from Raj and Romesh, which he published in *Relating to Reality*, he vividly records that despair. Raj wrote to Ashish, on Nov. 20, 1984:

"What a monstrous people we [Indians] are. I could understand looting, beating, burning, but the savagery was inexplicable. To have a gloating mob making fires and popping men, women, and children into it with glee, I cannot come to terms with. Hitler took a long time in preparing the world for his horrors, but here it suddenly sprang up from nowhere. How can one ever recover from this madness—or is it not madness but just the human condition? I don't know any more."

By September, 1986, Raj was in London undergoing chemotherapy. She wrote to Ashish that it was the stress of that earlier period that had caused her cancer:

"I keep thinking of what you said to me the last time we met—that I had given up and it was wrong. You are quite right. I seemed to have given up on the essential goodness underlying life, something I had always believed in....They say stress is a vital cause for the suppression of immunity which then allows cancer cells to proliferate in abandon—stress starting from six to eighteen months before the onset of the disease. I had always imagined that I was free of stress. What fond illusions we hold of ourselves, but I have been probing deeper within me and know that the aftermath of Mrs. Gandhi's assassination and the nature of the killings—just the thought—used to wake me up in the middle of the night with my body wracked with uncontrollable sobs..."

Raj returned to New Delhi, dying there in April, 1987. Romesh passed away in August of that year. Arriving at Raj's bedside shortly after death had claimed her, Ashish was still able to say goodbye, as he tells us in *Relating to Reality*:

"I reached Raj's bedside after she had gone. The family thoughtfully left me with her for a few minutes. How would she fare? I wondered. And then I found her: happy, joyous, immediately scolding me for my grief."

Ashish further tells us that "...it was not until the following summer that I made contact or, rather, they made contact with me. My party was travelling through the hills and had stopped for the night on the banks of the Mandakini river in Garhwal. Tired by the long drive and by the surfeit of sense impressions, I fell asleep—and there were Raj and Romesh, smiling, happy, and urging me to meet a particular friend of theirs."

Thus unfolded the drama of Ashish's life, among the initiated and the uninitiated alike, both in the thoroughfares of life and from the heart of the unitive vision. Ashish attracted so many people into his life; it was not hard to see why he had attracted myself and so many disciples to the ashram. What, I was beginning to ask myself, was this peculiar quality of guru-dom that drew us to him? I put the question to him frankly. He responded by inviting me to read an article on the subject that he had written for UNESCO the

year before I met him. That article comprises the next chapter of
this book.

Krishna Prem, *Initiation*, 22
Ouspensky, *Miraculous*, 97
Ashish, *Relating to Reality*, 326.
Ibid., 361-362.
Ibid., 363.
Ibid., 364.

10 ✳

The Guru as Exemplar of and Guide to the Term of Human Evolution
By Sri Madhava Ashish

The primary meaning of the Sanskrit word *guru* is "heavy" or "weighty." By derivation, it comes to mean "great," "respected," "venerable."

In the pantheistic culture of Hinduism, all things are divine and all acts sacramental. And since such a culture does not draw hard and fast distinctions between objects and the divine content of objects, he who possesses the sacred knowledge, teaches it, teaches the sacred language in which it is enshrined, teaches the sacred texts, and initiates in the sacred rites, is the guru, great, respected, venerated and worshipped as identical with the knowledge he expounds. Similarly, no absolute distinction is made between mundane knowledge and transcendental knowledge, because the divine is both immanent and transcendent. The teacher of a craft is thus as much guru as teacher of the spiritual philosophy.

In the context of this study we are concerned neither with the instructor of practical skills nor with the exponent of academic systems of thought, but with the guru as mahatma (great soul), sage, saint, or seer, who on the basis of this experience teaches the way to transcendental knowledge both by exposition and demon-

157

stration. Such exposition is called his 'philosophy,' but the San-skrit word translated as philosophy has different connotations for the Hindu from those currently associated with European phi-losophy.

Philosophy is a word which formerly had a much wider signifi-cance than it now has and included under the heading "natural philosophy" all of what we now call science. Gradually, however, the term has become limited to speculative reasoning about the ultimate nature of the universe in its various aspects. It is true that a follower of Hegel would give quite a different answer to the ques-tion, "What is Philosophy?" to that which will be given by, say, Bertrand Russell, but in a general way we may say that philoso-phy means, in Europe, speculative reasoning about the universe, either on a basis of accepted principles *a priori* held to be valid, or on a basis of observed facts, and is an attempt to arrive at an under-standing of the universe through the use of the discursive reason.

The classical systems of Indian philosophy, however, start on a different basis altogether. The Sanskrit word which is usually translated as "philosophy" is *darshanam,* which literally means "see-ing" and, in fact, the classical Indian philosophies start neither from *a priori* principles nor from observed facts, as usually understood, but from some transcendental experience in which the truth about the nature of the universe is directly perceived. What is usually called philosophy is an attempt to give a coherent and logical ac-count of the world as thus perceived in such terms as shall be both intelligible and convincing to a given hearer with his own particu-lar temperament. It is a rational demonstration of the truth seen by the original *rishi* or "seer," and with it is taught a practical method, by practising which, the pupil may gradually acquire for himself a realisation of the truths so demonstrated.

It is this claim to direct experience on the part of the teacher and to the possibility of such for the pupil that makes the widest gulf between the Indian and European systems. In the latter, no hope is held out that the pupil will ever arrive at more than an intellectual understanding of the truth. Whether one believes with Berkeley that a spade is an idea in the mind of God, or with

McTaggart that it is a colony of souls, the practical result is just the same as if one believed with the crassest realist that it is just a spade. Whereas, when the author of the *Bhagavad-Gita* says that "all is *Vasudeva* (the indwelling spirit)," he is saying something that he means his hearers to verify for themselves and on which they will be able to base their whole lives and outlook on the world.

This brings us to the crux of the matter under discussion. If we confuse the seer's account of his direct experience with speculative philosophy; if we confuse mystical vision with mythological or archetypal dreams whose content comes from the collective unconscious, or think that the spiritual experience is a delusion of the disordered psyche in men seeking opiates against the stark reality of a life that ends in death, and that the death of the body is the death of the man; if we think that the guru, sage, saint, or seer is possessed by the "wise old man" archetype or is suffering from some sort of megalomania; if, in fact, we are crass realists and believe that everything is just what it is, without reason, cause, purpose, or direction, and that anything perceived without the use of the physical organs of sense and without the brain is, *ipso facto*, hallucination, then we are blind, proud, stubborn, opinionated fools, lacking intelligence to inquire into obvious mysteries, lacking humility to suspect that others might conceivably be able to perceive facts which we are incapable of perceiving, and lacking courage to free our minds from the fixed opinions with which we screen ourselves from the impact of reality.

The experiential nature of the seer's perceptions does not challenge our philosophical ideas so much as it does the values on which we base our lives—not our pious values, but the ones like self-opinion and the importance given to feeling comfortable. It makes it easier for us if we can titillate our minds with his philosophy, give it a name, call it 'pessimistic' or 'obscure,' and turn with relief to our Sunday newspapers which tell us how science is solving the world's problems, a science which regards even the commonplace ghost as "unproven."

This common and quite inadequate attitude is peculiar to the "modern" world—the world most benefited by science and so most vulnerable to the materialism that goes with it. It seems, curiously enough, to represent a shadow cast by one of science's real contributions to the progress of the human race. By establishing the validity of experimental pragmatism when applied to the data of sense experience, science, as a historical movement, won its battle against religious prejudice and mythological thinking. Its antagonist was not merely the vested interest of institutionalized religion, which for centuries had cramped and distorted the development of thought, but the whole mode of primitive, mythological, and superstitious thought, the kind of thought which is still common in peasant and tribal societies. The development and diffusion of the scientific method, with its repercussions on philosophy, has had the effect of making our thought less mythical in content, more practical. We ask real questions and demand real answers. Our minds do not stop at the emotional resonances of the religious "God," by whatever name called, but we ask, if we ask at all, for direct experience of the being or state of being which for millennia has been symbolized by the word "God," even if we now call it the nature of reality.

We need not pride ourselves on this new ability. Men have sought and obtained such direct experience since there have been men on earth, and they did not have the disadvantages either of our rationality which we oppose to the objectively undemonstrable spirit, or the mass of scientific knowledge which clouds our perception of the magical qualities in nature. What they saw, however, they interpreted in the terms in which they thought; and much of their terminology no longer seems valid to us unless we voluntarily make the effort to translate their concrete symbols into our abstract ones. Some progress has been made in this direction by psychology in its discovery that the "unconscious" psyche of sophisticated people often uses the same sorts of mythological terms and symbols as did earlier men. In other words, our capacity for direct appreciation of the mythological outlook may be dormant, but it is not dead.

It is inadequate to regard this development of the conscious mind merely as a veneer of sophistication over an essentially primitive psyche. The man who uses his conscious mind to penetrate and integrate the primitive elements in the psyche does not go wild or run off in search of the simple life in savage surroundings. He becomes more, not less, civilized; more, not less, human.

Though the unitive experience has frequently been gained by uneducated and relatively inarticulate men of peasant or tribal stock, it is by no means limited to them. Some of the greatest minds of their times have known it, and some of them have been highly articulate in their attempts to interpret it, even though a few, like St. Thomas Aquinas, found their eminent articulateness stopped by it. However, their interpretations were made in relation to the then current extent of world knowledge and therefore fail to provide satisfaction to many people of the present day who may be genuinely distressed at their inability to reconcile the demonstrations of saints with the demonstrations of science. Even though neither demonstration factually invalidates the other, few men are able to perceive the discrepancies that exist between facts and their interpretation—discrepancies that frequently underlie this problem of reconciliation. This is particularly the case where such discrepancies are made apparent only on the evidence of powers of perception which the questioner has not yet learned to use.

Although the scientist's facts may be objectively demonstrable, he takes into account only that aspect of his subject of study which can be made perceptible to the organs of sense, and he excludes the inner or subtle aspects of form from his frame of reference— many scientists deny that there is any evidence for their existence. His conclusions as to the significance of his discoveries are therefore inadequate, and when he extrapolates from his conclusions onto areas which come outside the self-imposed limits of his discipline, they may be entirely false.

Lest it be thought that this criticism of the outlook engendered by the scientific method is unjust, one may cite a review by Claude Alvares of the book *Chance and Necessity* written by the Nobel laureate, Jacques Monad: "All systems rooted in animism, all religions, all philosophies, exist outside objective, non-purposive knowledge, outside truth, and are strangers to and thus fundamen-

161

tally hostile to science....Our philosophers might just as well be dismissed, as they are no longer valid interpreters of truth." In his true enthusiasm for an uncomforting view of life, Alvares exceeds his competency to pronounce on the role of science in its contributions to the totality of knowledge. There are vast areas of objective experience outside the range of the material sciences which are as much parts of "truth" as is the nature of the sort of matter which scientists have so far investigated.

We have no reason to suppose that men in the past who wrote learned theses based on inadequate or faulty knowledge of the material world were less intelligent than men in the present who write equally learned theses based on less faulty knowledge. Similarly, we have no reason to suppose that the level of mystical experience attained to today is any different from the levels of such experience in the past. But, because the attention of mankind has been turned towards inquiries into the material structure of the universe, development of inquiry into its inner nature has lagged behind. We have not yet learned to adapt the intellectual disciplines gained through outer inquiry to the less easily marshalled phenomena of the inner worlds.

So great has been the prestige of the scientific method that it is only now, when men have begun to taste the bitter consequences of the materialism engendered by the scientific outlook, that there is a widely felt need for a reinterpretation of life's significance. When men turn away from the sterile evaluation of life which has arisen from the scientist's unjustifiable extrapolations from his discoveries, we may expect developments in this field which will lead to reassessment of mystical experience with corresponding effects on the social ethos. These will to some extent balance the degradation of the old religious ethos which occurred when scientific empiricism supplanted mythological and superstitious thinking. For this to be effective, however, such reinterpretation must be a renewal of the eternal values of life based on direct mystical experience. No syncretistic re-hash by an oecumenical council will achieve any real change. To such men of mystical experience, the present accumulation of knowledge about the material universe will be a basis of fact with which their equally factual perceptions must be reconciled. The human psyche cannot indefinitely tolerate our adherence to any one-sided view which opposes its need for integrity. Knowledge of the material universe may continue to be amassed, but the striving for total knowledge which is implanted in the soul of man demands that knowledge of existence be balanced by knowledge of essence.

As world views stand at present, we are divided roughly into two groups, the scientific and the religious: the people who accept the scientific view that reality is physical and that all things can be reduced to objectively measurable systems of energy, and the people who accept the supremacy of consciousness, the autonomous nature of the psyche, and the evidence for a non-physical reality. Each group reviles the other on the assumption that if one is right the other is wrong. But both views are expressed by the same human psyche, and, though the progress of human thought is often marked, and even promoted, by swings between such extremes, the psyche itself demands the reconciliation of extremes and their fusion into the wholeness which it seeks.

This apparent digression into the joust between science and religion is in fact relevant to our subject because it bears on the world attitude towards the seer as guru or spiritual teacher, and so on his practical, as opposed to his actual, status. To people for whom reality is what is perceived through the physical organs of sense, the seer is an anachronism, a purveyor of antiquated illusions. To the ordinarily religious people, he is the saint of their particular religion who affirms what they believe to be the uniquely valid tenets of their faith.

The Indian attitude towards the mahatma, sage, saint, or seer, is similar to that of any predominantly peasant society. From familiarity with the traditions of his culture, the Hindu already knows the mahatma, and he may also know him in fact. Mystical experience is perhaps not so rare amongst peoples whose teachings and customs are infused with perception of the immanent divinity as it is amongst those whose upbringing persuades them to view all things as grossly and solely material. The Hindu is taught that the mahatma is the embodiment of the highest, world-transcending knowledge, and that the pursuit of such knowledge is the greatest and most noble aim in life, ordained from the beginning as the ultimate goal of all men. He therefore reveres the Mahatma with that awe in which admiration and fear are mingled. The Mahatma is admired as a numinous figure, endowed with magical powers, whose blessings are insurance against misfortune, and whose teachings promise what may be variously interpreted as escape from or transcendence of suffering. His knowledge is essential and thus superior to any knowledge of temporalia. He is emancipated from desire, liberated from rebirth, and he neither seeks gain nor fears loss. He is also feared because, united with the universal spirit, he stands outside caste, religion, race, and social restraints in general, and therefore appears as a threat to the householder whose security lies in conformity to the established order.

Each mahatma who arises currently represents the eternal source of the *dharma* or code of sacred conduct, established by gods, sages, and prophets in time immemorial as the mundane counterpart to the divine harmony of being. In the setting of mythological thinking the mahatma therefore appears as a recurrence of a timeless beginning and consequently tends to be identified with one of the eternal gods or one of the sages of mythic antiquity. For this reason, men of actual spiritual attainment, whose inner and outer experience has liberated them from the conditioned thinking of the societies in which they arose, are mythologized by their devotees and publicly represented in a fashion that conforms to a culturally recognized pattern. On the other hand, men with equally valid experience, but whose minds have not been freed from behavioral rules, themselves conform to those modes of behaviour which their culture prescribes for the seer.

What is the seer in himself? To answer this question we have to turn to the statements made by seers in their attempts to interpret the "ineffable" vision, and ourselves attempt an interpretation which is consonant with our present understanding of the world. Consciousness and the desire to "conscire" are inseparable. Being desires to be. But, prior to the manifestation of a universe, the diffused awareness which inheres in unmanifest being can have no particularized knowledge of the content of being. Driven by its own desire, and from the energies of its own desire, the self-nature of being first establishes itself as the separate units of the atomic world. On this basis it then elaborates forms as vehicles for progressively higher modes of conscious function. Finally, in its highest and most elaborate form, namely that of man, it achieves an intensity of individualized awareness through which it is capable of obtaining both particularized knowledge of qualities inherent to its nature and knowledge of its prior state of unity out of which all energy, all form, and all awareness have sprung.

Inherently associated with consciousness, the urge to self-knowledge is the driving force within the evolution of forms, driving all creatures along the pathways of desire and, finally, urging men to discard their separate selfhood and to complete the cycle of creation which begins and ends in unity, a unity which the *Vedanta* of Shankaracharya describes as "not two" or inseparable. Having exteriorized its own qualities in the differentiated forms of the manifest universe, through its out-turned awareness in its creatures, the spirit first appreciates its qualities in existence and then, turning inwards through man, rediscovers its undifferentiated essence. The cycle is complete. The term of the evolution has been reached. The spiritual experience is thus the natural and logical term of the progressive movement within consciousness through which the divine endeavor achieves its goal. Through its creatures, individualized in its human vehicle, the universal consciousness achieves awareness of its own essential nature.

In the unitive vision the identity of the individual with the universal is experienced, and it is perceived that this identity encompasses all being as an eternally valid fact. It has not come into being with the seer's attainment to the vision, but simply is. What comes into being, or, more truly, is developed in the seer, is the seer's capacity to perceive the identity. In this context it seems meaningless to say that any individual man ever attains anything. The spirit raises its human vehicle out of its own being and, through this vehicle, achieves knowledge both of the qualities it has made manifest to itself and of the undifferentiated and unmanifest being within which all qualities inhere. Our life is its life; our awareness is its awareness; our desire to live, to experience, and to know, is its desire. And the motivation which urges men to turn inwards to self-discovery is the driving motive behind the whole universe, a motive that seems to be as inherent to the nature of being as is consciousness itself.

The seers of the unitive vision are established in the unmoving centre of the world wheel. The unchanging Real which is their essential being was before all things, is now, and ever shall be after all things have ceased to exist. Within it, past, present and future blend into an eternal simultaneity, a simultaneity which is unaffected by the Einsteinian denial of temporal simultaneity because the former has nothing to do with the "simultaneous" perception of objects through the organs of sense. That in the seer which stands in the center always stands there by virtue of its nature. The worlds of form 'evolve' not outwards but inwards, enclosing, encircling, or integrating the eternal stasis within the circle of time. It is thus that within his being the seer links eternity with time, links them with full and constant awareness that the sequence of temporal events floats within eternity.

It is in this context that the seer as guru or teacher most significantly comes within the purview of these studies on philosophy and time. He shows the road from time into eternity, drawing other men towards him, as if the eternal in him called to the eternal in others. He does not go forth with missionary zeal to persuade others of the validity of his message. He is his message. Like calls to like, and those who have grown close enough to the eternal in themselves are attracted to the eternal in him.

From the above discussion it should be clear why the Hindu identifies the guru with God, whether by guru he means the particular individual through whose attainment the spirit now stands in full and non-illusory knowledge of its own nature, or whether he means the as yet unrealized potential within each one of us through which, if realized, the spirit will achieve self-knowledge.

The latter, like any other unintegrated content or capacity of the psyche, urges towards inclusion in the awareness of the individual; urges, guides, and, when integrated, is the capacity for knowledge of the self-nature both of man and the universe. Prior to its development, for practical purposes we do not possess it, and we become aware of it only in another man in whom it is realized.

To say that it is the spirit that attains its own goal and not the individual may seem to deny significance to persons and personal values. It is true that undifferentiated universal consciousness is so diffused as to appear impersonal, but if personality was not rooted in it as an inherent quality, there could be no person in man. By person we are not referring to the negatively toned mask of behavior characteristics denigrated when we speak of a personality cult.

We refer to the warm and living actuality of the man behind the mask, the indwelling spirit of man. When this person, this indwelling spirit, develops his full capacities and achieves the knowledge of his essential nature, he is not less human, but fully human. His knowledge and experience of the actual unity of being calls forth the compassion which is the underlying 'feeling-togetherness' of a unity which has expressed itself in parts. When he turns his attention towards his source, the objects of physical sense perception melt and vanish before his vision, and he stands in that same timeless void in which past, present and future co-exist inseparately. This is the "void" from which all worlds emerged, in which they stand, and into which they will be withdrawn, just as for the seer they are now withdrawn. When, however, he turns outwards and is again aware of the worlds of form, he looks out as an individual through the limitations of his psychosomatic complex, limited by the accidents of birth, education, intellectual capacity, life experience, cultural conditioning, and the extent of world knowledge at the time.

Furthermore, the society in which he resides may exert pressure on him to modify his statements. In early Christian and Islamic societies seers have been martyred because the truths of their experience were considered heretical. Indian seers were more fortunate; the code restricts behavior but permits the mind to range free. Behavior contrary to the code is tolerated if the practitioner removes himself from the social order and lives as a wandering mendicant. While this liberality may have led to an undisciplined proliferation of views, not all of which were based on experience, it has also assisted in preserving interpretations of mystical experience which are relatively free from the distortions that stem from religious coercion. Such limitations restrict the seer's interpretation of what he sees inwardly, just as they also restrict our interpretations of what we see outwardly. Nevertheless, despite differences in interpretation, the underlying similarity of the mystical experience gained by many seers is abundantly clear.

An example of this sort of limitation can be given from the life of Black Elk, a seer of the North American Sioux, who obtained a remarkable vision as a boy of nine, but could do nothing with it until older men with similar experience helped him to express it in the form of a ritual consistent with other rituals of the same tribe.

Another example can be taken from an account of the life of the south Indian Mahatma, Sri Ramana Maharshi, who similarly achieved the mystical experience as a youth. After his attainment he remained silent in a cave for some years. During this period a group of educated devotees frequently met in the cave and would discuss Vedantic philosophy together while sitting in the Maharshi's presence. According to one of the men who took part in these discussions, when the Maharshi broke his silence and began teaching, he taught in precisely those terms of orthodox Advaita which he had heard discussed. Neither this man nor others, including the present writer, who had the fortune to meet the Maharshi, could doubt the reality of his status. But it appears that as a boy he lacked a framework of intellectual concepts in which to express his experience, and found the Advaita philosophy satisfactory when he heard it discussed.

Whether ancient or modern, Hindu, Buddhist, Moslem, or anything else, liberated from social values or bound by them, it is to the seers of mystical experience that we owe whatever validity there is in the religious and philosophical teachings of the world.

They have "seen" the one, timeless truth on which depends the validity of all the lesser and contingent truths of this world.

The significance of a seer far transcends his place in his local culture, for by virtue of his experience of the transcendental unity from which the whole of being derives, he represents the goal of all religions, the term of the evolutionary process, and the perfection of man. He is not merely the saint of a particular religion. Such differences as may appear between the Hindu mahatma, the Islamic *wali*, the Buddhist *arhat*, and the Christian saint are accidental to their essential identity. All seers are essentially one, and their vision is one. Different though their temporal forms may be, in themselves they are the same.

Thus, any seer's mythic status within the sacramental framework of his culture in no way affects either the validity of his mystical experience and metaphysical knowledge or his significance, both to his own society and to the world at large. In discussing his essential significance, we are therefore concerned with him as a universal, rather than a local phenomenon. He is not a mere visionary, in the sense of someone who is susceptible to having clairvoyant perception. He "sees" and experiences the essential unity of all things, and he integrates this experience into his being so that, in some sense, he lives in and from a constant awareness of the unity. The fact of the unity is his message; and the method by which men may attain his integral perception is his teaching.

The seer is the exemplar of the goal of life because the universal desire for self-knowledge has achieved its goal through him. All men have the ability for such achievement in potential, for the simple reason that they are part of the universe; and man is the one part of the universe which can know the whole, and know by his own experience his identity with the whole of being. When, therefore, the seer teaches, he calls forth this hidden capacity in other men, in the same sense that a school-teacher leads forth (educates) the unrealized capacities of a child's intelligence. If devoid of intelligence, the child could not respond. In practice, children ordinarily respond only to teaching levels within the range normal to the capacities of their age-groups. Similarly, men respond to the seer by virtue of their having the same capacity in potential which the seer has made real, but the level at which they understand or interpret the teaching depends on the extent to which their potentialities have been developed.

The outer teaching "rings true" to men when it resonates in harmony with their innate capacity to experience the truths expressed. But since relatively few men have done anything towards developing this capacity, and since the teachings both from within and from without frequently conflict with the social and religious codes imposed on them in childhood, few men, again, can recognize and respond to the true teaching. They are presented with statements of fact which to them have no factual basis, because they have not developed the capacity to see or feel the demonstration of their truth in the being of the teacher. Nevertheless, the capacity is there, and it is usually true that inner responses are stirred by outer teachings long before the student's capacity is developed to the point where it can be trusted as a source of direct guidance. To draw yet another parallel from education, it is usually only in post-graduate work that a student can be trusted to apply the methods he has learned to independent studies and so to demonstrate that he has made them his own.

In the *Vinaya Pitaka* it is told of the Buddha that immediately after the enlightenment he doubted the possibility of conveying his knowledge to others. Anyone achieving similar enlightenment in the present day might feel the same way. The shared and relatively stable continuity of objective reference which fills the field sensed by the physical organs is declared the only reality, while private experience is denigrated as subjective and, by opposition to the publicly shared experience, unreal and illusory. Few people accept the truth of Whitehead's statement, "Apart from the experience of subjects, there is nothing, nothing, bare nothingness."

All experience is private to the observer. Even the world of everyday life is privately observed by each one of us, and our perceptions are correlated by agreement. It is only because the unitive experience is as yet relatively rare that it is not commonly accorded the same validity as that of the everyday world. To the seer it is so convincingly real that he needs no confirmation of its nature; and this reality has been verified by mahatmas, saints, sages and seers from time immemorial and continues to be so verified. Furthermore, in discovering our identity with the universal substratum of consciousness, we discover the metaphysical unity which makes possible any sharing of objective content. If there were a plurality of separate consciousnesses, no two such consciousnesses could share experience, for they could have no grounds on which to build the supposition, which is what supports the whole scientific outlook, that all men perceive phenomena in much the same way.

However, the mystical experience is not shared in quite the same manner. Even if two seers were to get together to compare notes, they would not expect to find similarity in any objective content there might have been to their experiences. They would look for agreement in the significance of the direct knowledge or symbolized knowledge obtained. The visual or other objective content often associated with the unitive experience is different for different people according to their type, their cultural background, and the religions and philosophical ideas they have assimilated. This variation is inherent to the situation. In a realm where there is no form, any objective appearances are symbolic representations of the meaning with which the experience is filled; and these symbols are in some sense called forth or projected from the nature of the experiencing subject. They are symbolic interpretations of the essentially formless meaning within unmanifest being.

The problem becomes deeper when the seer returns to the 'normal' waking state and attempts to interpret what his nature has already shown as a symbolic interpretation. While the latter has at least the validity of what C.G. Jung calls the archetypes of the collective unconscious, the validity of the seer's reinterpretation will depend on the individual's mental capacity to handle the symbols of transcendental concepts and the adequacy of the philosophical systems with which he is familiar and to which he can relate his perceptions. This may lead us to bark our shins on a stumbling-block, for we are apt to assume that spiritual teachers, especially those who teach from experience, express the unadulterated truth, whereas we now discover that what they express are interpretations of the truth. We need to come to terms with the fact that all statements about the transcendent unmanifest are necessarily symbolic interpretations, and that the use of a vocabulary of abstract terms is no less a symbolic interpretation than the use of concrete symbols, nor does it necessarily express more truth.

In fact, limitations to the seer's intellectual capacity and his ability to express himself coherently may present more problems for the disciple than for the seer. The seer may often rest content with a vocabulary that is meaningful to him. When a Hindu seer speaks of the *Brahman*, he knows what it means to him in terms of experience and may not attempt to correct a listener who thinks he is talking about a specifically Hindu concept. On the other hand, we hear of a Zen master attempting a special study of philosophy in order to help his pupil.

What the Seer may say in his interpretation of the unitive experience is truly of less significance than what he is, for what he is validates what he says. His status is neither dependent on his learning, nor even on his capacity to articulate his experience. For anyone who has eyes to see, he demonstrates the truth in his being. The problem for the unenlightened man is how to perceive what the seer demonstrates. This is the problem that may face anyone seeking a teacher of the method by which the unitive experience may be obtained. How is one to distinguish between the charlatan, the scholar, the seer of distorted psychic vision, and the true seer?

All religious systems consider it statutory that their spiritual disciplines should be performed under the guidance of an approved teacher. Hinduism differs only in that it assumes the guru to be a true seer who has experienced his identity with the universal spirit; and its code of conduct prescribes an attitude towards any person accepted as a guru which equates him with the spirit. Where such rules are not framed solely in the interests of institutionalized religion, the principle behind them is valid. Were it not for the constant reassurance of the man who has been on this road before us, who stands by our side, affirming, encouraging and goading, which of us would dare, like the heroes of romance, to lose ourselves in order to find ourselves? And in a modern, non-sacramental society, men need reassurance that there really is something to be discovered and that the venture is not equivalent to madness. But, since the teacher is commonly within the socio-religious system, and since the motivation of the pupil is more often dissatisfaction with worldly life than a true inquiry, men publicly accepted as teachers of the spiritual way may factually be little more than worldly-wise priests with stores of appropriate sayings from holy writ. One can find many benevolent, ascetic and dedicated men with great knowledge about the transcendent being, but with no direct knowledge of it. And there are professional teachers, both in India and elsewhere, who openly claim a status they do not possess, for the saintly garb is no guarantee that its wearer does not lie.

Hindu texts give descriptions of the true guru's distinguishing marks, some of which would seem to restrict the status to certain ethnic groups with particular physical characteristics, while others are applicable to a traditionalistic society where a specific dress and way of life may be laid down for anyone obtaining mystical vision. But since there are many levels of mystical vision, and since people without such vision may also follow the same way of life, there are factually no external signs by which the true teacher may be distinguished from the partial or the false.

The one reliable guide is 'the guru residing in the heart.' But we can rely on the voice of this teacher only when we learn to distinguish his 'voice' from the many voices of the as yet unintegrated psyche. Unless we have begun the task of awakening in our own hearts the capacity for the experience we seek, our hearts will not respond with recognition, and we shall be incapable of recognizing whether a man of apparent saintliness is speaking from learning or from experience. In our worldly professions we develop a fine sense for whether or not a man knows what he is talking about. We have to develop the same power of discrimination in this field. Outwardly the seer is a man, waking and sleeping, eating and defecating, like anyone else. While one expects the emotional maturity of a man who has come to terms with his own nature, his mental capacities may or may not be above the average. If he teaches, he may say nothing which has not been said before and could not be learned from books. No external characteristic, no sensible sign, and no supernormal phenomenon necessarily differentiates him from the ordinary man. Outwardly he is ordinary. Inwardly he is exceptional because he has developed an actual capacity which in most of us is still unrealized potential. The development or integration of that potential capacity for unitive awareness constitutes the final step in the evolutionary progress of man. It is the one remaining power of being whose integration within the human soul produces the whole, complete, or perfected man.

Our aim, however, is not to win the capacity to distinguish true seers from false, but to follow the seer's path inwards and see for ourselves whether our experience corroborates his. We need give no name to the experience. We need neither philosophical hypothesis, scientific theory, nor religious formulation. All we need is the resolute courage to turn inwards to find direct experience of the roots of being, or, if we prefer to put it this way, to see whether our being has experienceable roots.

If we are at all intelligent, we do not need philosophical proof that God's existence can neither be proved nor disproved. The self-evident fact both of the universe and of our capacity to perceive its phenomenal appearances should be sufficient evidence to support any direct investigation into the source of the awareness by which we perceive. And since the investigation is of awareness and not of the material correlates of awareness, our sole course is to turn within ourselves. Our body forms the walls of our laboratory; our feelings, the power by which we operate; our dreams and visions, the data of the process; our thoughts, the regulators and channels of power; and that which is beyond thought, the awareness of being aware, becomes both subject and object of the investigation.

If we do not know that we are repeating an inquiry that has been successfully accomplished by many men before us, we shall be liable to stop at the first obstacle and come out with something like Descartes's *cogito ergo sum*. This barrier of the thinking mind is the first bottleneck, corresponding to those between waking and sleeping, and between embodied living and disembodied living, rites of passage through which each man must pass alone, momentarily unsupported even by knowledge of his own identity.

No purpose would be served by adding one more to the many descriptions of the way, because the differences in individuals result in such varying approaches that we are all, in some sense, pioneers. Other men have blazed trails through the jungles of their minds, but we have never before travelled this road through our own. And if we find features in our country corresponding to features in theirs, it is not the fact that we have read or heard about this that gives it its validity; there is simply the pleasure of a shared experience. For instance, when the mind is truly stilled, the quality of the experience shows us why the author of the *Srimad Bhagavata* describes the streams of *Braja* as "clear as a Yogi's mind."

We need only to follow our noses—inwards—in order to arrive at a confirmatory experience of man's essentially immaterial nature which carries such overwhelming conviction that material assessments of man are seen as sheer ignorance. But the disciplines we follow must be strict. If we waste our energies on temporalia, we have no one but ourselves to blame if our inquiry ends where it began. We must expect that many elements in our natures will, like the crew of Columbus, rebel at our journey over the edge of the world. And we must expect that any conviction we find will be shared only with others who have braved the same crossing. We become like people with an extra sense whose data can be shared only amongst themselves. Those who lack the sense reject the data. We shall be called self-deluded, and our experience called hallucination. Yet he who knows his essential unity with all things can never be essentially alone.

Encompassing coincidence and what C.G. Jung called synchronicity, there is a harmony of being which brings it about that, when we search for the answer to our question in the one place where it can be found, namely in our individual focus of the universal awareness, outer correspondences are activated and come our way: books, people and other events meaningfully related to our search. This does not imply that we need never make effort to gain information. Opportunities are offered which, if taken, bring results appropriate to our needs. People looking for the teacher in the wrong place are easily duped by charlatans who claim them as their disciples.

Even if our fortune brings us before a man in whom we sense the presence of genuine knowledge and experience, we have no means of assessing his actual status and would be wasting our time were we to make the attempt. It often happens that our hearts and minds respond to the man who is only so far ahead as to be still in touch with us. We may draw inspiration from the presence of men who have gained the supreme knowledge, but the best guide in practice is often the man who is still working on or has just conquered the problems we are beginning to face.

Note that we speak of the heart and of feeling, and not of the mind alone. The experiential knowledge we seek is not a cognitive abstract, nor is it something we can get, look at, and file away for reference. By its very nature, the search for the whole demands wholeness in us who seek, and feelings are an important and often neglected part of the whole.

If we place ourselves under the guidance of any teacher of the way, we are not asking for religious or philosophical instruction, though both may be included in the discipline he imposes on us. We wish to follow him on his inner journey, share his experience, and, like him, discover the unitary consciousness within which we, together with all beings, are sustained. The obstacles we shall encounter are hidden in our own natures behind those self-assertive demands and opinions by which the immature—and all men are immature who have not achieved wholeness of being—attempt to conceal their inadequacies of character. They are obstacles, because anything which drives us to assert our individuality thereby separates us from perception of the transcendental unity.

And any fear of self-loss which makes us cling to externalities for reassurance, by asserting the importance of the outer universe prevents perception of the inner. If, therefore, the teacher produces emotionally charged situations which involve us, we must submit to them, for by using his own emotions he demonstrates to us the inadequacy of ours.

We shall attempt to protect ourselves from perception of our immaturities by permitting our own faults to be projected onto the teacher. If we fail to recognize what is happening, we shall eventually become so dissatisfied as to go off in search of a 'better' man, and, as a person who has failed in one marriage is apt to fail in another for the same reasons, we shall be liable to repeat the process of an initial enthusiasm followed by discontent when we balk at facing the same faults.

The principles outlined above can clearly be applied to ordinary life experience. We should be able to see that the true teacher is life itself. If we can accept both rational criticism of our faults and emotional and seemingly irrational demonstrations of them from a man we respect and love, without self-defence, self-justification, or projecting our own faults onto him, then we should be able to accept them from anyone. Life produces real situations which the teacher imitates. The teacher weighs the ties of dedication, loyalty and affection against the emotional strains he subjects us to, and he may take compensatory steps to offset shocks that prove too severe. Life appears to operate more impersonally.

But if we examine the shocks life imposes on us and we see what lessons we have or should have learned from them, we can often perceive how they have acted on us towards producing maturity of being. However, since most men's views of maturity stop at a superficial adaptation to the practical affairs of living, it frequently happens that we cannot begin to see the teacher in life itself until we have gained a more adequate view from a human teacher. However, whether or not anyone applies this technique to us, it is in the midst of emotional turmoil that we can most easily recognize the one part of our being which is essentially calm in its own nature.

This attitude towards life experience is not an egotistical illusion arising from the idea either that the whole world runs round 'me,' or that the universe is designed to benefit the human race. The universe is divine. The divine awareness seeks its own fulfillment through itself and finds it through the human vehicle in which that awareness achieves its highest intensity. In order to bring it to its highest intensity, the mental-emotional complex of the vehicle must be matured. Life experience acts towards maturity.

We have stressed the importance of the unitive experience, because its reality is the sole guarantee for the significance of our enterprise. But if we set out in search of "an experience," we shall vitiate our efforts because such an attitude is egotistic and therefore separative.

It is true that some people have an overwhelming vision of the unity, sometimes without much apparent effort, while others achieve it, if at all, only after years of struggle. But the former may take many years to assimilate and integrate what they have seen, while the latter may integrate each step as they take it. Admitting the reality of the experience and the maturity and integrity that it demands of us, how are we to interpret its significance?

Hindu philosophy, as commonly understood, places such importance on the unitive experience that the highest goal of man is represented as self-loss of the individual within the universal. However, the equally Indian philosophy of Buddhism, while denying the survival of anything that can be humanly conceived of as personal characteristics, in its bodhisattva doctrine gives as an alternative goal—that of the individual who, refusing complete dissolution in the transcendent unity, retains an individual spiritual existence out of compassion for the suffering of all beings. And whereas the *Advaita Vedanta* of Shankaracharya, commonly considered the most representative and influential form of Hindu philosophy, stresses the unmanifest and transcendent reality to the detriment of the manifest universe which it declares illusory, Nagarjuna of the *Madhyamika* school of Buddhism declares: 'There is no difference at all between *Nirvana* and *Samsara*—meaning thereby that the unmanifest absolute and the worlds of form are of the same nature.

We are not concerned to evaluate these views either in support of or in opposition to the religious systems which claim them as their own. They are not given as examples of religious thought, but in order to demonstrate the different interpretations given by different men of what was fundamentally the same experience. Both views represent modes of apperception of the one truth. And we must have the honesty to admit that the ultimate truth may not be susceptible of any one definitive evaluation. All that can be said with certainty is that it is the underlying unity of being which supports all values. This could be formulated in the words of an elderly Indian sufi who, when asked, "What is truth?" replied: "That is very simple. What makes one out of two is true. What makes two out of one is false."

From the attitudes taken by seers towards their own perceptions, it would appear that we are here not so much dealing with two different interpretations of one truth, one of which must be more true than the other, as we are with the concept of there being two distinct interpretations, each of which, if accepted, leads to different results. All seers agree that the unity can be entered and that the individual who enters it is lost forever. From the accounts of seers who have approached that state, such annihilation would appear to be utterly blissful. Whether blissful or not, however, annihilation in the unmanifest being from which all things arose is the inescapable end of all existence. And the fact that the divine awareness joys in uniting itself with itself and includes the individual in its joy, may not, so long as we have not reached that state of transcendental being, appear to be adequate compensation for our involvement in a seemingly pointless system of repetitious self-creation followed by self-destruction.

Though each individual who achieves such utter annihilation presumably has his moment when he feels participation in the cosmic fulfillment which is attained through him, this achievement is obtained at the cost of its immediate obliteration. Nothing remains of the individual, and the universal awareness loses its focus of individual experience through which it achieved the self-knowledge it seeks. Both the achievement and the world-negating thrust which supported the achievement appear to make nonsense of the seemingly tremendous effort which has raised existent being to the point where individuals can attain such intensity of awareness and such intensity of directed effort that both world and individual can be neglected.

Though all seers accept the reality of this annihilation, not all of them describe it as the only or even as the highest course. The bodhisattva doctrine, mentioned above, which teaches that men may halt on the edge of the ultimate unity for the benefit of suffering humanity, has its parallels in all religious systems. This doctrine places annihilation as the highest goal which brings the greatest bliss to the participant, and it represents restraint from this goal as a sacrifice, motivated by compassion, a compassion that is no sentimental "do-goodism," but which derives from actual perception of the essential unity of all things. However, some seers go so far as to denigrate annihilation in the sense of self-obliteration in the infinite, calling it selfish bliss, and prefer restraint as the highest goal. The rationale for such preference is simply this: through the individual attainment the universal spirit achieves its goal of self-knowledge. If such a man passes into utter annihilation within universal being, the goal is lost at the moment it is found and the universal effort is vitiated. If he refuses annihilation, the spirit retains its self-knowledge in his being. Just as the unmanifest spirit needs its manifest form in order to know its inherent qualities, so it needs its essential knowledge to be held in individual forms if it is to be retained and the two aspects of knowledge fused.

In evaluating such restraint as the highest goal, the seer is not cushioning either himself or us from the apparent starkness of annihilation. Nor can we impute to him a wish for egotistic self-preservation. Only self-transcendence can achieve either goal, and only the self-restraint natural to love can achieve the restraint necessary to refuse the unifying pull of the transcendent being which is experienced as its love-desire. Indeed, such restraint is not the sacrifice of the highest goal, but the final sacrifice of ego-motivation. The seer who achieves this state is no longer in any sense a separate individual. The light of the universal awareness shines, unobstructed, through the vehicle of its own form.

This dual interpretation of the goal possibly accounts for there being two recognizably different attitudes taken by seers towards the world: those who sacrifice the bliss of self-annihilation commonly accept the bonds and responsibilities of affection here, while those drawn to annihilation commonly reject them.

Myth, folklore, the teachings of religions, the living experience of men engaged in this work, and the statements of seers themselves, all affirm the real existence of such great beings who, long after their physical deaths, continue to live and to guide others to their goal. No one who has ventured far along this path will dismiss these figures as illusory images of the "wise old man" archetype, as, apparently, would the school of C. G. Jung. Nor, for that matter, will anyone who has met an embodied seer dismiss him as being possessed by such an archetype.

Anyone who undertakes this work in all seriousness will find himself compelled to accept the objective reality of subtle planes of being. They constitute both the realms of after-death existence and the subtle components of physically embodied existence. Anyone who withdraws his attention from the organs of sense inevitably finds his powers of sense registering phenomena of another sort. And though the data supplied by the sense powers are unreliable, in that they tend to be mixed with the projected content of the seer's "unconscious" psyche, analytic sorting of such data brings to light sufficient evidence for the same sharing of experience as constitutes the criterion of reality for the world perceived through the physical organs.

Furthermore, anyone who takes the trouble to do so can gain sufficient experience of the physical and psychological effects produced by disembodied men impinging on this physical world to convince him that the shared experience of subtle states of being is neither collective hallucination nor mere experience of the collective unconscious.

181

The seer has passed through these realms and, though he may discourage us from egotistic fantasies of development and exploitation of psychic powers, he knows the value of paranormal experiences which shake our habitually materialistic outlook. He introduces us to a path on which, if nothing unusual ever happens, we may justly doubt either our own progress or the efficacy of the method we are practising. The effect of mystical experience is not limited to the individual to whom it comes. The individual becomes the source of a world view which affirms that life is meaningful and purposeful only when the direction of events along the dimension of time is related to their significance in the dimension of eternity.

We have spoken of the seer as the exemplar of the goal of life and as the sum of human perfection, yet so described his characteristics as to include inarticulate men of average intelligence. Though we can easily accept that there may be human qualities of greater general significance than intellectual brilliance, it is hard to accept a view of human perfection in which there is no visible luster. It is true that the human eye is a window into the soul which gives us a measure of the soul's radiance, but it is the tongue that reveals or betrays our highest human qualities. To the uninitiated a rough diamond may pass unnoticed. Let but one face be chipped, and its qualities as a gem become apparent. Not until many facets are skillfully cut and polished is its full beauty and brilliance manifested. Nevertheless, one recognizable diamond, even uncut, is of more value than highly polished glass. And one real seer, even if inarticulate, is of more value than all the highly polished prelates of the world.

The above analogy suggests that there may be seers with many or all of the facets of their personalities highly developed. And so there are. But one must beware of fantasies on this subject. Before hunting a presumptive seer with shining facets one must learn to distinguish diamond from glass.

When the divine awareness achieves knowledge of the divine self-nature, it achieves the term of the movement by which it evolves itself out of itself. By the fact of his being, the human teacher or guru exemplifies the term of the evolution and, by virtue of his example, arouses and activates his counterpart within our hearts.

The guru lives in us as the urge to wholeness. We see him in men who have found the whole or part of that whole. We see him in the whole of life that grows towards wholeness. We find him in that unity which contains the whole.

The wonder with which we view the guru's path as it unfolds before us, the spontaneous respect we feel for him whose calm eyes affirm that our turmoil can be calmed, the love that wells up in our hearts for him who supports us in our moments of despair, and our overflowing gratitude to him who gives us so much of his knowledge, of his guidance and, above all, of himself—all these are natural responses of the human heart towards the man whose very being declares the truth of his attainment and the factual efficacy of his teaching. By being what he is, he has shown us the way, for he is in himself the demonstration of an objectively undemonstrable attainment.

Praise to the Guru who showed me the impartite Spirit which pervades all animate and inanimate beings.

Praise to the Guru who cured my blind ignorance with the eye-salve of know-ledge.

Praise to the Guru who is Creator, Preserver and Destroyer, and is even the Supreme Being himself.

Prem, *Outline Sketch.*
Times of India, 15 Oct. 1972.
Whitehead, *Process and Reality.*
Herrigel, *Zen in the Art of Archery.*
"Guru Gita," *Nectar of Chanting*, 16-17.

11

Pastor: Meetings with a Remarkable Channeled Entity

When I was a busy corporate manager in Chicago, "channeling" or mediumship and reincarnation possibly came at the bottom of a list of things I was interested in, or thought that I ever would be interested in.

This notwithstanding, what follows is an excerpt from a "channeled" talk that, some ten years into my correspondence with Ashish, I found myself listening to with a group of twenty persons mostly members of my Gurdjieff group, in my condominium in Fort Lauderdale, Florida.

'What? Are there some sick souls up there? Can a soul be sick?'

Of course, it is not a matter of the same type of healing. We must understand that when the souls which pass through incarnation on planets like the earth, where we know that torture is a daily occurrence, where we know that we can die suddenly in an accident, where we know that we can die in a very traumatizing way or can have lived a very traumatizing life, come out of this conditioning, they will, in a way, be somewhat like lame ducks....All this has to be corrected, and the doctor of the soul at this time intervenes and rectifies the substance, first rectifying the etheric body which during the three days following death continues to exist....It is at that time that we put these souls in what we could really call a cosmic hospital or celestial hospital, and these individuals go around acting out their problems.

These words were issuing from the lips of a young woman from Switzerland, whom I'll call Charlaine, who sat facing us in a straight-backed chair. Her eyes were closed. She was merely a medium, or "channel;" allegedly, the words weren't coming from her at all but from a discarnate spirit guide who spoke through her and whom (at his request) I'll call Pastor.

The passage I quote above is only a fraction of what "came through" that afternoon. I chose those particular lines because eventually Ashish would comment on them, as the reader will discover later in this chapter. Charlaine "talked" for four hours and fifteen minutes that day, pausing in her slow careful monotone only to answer our questions, and never even getting up from her chair. This was the second of what would end up being nine sessions given primarily before members of my Gurdjieff group in my condo in Fort Lauderdale. I would later attend several additional sessions, a number more in my condominium, and the rest among Theosophists and other interested parties in Switzerland (in which country, along with France and Belgium, Charlaine gave a great many séances). However mystifying and compelling these séances in Fort Lauderdale were, one of those given in Switzerland would be the most explosive of all.

My interest in channeling had arisen in connection with my interest in esotericism and all related phenomena. Still, my encounter with Charlaine only took place because of what I once called "chance" and now call "synchronicity"—a happening due to laws of causality we know nothing about. In May, 1988, I'd received—out of the blue, unsolicited—the English translation of a channeled talk Charlaine (then unknown to me) had given at a chapter of the Theosophical Society in Cavallirio, near Milan, in Italy. At the time, my interest in channeling was such that I would have thrown the paper away unread immediately, had it not been for one fact: The group called itself the Gruppo Teosofico Sarmoung—the "Sarmoung" Theosophical Group.

The reader well knows the resonances that the word "Sarmoung" has for me! It had become for me almost an archetypal name for the secret, hidden societies of the Masters of mankind, in whose existence I still harbored a lingering hope, despite the frequent remonstrances of Ashish that, in pining after this place, I was merely avoiding the Self.

Still, even the presence of the word "Sarmoung" was not enough to make me read the paper, and I tossed it into a drawer unread.

Seven months later, I came across it, began to read it, and continued to read it. It was called *The Role of an Initiatory School* (into esoteric knowledge), and it was really rather interesting. The channeled entity who had dictated this paper through Charlaine was, as I've been calling him, Pastor. Whatever his reality, he could give a pretty good talk. I found out that Charlaine lived in Switzerland. The reader will already know that I maintain a condominium in a Geneva suburb where I spend several weeks a year. I wrote to Charlaine, telling her who I was and what my interests were and suggesting we meet in Geneva.

About a month later, the reply came back—not from Switzerland, but from Hollywood, Florida, right next door to where I live in Fort Lauderdale. It was from a man whom I'll call "Carl" (he has also asked that I use a pseudonym).

I would later find out that Carl was a wealthy Swiss real estate developer who lived in a suburb of Geneva himself and wintered with Charlaine in a condominium in Hollywood, Florida, every year. The two were not married, nor was there any romantic interest between them. Carl, who was fairly elderly, had a great many health problems; unable to find relief from established medicine, and being an ardent Theosophist, he had, after interviewing a number of highly recommended mediums in Switzerland and surrounding countries, hired Charlaine on a permanent basis to provide him with sometimes quite effective channeled medical advice from Pastor.

I would discover that Carl was no crank, nor was he in any way taking advantage of Charlaine. He is a successful, intelligent businessman who, well versed in esoteric lore, had the imagination, the courage and the financial means to retain this highly unorthodox method of receiving treatment for his many ailments.

I wasted no time in contacting Carl, and he and Charlaine and I became good friends. (Steeped as I was in the concept of synchronicity, it was not lost on me that Carl and Charlaine's condo in Hollywood, Florida, was about the same distance from my residence in Fort Lauderdale as their villa in a suburb of Geneva was from my residence in another suburb of Geneva!) As a result of our meeting and the resulting friendship, Charlaine held, as I've said, nine séances in my condo in Fort Lauderdale, including the one a passage from which I began this chapter.

Let me explain what happened during these séances. Charlaine waited in a room next to the room where she gave the séance, quieting herself in preparation. In her absence, the audience discussed possible questions to put to Pastor. Experience had shown that, whatever the question, Pastor used it as a kind of jumping off point to give a spiritual dissertation. Once we'd agreed on a question, Charlaine was called back into the room where the group was assembled. She sat down in her chair facing the audience. She closed her eyes and begin making various motions with her hands (she told me on one occasion that she believed this latter happened because Pastor was using her fingers to pick up the vibrations of the audience). Then she became very quiet.

Carl was usually the one who presented the question, although in some later sessions others, including myself, took on this role. Charlaine listened to the question. Then Charlaine/Pastor began a lengthy talk. These talks averaged about two hours, though, as I have mentioned, during one of the sessions I attended she spoke for four hours, fifteen minutes. The voice was Charlaine's, but the inflections and style of speaking were completely different. It was a personality other than the Charlaine I'd come to know. Sometimes, Pastor would address a statement or comment to someone in the audience and have a conversation with that person, but for the most part he gave a monologue. The question put to Charlaine in the second talk was a Gurdjieffian question that we'd put together. In this instance, since the audience of about twenty people was composed almost entirely of members of our Gurdjieff group, the question had a special significance for us Gurdjieffians.

The early talks to our group were conducted in French, Charlaine's native language. Some of us understood French and others did not, so we transcribed and translated these early talks into English. In later talks, Jacqueline, who was our group's native French speaker, did a simultaneous translation for the audience. In still later talks, Charlaine—whose English gradually become more proficient during the several years of her involvement with these talks—developed the confidence to channel in English the information she was receiving from Pastor.

I'd kept Ashish abreast of these developments. Both Madhava Ashish (and Krishna Prem before him) believed in the existence of a plenitude of other worlds and dimensions (it is only the Western belief systems that hold no such belief). Both Ashish and Prem believed that channeling could, and did, take place, and could represent contact with other, discarnate, entities.

That being said, Ashish believed that the nature of the other realms of reality was such that one could expect at best only an extremely garbled channeling "transmission." In fact, so garbled could be this transmission, for so many complex reasons, that it was practically not worth one's while to participate in a séance, especially given that too great an involvement in such a pastime could even impede one's spiritual development. As I've quoted earlier, Ashish had written, in *Man, Son of Man,* that "all information coming from or through the subtle or 'astral' realms is liable to deformation or alteration, the cause of which is usually considered an objective property of those realms themselves."

I'd sent Ashish a copy of Charlaine's channeled Gruppo Teosofica Sarmoung talk, along with an explanatory letter.

A.   The guide could be any ordinary person, or just a split-off bit of Charlaine's personality. And one has to guard against her getting mixed up because people make demands on her and she wants to please, even when herself feeling put off it. I am not particularly happy at the level of communication. If you want to keep up the contact, you must be very sure of keeping your head. This is the problem. To be safe from any mistake she may make, you have to have the capacity to know/feel the truth or falsity of whatever she brings. In which case your need of what she may bring is reduced. The responsibility for being or not being fooled is yours, not hers. Blavatsky was genuine, but that didn't stop her from delighting in fooling others. [March 2, 1989]

By mid-March of 1989, I'd printed up translations of two of the séances that had taken place in my condo and sent the texts plus tapes off to Ashish. Because I'd come to know Charlaine well, I was convinced there was no intentional fraud involved. I had also witnessed, as had the others, that the entity, when it spoke through Charlaine, manifested as an entirely discrete personality.

I wondered whether that personality was some split-off part of Charlaine's personality or something completely separate. Although I'd previously seen other demonstrations of channeling, what the others and I witnessed in this instance appeared in some sense to be a more genuine voice from another place, and in that respect, miraculous—not unlike, I thought, the communications of Djwhal Khul as channeled and written down by Alice A. Bailey.

I put these various issues before Ashish.

A.   The problem of fraudulence. The nature of such communications is that they are inherently unreliable. The person may be as genuine as you could wish, but she has by definition and by admission no control over what comes. Even H.P.B., who was exceptional, occasionally got things wrong.

The big problem is that, while the audience must accept responsibility for the acceptance or rejection or modification of what comes, they usually lack the criteria for assessment. Generally, it is better to be gullible than to be coldly analytic on the basis of current establishment standards which, being materialistic, accept nothing of the sort. Gullibility leaves one open both to the truth and to fraud.

One must therefore accept that one may be misled, and that it is better to be misled and to learn from mistakes than to avoid mistakes and to be shut to the truth.

189

Personality: That what comes through is unlike the waking personality is no guarantee that it does not come from the person. There are numerous recorded cases of multiple personality, each one speaking separately in trance—often hypnotic trance. Typically, each level of personality is aware of the behavior/thoughts of the one below it, but not of the ones above it. Ultimately, of course, the higher Self in all men is the same, but this is not of much help in practice.

You must forgive my amusement at your reaction to your first experience of psychic communication. It confirms Gopalda's dictum that an interest in the occult is one of the necessary attributes of the seeker, and my own view that one needs experience of the occult to persuade one that the subtle worlds are real and not just metaphysical speculations. [March 30, 1989]

I'd told Ashish: "Charlaine told me she sensed an entity near to me who she assumed was my spiritual guide. This sounded an 'alarm bell' in me, because it smacked of flattery."

A.   You are right to beware of flattery. You should also be awake to the fact that Charlaine may unintentionally pick ideas and thoughts out of your head. This can be positive evidence of thought transference. [March 30, 1989]

I'd also asked, "What is the significance of those coincidences regarding where we all live in South Florida and Switzerland?"

A: The Geneva and Florida coincidence is only an example of how properly directed work brings you into contact with the people, experiences and so forth that one needs. [March 30, 1989]

A month later, Ashish, having read the transcripts, had a great deal more to say:

A: I have read Charlaine's talk twice, first to myself and then aloud to the group. I find that reading aloud is a powerful test.

I appreciate the difficulties inherent in translation. In this sort of work, the success really depends on how good a grasp of the subject one has, the attempt being to write what she means and not merely a word-by-word transliteration. In reading aloud, I found I had to abbreviate; there are too many words which bemuse rather than elucidate.

The content appears genuine. The rather poor passages, such as some of the descriptions of the inner worlds, are a bit too reminiscent of spiritualism, i.e., too literalistic. For instance, there are indeed hospitals for sick souls [this refers to the passage at the beginning of the chapter], but one has to be careful not to give these a more material being than the images of dream. However, the point that after-death-experience varies with the evolutionary level of the individual is not commonly appreciated and is therefore good.

The patchiness complicates the problem of whose teaching it is and who is repeating it. Charlaine may not have been exposed to Theosophy, Bailey, etc., but Carl has been and one wonders how much she may be picking up from his mind, for you say he is the dominant personality in the pair. Also, some psychic children can record in memory adult talk overheard, and then repeat it automatically, without understanding, so the fact that Charlaine consciously knows nothing is no proof that she is not repeating stuff heard in childhood.

Don and Kersy were reminded of one of Nisarga Datta's interpreters who, when interpretation was called for by a non-Marathi-speaking inquirer, would volunteer answers without reference to Nisarga Datta. It was not just that he knew Nisarga Datta's answers from long exposure to them; he would embark on a long lecture about Hindu philosophy in general. This could suggest that it is, indeed, only a Guide speaking—someone who has sufficient exposure to the teaching to have been deputed to pass it on through Charlaine. This fits the account given in the text. It also accounts for the patchiness. This squares with my impression that the given explanation is correct: The Guide is speaking most of the time on the basis of teaching he has received.

191

One would like to have the opportunity to compare this regular stuff with what is said to come through when a Teacher speaks directly. One would expect it to be much less verbose. The guide is repeating things he has not yet made his own, and mixes it with descriptions of the inner worlds as they appear to his level of consciousness.

So you can see how difficult the thing gets. The important aspect lies not so much in the details of the teaching given, but in the sense of reality that comes across: Something is really happening, and something is coming through from a real though non-physical world. As you say, this encourages you to work harder. But your effort should be to find your own source of communication. Even then, certainty lies beyond, in what is eternal. The Eternal has its own certainty.

There are a few places in each of the talks I have read where there is falsity. If, as Gopalda put it, one can't write anything on this subject without saying something that is true, it does not follow that one can't write anything on the subject without saying something that is false—not, at least, when a Master is supposed to be keeping an eye on the talk.

I shall tentatively suggest that an attempt is being made to get something through, but that the channel is distorting the output. Mediums are inherently passive types and are therefore inherently liable to get things a bit mixed.

Have you discussed with Carl the question of the ambience of the place in which the talk is given? Charlaine does not react well to the wrong sort of crowd—naturally enough. The level at which these things work is sensitive to the atmosphere, which is why there is hymn-singing in ordinary séances, incense burning, pictures of saints or images of gods. If anyone present has the power, and the intention is not to have any old ghost blundering in to have his say, steps can be taken to ensure that only the desired class of entity can communicate.

Of course, anyone might say that the verbose and confused manner of speech is deliberate and profoundly clever, along the lines of the two monks, Brother Ahl and Brother Sez, in the chapter on Professor Skridlov in *Meetings with Remarkable Men*. People looking for personal immortality will not feel so threatened by this presentation, as they would be by a clear one. Under the cover of confusion, the message gets under their guard.

I first read the text to myself, making as many allowances as possible for the presentation and making things fit. Then I read it aloud to the group, and there were yells of protest. I was accused of special pleading. But all admitted that some of the analogies are good, and that the whole thing might appear differently with Charlaine talking in some sort of trance/dissociation.

With this sort of communication, one must expect good days and bad days. If you take every word that comes from her as gospel truth, you will run yourself and Charlaine into trouble. But it's a touchy business; you don't want to make her lose confidence in herself by showing too much distrust. [May 1, 1989]

My relationship with Charlaine and Carl continued to develop all through 1989. They returned to Switzerland after wintering in Florida, and I met with them there on several occasions, witnessing public demonstrations of the channeling of Pastor.

Probably on account of my experiences with Pastor, I'd grown increasingly interested in the subject of reincarnation and what significance it might have. It's not clear whether Gurdjieff believed that we all live many lives, though it seemed to some that the higher sort of human being could "crystallize" what Gurdjieff called a "Kesdjan body," which could survive for a time after the death of the body ("Kesdjan" is a term used by Gurdjieff to denote the "astral" body, as it is known in theosophical terms—a body of very fine energy, connected with the emotions, that interpenetrates the physical body).

Both Ashish and Sri Krishna Prem believed in the reality of reincarnation. They held with the Theosophists a belief in an obligatory pilgrimage for every soul or essence—itself a spark of the Universal Oversoul—through countless cycles of reincarnation in accordance with cyclic and karmic laws. According to theosophical doctrine, during these incarnations the essence evolved from the lowest mineral form, through plant, animal, human and superhuman states, to a level of consciousness that knows its identity with Universal Oversoul or Absolute—one ultimate reality.

Some years earlier, I had sent Ashish the following quote (from the *Hermetica*), to which I was drawn, in which TAT is the pupil and HRM (Hermes Trismegistus) is the teacher, and had asked him what its significance was.

"TAT: 'Father, God has made me a new being, and I perceive things now, not with bodily eyesight, but by the working of the mind.'

"HRM: 'Even so it is, my son, when a man is born again; it is no longer a body of three dimensions that he perceives, but the incorporeal.'

"TAT: 'Father, now that I see in mind, I see myself to be the ALL. I am in heaven and in earth, in water and in air; I am in beast and in plants: I am a babe in the womb, and one that is not yet conceived, and one that has been born; I am present everywhere.'

"HRM: 'Now, my son, you know what rebirth is.'"

A: You appreciate that the "rebirth" talked of in the quotation you give is, of course, not reincarnation, but the "birth" of the higher being in man, which is what knows its identity with others. Perhaps this is what G was really talking about when he spoke of the "creation of the Kesdjan body." The energies of transformation are what builds that "body" and "gives birth" to the level of awareness which sees all things as one. [June 28, 1981]

Ashish was also to speak eloquently on reincarnation in dreams:

A.   As for the stuff about previous incarnations that sometimes appears in dreams, the most it can do is to give a person a sense of meaningful continuity in life. We are not ephemeral beings who appear by the chance processes of conception and disappear through death. These bodies are ephemeral, but our essential being belongs to the eternal. As the Orphics said: "I am a child of earth and starry heaven, but my race is of heaven alone."

As part of this, a troubled person can be relieved by the belief that his present difficulties are explainable in terms of misfortune or misdeeds in previous lives. Facts are unimportant. It is the personal myth that counts. Irrespective of the truth about previous lives, what troubles one now must be dealt with now. Neither blaming past conditions nor hoping for better ones in future lives will help. I have read only one recorded case of a nurse who appeared totally changed through hypnosis/reincarnation experiments, and that could have been due as much to the confidence engendered from the attention paid to her, as to the "therapy." All the rest are agog to have "experiences"—"ain't it wonderful!"—and have something to add to their meager ego identities.

I don't deny that experiments with drugs, breathing, and all the rest, are exciting, stimulating, encouraging, affirmatory of their being "something more," and in general great fun. But one must not go overboard and confuse such fun and games with serious work. Play by all means; but know where the Work lies.

It is devastating to be told that one's progress is completely blocked due to complications from past lives, and I would ignore any such interpretations from dreams or otherwise. But it is quite different if one is told that, for instance, cleaning out emotional blocks from infantile traumas will open up the possibility of inner progress. The same thing has been said but in the second case it is presented as part of the ongoing work. In any case, in this work the power to persist in one's efforts is really of more importance than what results from those efforts in terms of recognizable progress. [Jan 8, 1991]

The talks Pastor gave through Charlaine included numerous references to reincarnation. It turned out that Pat, another of Ashish's students from America, had brought him a recent book on the subject. I, in turn, had sent Ashish a book on reincarnation currently in vogue in America, *Many Lives, Many Masters*, written by the psychiatrist Brian Weiss. In this book, Weiss recounts how, while well into his first experience of administering "past-life regression" therapy—the sessions had begun as conventional regression-into-childhood therapy—Catherine, his patient, suddenly began to speak in a deeper, calmer voice, allegedly from "between her lives." The voice purported to belong to one of a number of "Masters" who described themselves as "highly evolved souls, not presently in body."

Weiss was astonished to hear this "Master" go on to describe a personal tragedy that had taken place in his life and that he had shared with no one but his wife. Years before, when Weiss was a physician not yet decided on psychiatry, his first son, Adam, had died at the age of twenty-three days from "total anomalous pulmonary venous damage with an atrial septal defect," the extremely rare medical event of a "backward" heart.

The "Master's" voice channeled through Weiss's patient further told the psychiatrist: "Your father is here, and your son, who is a small child. Your father says you will know him because his name is Avrom, and your daughter is named after him. Also, his death was due to his heart. Your son's heart was also important, for it was backward, like a chicken's. He made a great sacrifice for you out of his love. His soul is very advanced....His death satisfied his parents' debts. Also, he wanted to show you that medicine could only go so far; that its scope is very limited."

Weiss knew there was no way Catherine, his patient, could have known his father's Hebrew name was Avrom, or that Amy, Weiss's daughter, was named after her grandfather. He writes in *Many Lives, Many Masters* that "After Adam's death, I firmly decided that I would make psychiatry my profession. I was angry that modern medicine, with all its advanced skills and techniques, could not save my son, this simple, tiny baby." This unique personal "communication from a Master" radically altered Weiss's life, prompting him to publish not only *Many Lives, Many Masters* but also a second book, *Through Time into Healing*, in 1992.

I'd commented to Ashish on how astonished Weiss had been by all of this.

A.   All this reincarnation business is curious. Ian Stevenson's book [*Twenty Cases Suggestive of Reincarnation*] is "clean"—straight reporting of facts remembered in this life, without the suspicion that a psychiatrist has been grubbing around in the client's psyche. The book Pat brought (someone here is reading it so I can't refer) started off all right, but one got more and more suspicious as one went on; too many pirates and violent lives. O.K. History is full of violence, but there seems to be an overdose.

In many instances, I think, the writer's own suspicion is correct, namely, that deeply repressed and rather frightening material (frightening to the patient) is easier to bring up to consciousness when it is dressed up as having happened in a former life for which the person can feel in no close way responsible. This is the same mechanism as the dressing up of unwelcome messages in relatively pleasant symbols and so getting it past the dream censor. In that book, about the only two cases I felt might be actual past lives were the woman who had been a Dutch painter who hung himself in remorse, and Sol with sinus trouble who had been very unhappy over his mother's illness as a boy and then wept at the Wailing Wall in Jerusalem. But even in Sol's case, there is ground for doubt that he was specifically connected with J.C.

I shall have to read Weiss again to form an opinion. The credentials only show that he is not a failure in the world who sees a chance to cash in on people's gullibility. They add nothing to his story, one way or the other. The dull repetitiveness of the lives supports the possibility of their historicity; but from the psychologist's viewpoint it could suggest that there is something not dealt with here and now, as would be the case with repetitive dreams. The question is not really very important in comparison to the importance of their therapeutic effect.

I find his supposed "Masters" entirely unconvincing. They are at best only "Guides"—a subject to discuss in reply to your question—if they are not his own mental constructions picked up by the girl in trance. Previous life information that turns up, unasked for, in the context of specific locations, whether backed by dreams or not, can easily be believed—e. g., the woman who knew her way around Rome on her first visit. Also, memories that float in without help from hypnosis, drugs and analysts. But as soon as hypnosis, drugs, etc. come in, with nothing in the patient's waking experience to confirm or deny, one is left only with the fact that it is therapeutically useful, and the question of their being real past lives ceases to matter, except to the patient who needs to believe it.

Then how should we regard these images? My guess is that they are as real as any remembered images of life are real, but that one does not need to assume that they are the past lives of this particular person lying hypnotized on the couch. They can be anyone's past life experience, drawn from the store of lives in the collective unconscious, and selected for therapeutic use on the patient in the same way that dream images are selected. It is commonplace that not all dream images derive from one's own waking experience in this life, and I see no reason for supposing that they must derive from this individual's past lives, even if there are not obvious reasons why they should not be. Moreover, once the person has seen those images, one cannot hope to confirm or deny by taking him/her to the location of the dream/vision, because he can obviously recognize what he saw in dream.

It is clear that my objection is centered on the fact that the visions occur under hypnosis, a state in which, as is only too often seen, the hypnotized person's mind is affected by what is in the hypnotizer's mind. Under hypnosis you might be able to re-experience the traumatic experience you seem to have had in infancy, and you might see it as if it occurred in a previous life. If it helped you get over the problem, what else would matter? As Gopalda used to say, "You may have been the emperor of China in your last life. But how does that help you now?" This does not deny the usefulness of knowing enough about reincarnation to get this life into perspective, and to benefit from a sense of continuity. In fact, you should be more concerned with seeing the one life in all, including the sense in which you have lived all lives, than with which particular lives were specifically linked with the one now referred to as Sy Ginsburg.

Increased interest in inner things? As Weiss discovers, once you dare to start talking of them, you find all sorts of ordinary people admitting to having them too. So it is very difficult to know whether there is a real increase, or whether what was there all along is now allowed to come to the surface. It is the latter alternative we are really concerned with. Two things have happened which affect the issue. Physics has broken through the barrier of matter and has accepted that there are no ultimate particles of matter. This does not mean that scientists all over the world immediately accept the findings of mystical vision, etc. However, the other thing that is happening is that the utter emptiness of life without spiritual significance is not only threatening the very structure of society and questioning the values of political systems and their ideologies, but is also making people, including scientists, question the premises of scientific materialism. All sorts of things which were not respectable and whose study would lead to a scientist losing his job and getting no one to publish his papers if he studied them, are now open to discussion. And because the subject is full of the sorts of pitfalls I mention and because people think they can approach it all in the same analytic fashion as worked in the material world, a terrible lot of trash is and is going to be printed.

This sort of thing will find its parallels in astrological periodicities. But that is, as it were, on the level of macro-statistics which do not determine what any particular individual will do. In your own case, meditation, etc. and self-awareness exercises have made you more open to what is happening in this field. If your mind was shut, many of these things would not register. Your interest in the psychic (Charlaine, etc.) has opened a road in you. Spirits go to and fro on that road (i.e., visions of people). But there lies no certainty, and here lies no certainty. You must not be enslaved by the spirits: "Seek for thy Master in what lies beyond...the Hall of Truth... " The energy you have awoken has to be guided. Guide it by fixing your attention on "The star whose ray thou art." [May 1, 1989]

I have yet to speak of the most mysterious, even the most explosive, of all the séances channeled by Charlaine that I attended. This was a session that took place at Charlaine's house in Geneva. The reason for this European venue was that a colleague and good friend of mine, Nicolas Tereshchenko, had some very specific questions for Pastor; and since Nick, a retired surgeon, lived in Paris, the most obvious place for him to meet Pastor was at Charlaine's home in Switzerland.

Nick is one of the world's leading scholars of Gurdjieff's space odyssey/allegory *Beelzebub's Tales to His Grandson* (see next chapter), and he wanted to ask Pastor about some particularly mystifying details in that great book over which Gurdjieff labored for many years. I've previously mentioned that some followers of the Gurdjieff teachings think there is, for want of a better term, an "eternally conscious essence" of Gurdjieff, which can make itself known to the pupil if the need is great and is a valid one.

I'm not exactly sure if Nick subscribed to this belief, but his intention was to at least try to find out from Pastor what Gurdjieff meant by a particular concept expressed in *Beelzebub's Tales.*

The private session took place on November 21, 1989. In 1984, Charlaine's psychic talents had come to the attention of a prominent Theosophist from Geneva, who had then helped Charlaine to develop her psychic abilities. This had culminated in the appearance of Pastor, who claimed to be a minor initiate in what is known in theosophical circles as the "spiritual hierarchy." By November, 1989, then, Charlaine had in one way or another acquired some knowledge of Theosophy. But she still knew virtually nothing about Gurdjieff or the Gurdjieffian teachings.

Here is part of what transpired on that night, with Charlaine, in a light trance, speaking as Pastor:

Nick: "Mr. Gurdjieff calls the 'heptaparaparshinokh' one of the primary cosmic laws, but he does not give, it seems to me, all the data necessary to understand it well. What must I know, in addition to what is given in Mr. Gurdjieff's work, in order to really understand this law in depth?"

Pastor: *The initiate you are talking about is a being who has been composed. Of course, he came on earth with his own spiritual dimension, but, in fact, the Masters he has met have not created in him the spirituality he could radiate. We must know that he has been composed as far as the kind of intellectual radiance, as far as the kind of* alchemical radiance which he could propose to people and to which he has initiated people.

This is to say that if the being you are talking about, whom you call Gurdjieff (although for us he has another name), had known totally free spiritual enfoldment, he would have given of his own being, of his own initiatic level. And what he would have given would have been, believe me, something entirely different. However, there was written in his stars, in his destiny, the fact that he would have to take on one destiny, to offer one message. And this was in direct resonance with the disobedience he had committed a very long time ago, a very long time ago in history.

This means, in fact, that his work was a service and at the same time also a karma, a kind of reverence he owed to humanity but especially to the Lodge to which he belongs. This is why he could not do anything else but to return to this Lodge, to return to see his Masters whom he had disobeyed. And by the way, disobedience, originality, is something that characterized him even in the life he has known as Gurdjieff, all the way to the end of his days.

It is by this note that we could discover his disobedient nature or, if you wish, the final impact of his disobedience. Although I speak of disobedience, we must not see it as being an error. It is simply something that happens. It is almost unavoidable in the development of the initiate. I would say it is even desirable, because it is where we can see that he really exists, that he is building himself, that he is beginning to understand the universe and he is beginning to appropriate the divinity. Therefore, it is desirable. But of course this commits the individual to a certain kind of karma; this is also certain.

So, to get back to the question, I would say that the teaching he gave rests on one hand on the spiritual dimension he himself was, which he has developed throughout history. But at the same time his teaching was largely composed by the Masters he had met who ordered him to say things this way, to do things that way, and to give until such point and no further. This is why we can discern randomly in the texts, randomly in the lines, that something is missing. Not because something is really missing, but rather because he did not have the permission or the command to give the complement of information.

This communication was totally unexpected and surprising. It was not, however, without meaning for Nick and myself. The question whether Gurdjieff was an "enlightened Master"—whether he was enlightened, and what constitutes a Master—is a problematical one for those of a spiritual bent. Not only was Gurdjieff no "plaster saint," but there is no question he was a hell-raiser in his youth and indeed ever afterward.

So it was remarkable that Pastor should have uttered lines like, *And this was in direct resonance with the disobedience he had committed a very long time ago, a very long time ago in history.* Disobedience is a trait that characterized Gurdjieff even as Gurdjieff, from the beginning of his days to the end. One of Gurdjieff's prime teachings—one for which I, along with many other Gurdjieff students, had the greatest admiration—was that one should never "do the expected thing " It was practically an admonition to constantly disobey. With this admonition, Gurdjieff had justified his habit of always saying and doing the opposite of what you might expect—especially if it might bring the necessary Gurdjieffian "friction" into your life to help you "wake up."

How could Charlaine possibly have known all this?

Pastor seemed to question Gurdjieff's full status as a Master. Ashish had often remarked that Gurdjieff was not only not an ordinary human being, but he was not even someone who during this lifetime had developed the guru-like qualities we usually ascribe to people who have attained spiritual development (such as Nisarga Datta, or perhaps Ashish himself). Ashish believed that the being we call Gurdjieff in this lifetime had attained his high level of development in previous lifetimes, and had been "sent back in" to this lifetime to help humanity. Ashish revered Gurdjieff as a bodhisattva—someone who had finished with his/her cycle of incarnations before this birth and, not obligated to come back, had come back anyway, just to help.

But Pastor was saying that however extraordinarily high the level of "objective consciousness" of the being we call Gurdjieff, there was something seriously flawed about his cycle of reincarnational lives, he was under certain compulsions and not an entirely free soul, that *his work was a service and at the same time also a karma, a kind of reverence he owed to humanity but especially to the Lodge to which he belongs. This is why he could not do anything else but to return to this Lodge, to return to see his Masters whom he had disobeyed.*

As far as Nick and I were concerned, these communications served simply to underscore how very meager was the understanding of us mere mortals about what being a "Master" really entailed. Ashish had often said that it was a mistake to "create" a Master in one's own image of how a Master should behave, in the same way as it was the common error of humankind to mistakenly try to create a God in its own image—the image of behavior *we* think is appropriate, rather than the other way round.

It was for these reasons that Ashish did not much care for the opinion of a Theosophist who had written to the journal *Theosophical History* criticizing any claim for Gurdjieff's status as a Master on the grounds that he smoked, drank, was not a vegetarian, and was sexually active.

A: The Theosophist can have her "gentle, pure and holy" Masters, but she has neither the right nor the equipment to claim that that is the only sort of Master there is. Jesus consorted with Publicans and wine-bibbers. He broke the rules of the Sabbath. He violently drove out the money-changers from the Temple. Jesus, the Buddha, and Mani hobnobbed with prostitutes. HPB used foul language—"swore like a trooper"—and smoked continuously. Even the "mild and gentle" Apollonius of Tyana, when he had a clairvoyant vision of the assassination of the Emperor Domitian, reportedly leapt to his feet crying, "Strike the tyrant; strike!" (G. R. S. Mead, *Apollonius of Tyana*, London: Theosophical Publishing House, 1901, p. 115)....We want to wean people away from the stained glass portrait of the saint, to learn from their observation of life that drink, sex, meat eating, etc., are not evil in themselves, but are good or evil according to the way they are used. She called G a *dugpa*, something she has no right to ascribe to G or to HPB who many churchmen condemned for her "satanic" phenomena. We have to get away from judging saints by their conformity to preconceived notions of social morality, and attempt to feel the real qualities of the Spirit in the man. One cannot even claim there to be safety in sticking to the pure and holy, for there are pure and holy frauds. [March 2, 1989]

Of particular interest to Nick and myself was Pastor's comment on *the disobedience he* [Gurdjieff] *had committed a very long time ago, a very long time ago in history.* In the chapter on *Beelzebub's Tales to His Grandson*, I speculate on the possibility that Gurdjieff's allegorical space odyssey is quasi-autobiographical, Beelzebub the traveler in time and space being a proxy for Gurdjieff himself. Beelzebub's sixth visit to planet Earth in the late nineteenth and early twentieth century parallels Gurdjieff's life. But, at the outset of the book, Gurdjieff writes of Beelzebub as having been "banished" from the center. Nick and I asked ourselves if it were possible that the being we know of as Gurdjieff could really have been expelled for "disobedience" from the unity of being in the very early history of the universe. Did this, perhaps, indicate a lack of objective consciousness? Of course, there was always the possibility that Charlaine, her lack of knowledge of what was contained in *Beelzebub's Tales to His Grandson* notwithstanding, had telepathically picked up our own thoughts about Gurdjieff. Again, we didn't think so, because Pastor's interpretation of G's life cycles was not entirely flattering, and we had no unflattering thoughts about Gurdjieff in our minds.

Pastor had more to say. Though not offering to serve as a conduit, the channeled entity suggested to Nick that he should reach out and try to speak directly to Gurdjieff himself:

If you want more, call Gurdjieff, be truly Gurdjieff's disciple. Then, if you show yourself to him as his disciple (and when I say "his disciple," it is not in the meaning of membership), I would rather say show yourself as a cup that strives to join another cup in order for that cup to tip over and fill it. Then you are out of the conditionings the Masters, who composed Gurdjieff, who composed his service, insisted upon. You are out of the orders, which conditioned Gurdjieff. There-

fore, he does not have to keep his word either to the Masters, or to the plan, or to the necessity of the present civilization. There is simply a Master and a disciple. And the one who will be the limit of the transmission of the teaching will not be the Master but will be the disciple. So, if you want more, call him.

However, you will tell me, "But I cannot call Gurdjieff. How can I get in contact with Gurdjieff? Does it mean that I must become either telepathic or that I could receive a teaching myself?"

Then I will tell you that there are a thousand and one ways to be in correspondence, whether with a Master, with a simple initiate, or with the mind of the Hierarchy, or with the mind of the Solar Hierarchy, or with God's mind, let us suppose. There exist a thousand ways.

But, generally, the method the Master uses is the one the Egyptian initiate used to use, and it is what they used to call "the prophetic dream" or "the sacred dream." This is to say that we must put ourselves into a deep meditative state, during which we do not predestine ourselves to meet the Master or find the answer to this or that question. We try to simply open ourselves, to be an absence, to be a cup waiting to be filled.

From the moment we begin to be in that state, and supposing that during all the subsequent days we have called the Master or we have called the Hierarchy, and we have sent the question or we have sent the enigma that preoccupies us, at the moment we present ourselves in the universe with this openness, the answer automatically comes.

The answer comes in different ways: either through a symbolic dream, or by an apparition who says something, or by a film which seems to unfold and explains everything, or simply as if nothing appeared to be happening but the individual finds himself to be guided toward a book which contains the answer, or he picks up for the nth time the same book he was studying and inside a sentence, because of his multiple vision, he succeeds to decode the mystery and to obtain the answer. So the way of administering the answer will depend entirely on the disciple and on the subtlest antenna, which reaches him in the easiest way. This is to say that you must not expect to hear something, to read it in a book, which appears, or to see Gurdjieff or his superiors appear and speak to you. It can happen in an entirely different manner.

Charlaine ceased to publicly channel some five years later, in 1994, on the instructions of Pastor, who had, he said, completed the messages he wished to transmit. What remains in the public archive about the channeling of Pastor by Charlaine is a book of channeled utterances, *La Conscience Cosmique, ou, l'Homme Transfiguré* [*Cosmic Consciousness, or, Man Transfigured*], published by Éditions Fernand Lanore, Paris, 1990.

After this thoroughly mysterious Geneva séance of November 21, 1989, Ashish and I rarely again discussed the subjects of channeling and spirit guides.

Ashish, *Man, Son of Man*, 8-9.
Weiss, *Masters*, 98-99.

12

Beelzebub's Tales to His Grandson

Through whatever strange alchemy of my American business-man-hood, my intense interest in all that is esoteric, my love of Gurdjieffianism, and my life-long fondness for reading, I have come to be totally fascinated by Gurdjieff's strange, science fiction-like allegory *Beelzebub's Tales to His Grandson*. I even, beginning in 1995, instituted with a group of friends an annual conference ("All and Everything") devoted to the study of this great if bizarre 1,000+-page *magnum opus*. In this chapter, I would like to explain to the reader why I find *Beelzebub's Tales to His Grandson* so utterly compelling.

At first sight (this was my first reaction, more than 20 years ago), *Beelzebub's Tales* seems like a colossal leg-pull. In Chapter One—"The Arousing of Thought"—Gurdjieff expends 17,000 words and a complex vocabulary to tell us only that his personality stems from two principles: "In life never do as others do" and "if you go on a spree then go the whole hog, including the postage." It seemed to me that he must be making fun of all the academicians, literary artists and philosophers who had ever lived.

But this weird, over-complicated style—which Gurdjieff deliberately cultivated, believing that the harder you worked at something, the more likely you were to get something out of it—concealed a strange and startling story. Its contents resembled what the old-time science-fiction pulp magazines used to call a "space opera," but with this major difference for starters, that the hero of *Beelzebub's Tales to His Grandson* is Beelzebub, thought by some religionists to be the name of the Devil, by others to be the name of the chief among the fallen angels, second only to Satan—either way, not usually the hero of a book. The more deeply I got into this 1,238-page work by G, which he had begun in 1924, which he completed just before his death in 1949, and which had first been published in English in 1950 (except for the private issuance in 1931 of an early draft which he later extensively revised), the more I felt that I was present at far, far more than a cosmic leg-pull— though the leg-pulling elements may never have been far away.

Beelzebub's Tales is a vast allegory unfolding through the description of visits to and observations of the planet Earth over several thousand years, as recounted by Beelzebub who is here depicted as an old and wise space traveler. In the story, Beelzebub, exploring the universe in the spaceship *Karnak* for perhaps the last time, is accompanied by his attendants and kinsmen including his beloved young grandson, Hassein (often regarded as the allegorical pupil sitting at Gurdjieff's feet). During the lengthy unfolding of this cosmic journey, there is much time for conversation, and Hassein, who has become especially interested in the strange "three-brained beings" (human beings) who inhabit the planet Earth, has many questions for his grandfather about these creatures.

It happened previously that for a very long period of time Beelzebub had been exiled from the center of the universe to our remote solar system, where he took up residence on the planet Mars. From there he made six forays to the planet Earth covering various epochs, the first beginning in the days of Atlantis and the last ending in the early twentieth century. In between these visits, with the aid of a telescope, Beelzebub continually monitored activities on Earth from his base on Mars. To answer Hassein's many questions, Beelzebub reports his experiences during these six visits along with the results of his telescopic observations. It is these accounts to his grandson that comprise the content of the *Tales*.

I was eventually to realize that, if this cosmic tale has a peculiarly Gurdjieffian complexity, it nevertheless fit into a clearly recognizable literary tradition, and a distinguished one at that.

(A cautionary note: In the introduction to his *The Psychology of Man's Possible Evolution*, Ouspensky warns that although comparisons of literature are perfectly legitimate in the academic sense, they can sometimes be an impediment to learning. He writes: "I found that the chief difficulty for most people was to realize that they had really heard new things....when we hear new things, we take them for old, or think that they can be explained or interpreted by the old." But since Ouspensky's statement, while being true, can also be used as an excuse for not making certain formal literary judgements, I think it's important to make those comparisons here.)

I am no literary scholar, and for much of what follows I am indebted to literary friends, one of whom studied William Blake (whom Ashish admired) under the world's leading Blake scholar, now deceased, Northrop Frye. It seems that, in a very real sense, G with his *Beelzebub's Tales to His Grandson* belongs to the same literary tradition as the great English romantic poet and engraver William Blake (1757-1827). Blake is remembered primarily for his short lyrical poems such as *The Tyger* (beginning with the famous lines: "Tyger, Tyger, burning bright/ In the forests of the night,/ What immortal hand or eye/ Dare frame they fearful symmetry?"). But the London-born Blake was a visionary as well as a romantic poet, and apparently so immersed in the spirit world that as a child he saw God peering at him through the window, Ezekiel sitting on the front lawn, and angels hanging out of every tree. Hardly ever free of this divine company, the poet/engraver spent the greater part of his life writing long, convoluted, seemingly obscure epic poems, the principle theme of which was (as for John Milton in *Paradise Lost*) mankind's fall from God's grace—the "fall of man."

But Blake, partly because he was influenced by certain earlier esoteric writers such as Emmanuel Swedenborg and Jacob Boehme, took a radically different approach from Milton. In Milton's *Paradise Lost*, when Eve eats the apple and she and Adam are expelled from the Garden of Eden, man is radically cut off from God. For Blake, God and man are one, so that when man falls, so does God. It is this dual-natured fall that creates the physical universe, whereas in Milton the creation of the physical universe (e.g., the Garden of Eden) precedes the fall of man. In Blake, as he touches upon in his shorter poems and makes explicit in the longer "prophecies" such as *Vala: The Four Zoas*, man/God falls through seven stages or Eyes. This latter concept is derived from Jacob Boehme (it also finds expression in many of the sources cited by Blavatsky in *The Secret Doctrine*), but Blake adds a further twist, asserting that, as man/God fell, or "contracted," from divine perfection to the stony rock-bottom of earth, his organs of perception contracted as well. Blake writes in *The Marriage of Heaven and Hell*:

"Man has no Body distinct from his Soul; for that call'd Body is a portion of Soul discern'd by the five Senses, the chief inlets of Soul in this age."

This implies that, as we successively fell through the seven Eyes (stages) with our man/God-body/Soul contracting, including our organs of perception, we necessarily perceived ourselves/the universe in a successively more constricted manner. Less and less were we able, in the words of Blake, to see "eternity in a grain of sand, infinity in a wildflower," until finally we came to a halt at the present fallen state of man (what Blake calls the 'Limit of Contraction')—and are now lucky if we can see some sand and the occasional flower.

This may seem like a digression from Gurdjieff and *Beelzebub's Tales to His Grandson*. But Blake's insight implies that when, for example, I observe an ancient artifact dating from a period of mankind's life when we were, so to speak, 'less contracted' than we are now, I will be prevented from taking in the full being of that artifact by the fact that my organs of perception have shrunk below the level of perception of the organs of perception of those who created the artifact in the first place. Were we able for a moment to "put on" our ancient being—a more expanded one—we might be able to "read" this monument. But it would seem to be extremely difficult for us, locked in our present constricted state, to "put on" a chunk of that primordial expanded vision, at least not without going crazy after a brief moment of illumination.

Gurdjieff seems to be talking about attaining just such a moment of visionary perception, of 'putting on our primordial selves,' when, as recorded by Ouspensky in *In Search of the Miraculous* he tells the following story:

"In the course of our travels in Central Asia we found, in the desert at the foot of the Hindu Kush, a strange figure which we thought at first was some ancient god or devil. At first it produced upon us simply the impression of being a curiosity. But after a while we began to feel that this figure contained many things, a big, complete, and complex system of cosmology. And slowly, step by step, we began to decipher this system. It was in the body of the figure, in its legs, in its arms, in its head, in its eyes, in its ears; everywhere. In the whole statue there was nothing accidental, nothing without meaning. And gradually we understood the aim of the people who built the statue. We began to feel their thoughts, their feelings. Some of us thought that we saw their faces, heard their voices. At all events, we grasped the meaning of what they wanted to convey to us across thousands of years, and not only the meaning, but all the feelings and emotions concerned with it as well. That indeed was art!"

Ouspensky asks Gurdjieff: "Why, if ancient knowledge has been preserved, is it so carefully concealed, why is it not made common property?" and Gurdjieff answers that there are two reasons, the first being that "this knowledge is not concealed." He is perhaps referring to the vestiges of ancient knowledge that are all around us but imperceptible to us because our organs of perception have shrunk below the level where we might have been able to perceive them. (Gurdjieff's second reason, that this knowledge "cannot, from its very nature, become common property" since it is material, finite and quantifiable, is a little more problematical).

As every student of Gurdjieff knows, in *Meetings with Remarkable Men* the author roundly attacks modern literature, declaring that "a European's understanding of an object observed by him is formed exclusively by means of an all-around, so to say, 'mathematical informedness' about it." G is implying that this is an extremely limited, so to speak 'contracted,' way of looking at the world. By contrast "...the people of Asia grasp the essence of the object observed by them sometimes with their feelings alone and even by instinct....hundreds of illiterate people will gather round one literate man to hear a reading of the sacred writings or of the tales known as the *Thousand and One Nights* [because such tales are]...works of literature in the full sense of the word."

These attacks, which Gurdjieff also launches in *Beelzebub's Tales to His Grandson*, referring sneeringly to the "bon ton literary language" of our day, boil down in the language of Blakean vision to the assertion that works like the *Thousand and One Nights*, and the powers of perception of the Asian, are less 'contracted' than those of the contemporary European; Gurdjieff seems to be declaring that his fellow countrymen have retained their power of, so to speak, putting on the expanded vision of the Sixth Eye, or the Fifth (assuming that we represent the Seventh; Blake in his cosmology calls the totally unfallen state of God/man itself 'Atlantis' and doesn't relate any of the successively descending stages to particular civilizations on our planet—as opposed to Blavatsky, who does do this when she equates the "third root race" to Lemuria and the "fourth root race" to Atlantis).

No doubt Gurdjieff thought (without using these words) that if anyone perceived the world in a "less fallen" manner, it was himself. In *Meetings with Remarkable Men* he is at pains to tell us his father was a bard—an *ashokh*—the descendent of an unbroken line of bards going back to the epic poem *Gilgamesh* (and this before the decipherment of the Sumerian tablets telling the Noah-like story of Gilgamesh); in so doing, he points to his own vital, unbroken connection to those works of art dating back to primordial times. We are left to infer that it is G's own ability to directly sense the power of these artifacts that drives his own devastating attacks on modern literature.

Gurdjieff's huge epic novel *Beelzebub's Tales to His Grandson* is in fact, like *Paradise Lost* or *Vala: The Four Zoas*, a story of the fall of man—or, rather, of the progressive descent of mankind as seen through the unfallen eyes of Beelzebub observing our race through a telescope from Mars, then observing us at first-hand as he makes six successive visits to our planet's surface, the first being to the relatively expanded epoch of 'Atlantis.' In this way does *Beelzebub's Tales* take its place in the mighty literary tradition of the epic depiction of the fall of man. This is a tradition that goes back a long way—the story of Gilgamesh in a sense belongs in it, telling as it does of a flood followed by a new breed of man—and has persisted up to our day not only in *Beelzebub's Tales*, but also with works such as James Joyce's novel *Finnegan's Wake* (1939). About this latter modern masterpiece, literary critic Edmund Wilson writes that Earwicker, the epic hero, and Anna Livia, the epic heroine, are "the eternal woman and the eternal man, and during the early hours of heaviness and horror of Earwicker's dream, he is an Adam fallen from grace—to be redeemed...with the renewal of the morning light."

There is an odd way in which *Beelzebub's Tales* stands apart from practically every other epic account of the fall of man. Blake's *Vala: The Four Zoas* is incredibly hard to understand—so much so that whole generations of critics thought that Blake must have been demented when he wrote it, or certainly continually intoxicated, relying for this latter state on the English romantic poet's drug of preference, laudanum. The current view is that Blake was entirely sane, and that these later epic prophecies in poetry are hugely obscure because Blake was, after all, attempting to describe levels of perception far beyond his own, for which the concepts themselves, let alone the words, barely exist in the limited, 'fallen' thinking of contemporary mankind. Critic Northrop Frye quotes Joyce as saying that *Finnegan's Wake* required "'an ideal reader suffering from an ideal insomnia,'" adding, "in other words, the critic." This isn't an unreasonable statement when you consider that this notoriously hard-to-read book is about what happens when a man falls asleep, sinks during his dreams to the archetypal unconscious of mankind, communes with the entire human race, and then wakes up. Works like the above are hard to understand not because of any deliberate obfuscation on the part of the author, but because

213

their themes are transcendent and ineffable, and it is probably a wonder that the authors are able to express as much as they do. This isn't at all the case with *Beelzebub's Tales to His Grandson*. J. G. Bennett tells the story of how Gurdjieff, in writing *Beelzebub's Tales*, "himself used to listen to chapters read aloud and if he found that the key passages were taken too easily—and therefore almost inevitably too superficially—he would rewrite them in order, as he put it, to 'bury the dog deeper.'"

Even when I first read *Beelzebub's Tales to His Grandson*, this policy of deliberate obfuscation struck me as making sense. It seemed consonant with G's overall strategy as expressed in his words, "I wished to create around myself conditions in which a man would be continuously reminded of the sense and aim of his existence by an unavoidable friction between his conscience and the automatic manifestations of his nature." The very difficulty of *Beelzebub*, consciously created by Gurdjieff, was intended to create this friction.

Still, this whole matter of Gurdjieff's "burying the dog" did puzzle me a little, and in a letter to Ashish I asked him about it.

A.   G and his dog: When anything is presented in easily understood terms, there is the danger that people will understand with their minds only. Effort to understand involves the more essential depths of a man's intelligence. Therefore, G "buried the dog" deeply. In Dickens's *Pickwick Papers*, the fat boy tells horrible tales because he "likes to make your flesh creep." G hid his meanings because he "liked to make you think." As is well-known, G made the book deliberately obscure, "burying the dog deeper," as he was fond of saying, so that mankind would have to work hard at getting his meaning and therefore appreciate that meaning all the more. [Jan. 15, 1989]

My non-Gurdjieffian literary friends continue to raise objections. They tell me that it is essentially because works like Blake's *Four Zoas* and Joyce's *Finnegan's Wake* are about expanded realms of reality that they are so hard to read—our feeble, contracted organs of perception can scarcely open out to them, they say. When I remark that Gurdjieff seems to share the faculty of these authors of living in and creating an expanded world, which is why *Beelzebub* is so difficult, they reply that, if this is really the case, why does Gurdjieff have to consciously make the book even more difficult? Isn't the dog buried deeply enough already by virtue of G's having to describe the indescribable? They finish up by telling me that G as a writer is somehow blocked and not really able to penetrate to (or tell the truth in words about) those regions with which he may be partially in contact.

The above is, however, a view with which I disagree. As I've said, the more deeply I have gotten into *Beelzebub's Tales to His Grandson* over the years, the more profound and useful a book it has seemed to me, and I can only reply to my literary friends that, firstly, under "Friendly Advice" preceding the Table of Contents, G suggests that his book be read three times, the second time "as if you were reading aloud to another person." It has been specu-lated that hearing something read aloud, so that it enters the con-sciousness aurally rather than visually as in ordinary reading, per-mits the matter to bypass the intellect and impact upon the emo-tions directly, thereby having a much more powerful effect. A vital component of this is hearing and/or reading aloud the 500+ special words G constructed from a variety of languages, the sounds of which presumably have a special emotional impact on our or-ganism. These words, since they have been invented by Gurdjieff (or remembered from the arcane sources of his knowledge), ap-pear exactly the same in all the translations of *Beelzebub's Tales*, and there even exists a glossary that suggests a single, universal pronunciation for these sounds. I know of no studies that verify the impact of these special words and sounds. Still, I suspect there is something occult-ly true about these speculations. It's also said of *Beelzebub's Tales* that the contents of the subtitle of the book, *An Objectively Impartial Criticism of the Life of Man*, in which G chronicles all the stupidities of human life, have a profound effect on the reader. I know that much of the above must sound like special pleading; but academia has been relenting to some extent in its attitude toward G, and in 1999 a friend of mine received from the University of London the first-ever doctorate issued for a thesis on *Beelzebub's Tales* (the subject was drawing astrological analogies to Beelzebub).

Still, certain parts of *Beelzebub's Tales* often seemed uniquely strange, and I looked frequently to Ashish for guidance. More than once, I simply asked him what *Beelzebub's Tales* was all about, as in, "I regard *Beelzebub's Tales* as a largely autobiographical account by Gurdjieff. Beelzebub's sixth descent onto earth in the late nineteenth and early twentieth centuries is clearly autobiographical. Could it be that the five earlier descents, going back to the time of Atlantis, recount the appearance in past times of the reincarnating being we know today as Gurdjieff? What is your view?"

A.   Of course a lot of Beelzebub is G! But G didn't have a tail tucked into his pants and he didn't grow horns. Much of the book is sheer romance, but so delightfully mixed with the literary equivalent of "tricks, semi-tricks and magic" that it keeps the reader awake and constantly guessing at whether to laugh, to perceive a profundity, or both. [Jan. 24, 1989]

My questions often had to do with obscure matters, such as, "In *Beelzebub's Tales to His Grandson*, Gurdjieff writes about 'being-Hanbledzoin,' which he characterizes as the blood of the astral or Kesdjan body. He writes about its importance in the 'animal magnetism' that some people possess, and that the possessor of adequate Hanbledzoin has strong hypnotic abilities. Is this information of any value in one's inner search?"

A.   The circulation of the human blood functioned well for millennium before it was understood, and functioned no better on account of its being understood. When consciousness is held, the occult mechanics of energy transformation which builds potential selfhood into actual selfhood functions of its own accord. However, in this latter case, practical knowledge of method can improve the functioning. But method without holding self-awareness may result only in odd psychic powers. [Nov. 15, 1980]

Few pieces of esoterica are more bewildering than G's contention that our moon is alive, dynamic, and ever-growing as long as it can feed on certain energies produced by man. Quoting G in *In Search of the Miraculous*, Ouspensky writes: "The moon is a huge living being feeding upon all that lives and grows on the earth. The process of the growth and the warming of the moon is connected with life and death on the earth. Everything living sets free at its death a certain amount of the energy that has 'animated' it; this energy, or the 'souls' of everything living—plants, animals, people— is attracted to the moon as though by a huge electromagnet, and brings to it the warmth and the life upon which its growth depends..."

In *Beelzebub's Tales*, Gurdjieff takes the subject further than did Ouspensky, telling us in Chapter Nine that the Earth has two satellites, the Moon and "Anulios." We cannot see Anulios because we can no longer see reality due to our improper overall education and conditioning. Some speculate that Anulios represents G's fourth state of consciousness, what he calls the Real World, and which has analogies with Ashish's state of unitive vision. Gurdjieff's ideas concerning the dynamic "feeding" nature of our Moon (and Anulios) remain a subject of heated debate among Gurdjieffians. I've described our channeling sessions with Charlaine/Pastor. During the second session, we resorted to asking the following question about G's moon: "What is meant when we say that the energy released at death is attracted by and feeds the moon, if it is not crystallized for the creation of the soul?"

Charlaine/Pastor's answer was very long, taking up several pages of transcript, and at best not very clear. I felt prompted to ask Ashish for his opinion on this answer (I'd sent him the transcript).

A.   I have been trying to make sense of Charlaine's talk on the Nature of the Astral. Your editing certainly makes it easier to read. First, I don't think the question to have been a fair one. Who but Gurdjieff has ever spoken of the earth feeding the moon? The guide, not being a Master, should not be expected to be familiar with the G jargon. It is not surprising that the question is not properly answered, except on six: "The astral plane is the emanation of the physical plane." It seems clear that the word "moon" in the question sparked the associative connection with "astral," which is what the occult moon often means. And so you get a long and rather garbled talk on the astral in which the only interesting thing is the idea that the so-called astral body is constructed of energies supplied from the physical in the "astral plane."

When we were struggling with G's "feeding the moon and Anulios," G told Gopalda in a dream that he had turned the usual thing upside-down. This seemed to fit his image of a mystery-maker. Whether we got his statement right or not, the facts are that, while the subtle worlds are usually depicted as the channel for the ingression of divine principles, e.g., the ingression of self-awareness, it also works the other way round, where things that are not integrated in the human being are released into the intermediate worlds at death by a process akin to the manner in which we project unconscious psychic content in life.

This accounts for the seemingly material heaven worlds which are experienced by true believers—Christian, Moslem, Hindu and Buddhist. There are individual images and collective images. The astral plane is full of them. With all these believed-in illusions floating around, it does become rather important to show the other side of the coin, namely, nothing, nothing, bare nothingness. [July 12, 1989]

Certain modern "New Age" works, including some on UFOs and alien abductions, express the notion of humankind's crystallizing an essence which "feeds" other parts of the universe. The books of "astral traveler" Robert A. Monroe—*Journeys out of the Body*, *Far Journeys*, *Ultimate Journey*—tell of his meetings while in astral body with aliens who harvest mankind's sense of humor and export it throughout the cosmos (the human sense of humor is apparently a rare and sought-after commodity in our universe). Monroe meets a second set of aliens (this time discarnate) who tell him of a powerful, non-physical creator-entity—not God, but a creature created by God—whom they call "Someone," who invented a highly spirituality-enhancing substance called "Loosh." Seeing that the best-quality Loosh could only be fermented in entities living in physical, space-time reality, Someone created homo sapiens and Earth as a sort of Loosh farm. Initially, Loosh was harvested at the moment of the human entity's death. Then Someone figured out that the finest Loosh could be extracted only from humans who were alive and engaged in selfless, egoless acts, such as protecting their children. To distill the most potent possible Loosh, Someone began to put humanity through every sort of vicissitude. The entire history of our species, it would seem, stems from our being manipulated to produce top-quality Loosh!

This "feeding" theme, unrelated to the moon, can also be found in UFO literature. Certain UFOologists believe the aliens are harvesting the soul matter of mankind. This lies behind the alien abduction experience, they say—and not only are the aliens milking us, but they have been manipulating us throughout our history in order to ferment the highest-quality soul matter. I don't know what these occult reports and strange phenomena mean, but they seem to indicate that, with his notion of a 'feeding moon,' Gurdjieff touched upon a very real phenomenon of the astral plane (as suggested by Ashish), one that manifests itself in the universe in other forms as well—though in both cases our contracted organs of perception are probably picking up only a garbled and subjective version of the underlying reality.

Connected to the themes of the Moon and Anulios, and equally prominent in *Beelzebub's Tales*, is another strange if seminal Gurdjieffian concept: that of the Kundabuffer. Beelzebub tells Hassein that the moon was created by the collision of the planet Earth with a comet named Kondoor. As a result, organic life had to be created on earth for the purpose of emitting vibrations which could be absorbed by the moon and were essential for maintaining it in orbit.

A "commission" of divine beings, fearful the human race would feel so humiliated it would kill itself if it found out it had only been created to keep the moon aloft, implanted a special organ called the Kundabuffer in our species. This organ caused us to perceive reality "topsy-turvey" and build up a need for sensual enjoyment. Eventually, the commission removed the Kundabuffer, but not before homo sapiens had become hopelessly addicted to pleasure and pain, with these identifications being passed down to subsequent generations through improper education and bringing about the general confusion and "asleep" state that characterizes mankind today.

I asked Ashish: "Gurdjieff's proposed solution to the problems of humanity as pronounced in *Beelzebub's Tales to His Grandson* is his wish that an organ would be implanted into each human being, similar to the organ Kundabuffer, but which would cause him to 'constantly sense and be cognizant of the inevitability of his own death as well as the death of everyone upon whom his eyes or attention rests.' I see this as allegorical. Is there some way we can achieve this, apart from the implantation of such an organ? Can one expect further instruction from Gurdjieff through meditation, prayer, or channeling? How does one pray? How does one blank the mind in meditation, yet pose the question?"

A.   In one of the great Indian myths, a "wonderful being" asks a series of Sphinx-like questions. One question is "What is extraordinary?" and the answer is "All men seeing others dying yet thinking that they themselves will not die." Something like Kundabuffer, I take as a throwaway. Yet it is absolutely true that only when one is convinced in one's guts that this body will die can one summon the sort of passionate energy that seeks what does not die. Strictly speaking, one needs neither Kundabuffer nor George Gurdjieff nor anyone of his sort to pursue this inquiry. One needs only honesty, courage and the burning desire to know.

Indeed, one should not expect Gurdjieff to take notice of prayers for help from people who have not done their homework, i.e., people who have not pursued the inquiry as far as their makeup permits. It is when one is blocked, yet still persists in trying anything, that trying to contact Gurdjieff may bring results. Again, one must do this oneself. The objection to mediums or channels is that this method does nothing to develop one's capacity for assessing the value of what comes through. When one is trying to get answers for oneself, one may at least be aware of the futility of anything which involves cheating, because one could only be cheating oneself.

Thus, whatever one gets, one must take seriously, but also with sufficient lightness so that one learns by experience what sorts of messages with what attached feelings turned out to be true and what false. "How does one pray?" No, Sy, that won't do. It's too much like the man on the road who asked the way and, on being told, then asked to be taught how to walk. How can you ask a question of Gurdjieff without thinking of him? You are like the maharajah who was given a medicine which could cure him with one dose, provided he did not think of a camel while taking that dose. He could not but think of a camel and you could not but think of Gurdjieff. What you must not think of is how famous you might become if you said you got this message from G himself. [Sept. 19, 1995]

I had other questions for Ashish about *Beelzebub's Tales*. But, in the 1990's, these questions increasingly had more to do with my growing involvement in writing about *Beelzebub's Tales*, and even more so with the controversy engendered by the publication of a new edition of *Beelzebub's Tales* in 1993 which sought to stick closer to the French translation—considered by many to be a better rendition of the original Russian-Armenian manuscript—but, which, according to a number of Russian-speaking Gurdjieffians, was actually further from that original. There was a question whether a third English version should be prepared. Ultimately, the 1993 "revised translation" was withdrawn by the publisher, and a new edition was put out in 1999 that returned to the exact text of the 1950 edition approved by Gurdjieff (several hundred typos and minor errors that had plagued the earlier edition were corrected in this new edition).

I continue to read *Beelzebub's Tales to His Grandson* with supreme enjoyment, and recommend it to one and all.

Ouspensky, *Psychology of Man's Possible Evolution*, xii-xiii.
Keynes, ed., 182.
Ouspensky, *Miraculous*, 27.
Ibid., 36-37.
Gurdjieff, *Meetings*, 16-18.
Wilson, 234.
Frye, 354.
Bennett, 274.
Gurdjieff, *Beelzebub's Tales*, vi.
Ouspensky, *Miraculous*, 85.
Monroe, 162-172.

13

Matters of
Life and Death

S omehow, in the 1990's, where I gave classes or even if I formally participated in groups at all came to be of less and less
importance. It was occurring to me that this business of turning
inward could be carried out anywhere, even in the business world—
even on a battlefield. It was a matter of wanting to badly enough.

One Gurdjieffian technique that could be practiced absolutely
anywhere was meditation. In G's teachings, this was called "sitting." I'd practiced it, sometimes with impatience (but less and less
as the years went by), right from the beginning. Ashish always
insisted mightily on the importance of meditation, and in his letters he had much of a compelling nature to say on the subject; I
begin this chapter with a kind of compendium of some of the more
important comments that Ashish made on meditation over the years.

To pontificate for a moment: I've called the chapter "Matters
of Life and Death." The meditation that Gurdjieff advocated, and
on which Ashish elaborated in his letters, was essential to the inward turning of oneself to the richest source of life within us all,
and indeed within the universe—the Self.

First of all, to refresh the reader's memory, here is a brief summation Ashish made of the Gurdjieffian concept of "self-remembering"—about, in effect, the "Self"—back in the beginning of the
time that I knew him.

A. Observe an object, for instance, a candle. See the candle. See what is seeing the candle. Drop away the candle. What is left is that you are seeing or observing what is seeing the candle. In other words, you are aware of being aware. This is true self-remembering or self-awareness, avoiding the trap of illusory self-remembering. Analogizing this to the body, recognize first that there is the body. Experience the body. Then experience what experiences the body. Then forget the body. [March 6, 1981]

From this point on, I'll proceed in a Q and A format:

Q. You mentioned meditation and I have started to read about it and to ask people about it. It is obviously an important part of inner work. What more can you tell me about meditation?

A. Meditative work is, in part, like trying to get one's eyes to perceive the light beyond the glass—light that at first seems to be darkness. Yet even when one sees the outer scene, one's own reflected image stands between one and the real world, in much the same sense that one's observations of the facts of daily life are distorted by psychological projections.

The aim is to see clearly, whether awake in this world, awake in dream, or awake in the spirit. Dream images show us the nature of our distorting projections.

If one is fortunate, direct teaching can sometimes be given through the window of dream. But if we do not clean the window, even this will be liable to distortion. Much work lies in cleaning, and no cleaning is like cleaning a lavatory pan. Shame and disgust clean nothing. To clean it, one has to overcome one's disgust, eventually realizing that there is nothing to be disgusted about and yet disgust is probably an imposed reaction pattern dating back to infantile hygiene training.

When all is one, how can one exclude shit? And if one cannot face physical shit, how much less can one face one's own psychic filth—"filthy" because "I" cannot accept it as an essential part of me? Therefore, one does not dismiss shitty or sexual dreams as "just Freudian stuff." One tries to find the meaning. Often one is being shown that in some specific manner one is degrading the divine creative power of eros either by exploiting it for selfish ends or by thinking of it in negative terms. [Dec. 28, 1978]

Q.   I have been trying to meditate early each morning. We call it "sitting" in the Gurdjieff groups. Are there any special meditational techniques you could recommend as useful? For how long should I meditate? Should I continually try to lengthen the period?

A.   Meditation is important. It is why so much stress is laid on meditational practices which lead you to stop thinking, stop reasoning. You still use your mind afterward on what you find, on what you see or don't see, on what you feel or don't feel. But mere collection of outer information and views, no! If you form views, you may put them up as a hypothesis of what you think you might find, but don't go in with a preconceived notion. Build your understanding more on what you do find within, the few sure points that are there.

Now, lengthening periods of meditation. Yes, of course, if you can. Holding your mind in check all the time. That is important. Keeping it centered, not running around all over the place. I mean, whether speculating about the inner life or speculating on the stock exchange, it's still the same outer speculation.

It's holding steady, holding steady all the time until you can turn back within. Holding, as it were, until the door opens of its own accord.

This is one of the most difficult adjustments a man has to make. To realize that he is surrendering his outer integration to something that is greater, knows more, something that stands in its own right. Frightening? Well, of course, it's apt to be because it means letting go of the familiar and trusting the unfamiliar.

Other people who have gone that way can give you the reassurance that, "Yes, I have gone that way, I have stepped beyond. I stand there. If you find me mad, if you find me stupid, if you find me less human, than you may have doubts."

The assurance of the outer persona is only truly significant to you insofar as you receive support for your search, your own inner inquiry. As I've said before, other people have pioneered their way through the jungles of their own beings. No man has left tracks in yours. You, again, are a pioneer through your own mind, through your own being. You need support, you need to trust in that support, but your search must be for the mystery of where it is, within you, not outside in somebody else. Outside you only see the reflection.

If another person for you seems to glow, glow with the insignia of truth as it were, that is because you are seeing the reflection of what is deeply with you. Seek for the inner and you will see its reflection, outside; but seek for the reflection and you will not find the original. [Dec. 22, 1979]

A.   Meditation may be the one essential practice, without which nothing of significance will happen. But the requirements of total self-dedication cannot be met by an hour or two's practice. One cannot be totally "given" at some times of the day, and following one's own selfish interests at other times. The attempt has to be made to bring the totality of one's nature into harmony with one's perceptions of the nature of the source of being. And one has to see the operations of the spirit in the world around one. This, approximately, is what people like those you met here are trying to do. For some of them, aspects of life represent challenges—areas of anxiety and uncertainty—which correspond to fears and uncertainties in themselves. Anything one fears or tries to reject has not been acknowledged. This is not a matter of mere psychological adaptation. If, for instance, I am deeply reluctant to stand up and make a speech before a crowd of strangers, it means that in regard to such circumstance, I am not standing in the fearless center of my being, but am identifying with a peripheral anxiety or inadequacy. This is quite distinct from an objective assessment of my nature as not being of the sort that makes for a glib public speaker.

Since the center of one's being is elusive, it is often only by perceiving where one is not centered that one learns what sort of shift in identity is needed to bring one closer to it. Every such move towards the center in waking consciousness both intensifies the center's "light" and makes it more real—less of a potentiality and more of an actuality. This has its positive repercussions on meditation. And the effects in meditation have their corresponding effects in ordinary waking, in that one gains both greater perception of the un-given or un-integrated parts of one's nature and greater courage to deal with them.

Such people come here once or twice a year, basically to get encouragement. They leave full of hope and good intentions, and the next wave of worldly worries sweeps over their heads, or it may be a wave of egocentric ambition, or a clinging to status. Each man has his own set of difficulties which tend to obscure his vision of the spirit. The work is slow, but sure. [March 6, 1980]

Q.   Madame de Salzmann once told me that there are two energies. One enters our organism through the top of the head, and the other flows upward through the body from the genitalia. One needs to be aware of these energies and to keep them in balance. The subject inevitably leads to confusion amongst our group members.

A.   Your questions on meditation: I once met a famous tantric teacher and wanted to know his status. So I asked, "Do you hold that by arousing the power the right state of mind will be produced, or that by entering the right state of mind the power will rise of itself?" He replied, "The latter," and this is my own view. However, work on arousing the power seems easier than working on the mind for some people, because it is "tangible"—something that can be sensed. Also, if one is accustomed to the process, one is not so likely to be thrown off balance if it arises spontaneously and forcefully.

I suspect that the teaching about bringing the power in from above (despite G's teaching about transformations within the body) is simply a safeguard against taking the power to oneself and using it as one's own—the path of the black magician. It has to be seen

227

as the divine Eros itself, even if its concentration does occur through the body (in what sense is the body one's own?). With this caution, there is nothing against invoking the power to heighten the sense of aspiration in meditation.

I see no need to involve oneself in Yogic anatomy, so it makes no difference to me which direction the power is believed to take. It finds its own channels.

The first purpose of meditation is to still the mind—by directly controlling thoughts, watching them detachedly, by tracing them back to their source, by forcing the mind to stick to a mantra. Concentration on an image is another traditional help which I have not personally found useful.

These exercises can temporarily still the mind, but one remains, as it were, in the midst of stilled mental process which can and does start again at any moment.

If one holds quiet, the next thing to look for is a slight dissociation from the thinking process, which makes it relatively easy to stay in this quiet state. It is peaceful but eventually unsatisfying. This can deepen into the state I have described to you where the body passes into sleep and one is awake within it. Deliberately invoking sleep, while keeping in a position which discourages sleep, is an aid in this process. It also points to the fact that this movement is not, initially, anything that you can achieve by intention. In practice, you have to hold yourself in the quiet state and let yourself get tired.

To pass beyond this requires prolonged effort, aspiration, the help of the power, and, hopefully, grace—or what appears as grace, because one has no control over it. It is this last step for which the earlier work should prepare one for untermed periods of sitting. One may learn, as I did, to change one's position occasionally (not fidgeting) without disturbing the state of mind.

This is also one of the side benefits of getting accustomed to physical work, with all the aches and pains that must be tolerated and lived with. One learns to put up with a fair degree of discomfort before feeling forced to move. When the mind truly withdraws, the body and its discomforts are forgotten.

228

Another obstacle to long meditation is the sheer habit of sleeping a fixed number of hours, with the accompanying belief that one must have one's full sleep in order to be bright and alert in the competitive world. The actual need is about four hours, with possibly an odd ten minutes or so of withdrawal into meditation/sleep during the day. The point is that the state of true meditation is as restful as sleep and often more so. What one is really fighting is not the body's demands for rest, but the fixed mental belief that those demands must be satisfied. Supporting that "belief" is the conscious/subconscious knowledge that sleep is an escape from the world. Meditation is not an escape. [Dec. 12, 1988]

Also during the period of the 1990's, I had many questions of a general nature for Ashish about Gurdjieff and his teachings. Perhaps I was a little less "star-struck" by this Russian Master and mystic than I had been in the early years of my relationship with G and his teachings (I had, though, come to believe increasingly in the truth and power of those teachings). Whatever the case may be, I was now a little franker in my questions to Ashish about Gurdjieff:

Q.   What is the essence of Gurdjieff's teachings?

A.   As Gopalda and I have understood it, crudely put it is that mankind is faced with a problem of identity. We do not know who we are, where we came from or why we are here. We are led to see that the root of the mystery lies at the root of our own being, somewhere in our awareness. We discover that by being aware, we become more aware; our self-awareness becomes "real" and we "wake up." We ask: What is this awareness in itself? When the mind is not full of thoughts and the sense not filled with stimuli, what remains? G did not teach what happens when the inquiry is followed to this extent. He gave exercises, waited for results, and followed up the results (when they came) with personal instructions. One has never heard what he said to people like C. S. Nott who had experienced something. He did stop people from going after professional psychologists, and he did not approach dreams in the standard psychological way. However, as I have previously pointed out to you, he did not discourage people from dreaming in fact. [June 20, 1990]

G's system [of cosmology] is tantalizing, but mythological in form. G did not intend to provide a rational framework. As he says at the beginning of the book, he aims to destroy preconceived notions. Frankly, you will get a clearer approximation of the facts from the *Man* books. I think you will find G's ideas making more sense against the framework those books sketch. [Feb. 26, 1993]

Q.   Why did the 1924 auto accident that led to the closing of his institute happen to Gurdjieff, a Master? Could he not have prevented it?

A.   G and his accident? The embodied Master is still a man (Nirvanas gained and lost) with all a man's propensities for making mistakes. Don't impose idealist fantasies on reality. For you to imply that G was not a Master because he had an accident is as silly as Ethel Merston denying Ramana Maharshi's attainment because he had a badly set broken leg.

It was perhaps part of G's scheme of things that he seems never to have allowed any of his establishments to settle down into an institution with set habits. He seems to have done the unexpected on principle. The closing of the Prieuré fits the pattern of the rest of his life. In any case it would have closed with the war. [Jan. 24, 1989]

Q.   What does the future hold for the Gurdjieff Work groups and the Theosophical Society?

A.   The burning question for the TS (and for the G groups) is whether anyone exists within or without the movement who is, and knows that he is, connected with the Masters, who is dedicated to and is travelling their path, who is dedicated to them personally, whose mind is free from bigotry, who has at least an intellectual grasp of the transcendental truths, who has the capacity to refer directly to the Masters for guidance and inspiration, and who is ready to accept the immense burden of responsibility.

This may be a rather tall order, so tall that one suspects he/she would not be found without the Masters' intervention. One might not know of the intervention until it happened, and even then be in doubt. There is also the important point that they will not intervene unless the ground is ready.

Can the ground be prepared? Or must one wait for the slow process of human evolution, backed by the reincarnation of evolved groups who seed society with sufficient numbers to form the nucleus of a "new" movement? Without insight, how can one know the answer except by trial and error. One may talk, write, lecture, etc. Will people respond?

What sorts of people would respond, if any? Would they want to use the techniques to make their lives better, would they want the excitements of occult powers? How many want the thing itself?

You cannot afford to make your own work dependent on such matters. There is an insidious obstruction in the form of a need to feel oneself supported by group solidarity. In the context of current social aims, the path seems so strange and contradictory that one fears to be the odd man out. This reluctance to be responsible for one's own life aims causes a confusion between wanting to help others and to learn by helping them, and wanting the support of their agreement with one's aim. (One of the advantages of being in India was that there was social approval of the inner aim.) Emphasis must therefore be laid on finding one's own certainty. One wants the confirmation of the Masters, not the doubtful support of people who are even more muddled than oneself.

Though one does not question the value of the TS and the G groups, both as centers of the teaching and as experiments from which to learn, we should no longer be concerned with any sort of fundamentalism. Our concern is not to maintain the purity of the Christian teaching, the Muslim teaching, or the received G teaching. HPB and G have become public property, their teaching now forming part of the tradition, along with the writings of all the saints and mahatmas there have ever been. I am not proposing a confused eclecticism. One has to adhere to a particular discipline. But there is need to distinguish between the discipline and the non-denominational goal toward which teaching and discipline are directed.

In effect, your group is doing just what members of sects have always done: broken away in the effort to keep the essential spirit alive. But you must avoid the danger of looking back—the psychological equivalent of those young people who, instead of getting on with their own lives, make the mistake of trying to put their parents straight.

In principle, you do not need to call yourselves a G group. In practice you have to call yourselves something, and it is a fact that you offer G's teaching and his discipline. But I suggest that it is your emotional loyalty to the man that counts, and not the wish to preserve "his" teaching. The essence of his teaching is transpersonal. He could well say, "Look through, not at me," but it is none the less his figure which gives the glow of life to a teaching which otherwise might be frighteningly stark.

You are following your path and sharing it with others. Your efforts should be directed toward finding a personal connection with G and his brethren, rather than hankering after the support of an external organization. I agree that you need your group to keep you going. The membership and the turnover is fairly typical and represents both numbers in your society who are ready to start something and the numbers out of them who respond to this particular approach. Were you to get bigger in terms of numbers, you would be faced with the problem of appointing "teachers" who would be mere repeaters, lacking any personal crystallization.

When this happens, the organizational staff see it as their task to increase income and membership, irrespective of the cost to the quality of members and teaching. Your task is to follow your own path, make your own connection, and share your work with anyone who wants it. You must continue, even if no one wants to work with you. If you run after popular appeal, you will lose your way. If you genuinely work for G, the right sorts of people will be sent to you. [Dec. 12, 1988]

Q.   You said our efforts should be directed toward finding a personal connection with Gurdjieff and his brethren. What did you mean?

A.   To understand G and his brethren one has to become one of them. How can I understand someone who literally has a dimension to his being that I either lack or have only in an undeveloped form? That won't stop me from trying to understand, but I should know that the most important part of my effort to understand must lie in the effort to understand myself and to find the "higher Self" in myself. My capacity to learn to swim will not be improved by my understanding or failure to understand the man who wins my confidence by taking my hand, introducing me to the new element of water, and teaching me to swim. However, I shall learn a lot about him in the process. [Jan. 24, 1989]

Q.   Would you call P.D. Ouspensky spiritually achieved?

A.   You have seen how Ouspensky failed because he could not accept that it was G who gave validity to his teachings. Give me all the teachings about man and the universe, and I will accept them only if I can be shown one man who embodies and validates these teachings. One follows the teachings back to their source in the man whose truth affirms the truth of the teachings. [Oct. 23, 1983]

During the late 1980's—when I wasn't struggling to try to attain to some sort of beginning purchase on objective consciousness or the unitive vision—I was busy with what I suppose you could only call scholarship. Some would say, and did (my colleagues), that in engaging upon such scholarly activities, I was merely being the American businessman expanding his market share on Gurdjieff. Others would say, and did (Ashish), that I was merely fleeing pell-mell, as always, from the business of trying to expand my market share on my own Self.

I admit that it may well have been that one reason I was so fascinated by Gurdjieff was that he himself was a kind of quintessential businessman. In the Appendix ("The Material Question") that was later added to *Meetings with Remarkable Men*, drawn from a fund-raising speech G gave while in New York City in April, 1924, Gurdjieff expounded on his relationship to money. Into that relationship was mixed not a little contempt for this usually important commodity. Gurdjieff made no bones about "shearing the lambs" of American investors who were willing to invest, sight-unseen, in his spiritual and otherwise enterprises. He was not even above what amounted to the occasional scam (Ouspensky was forever uneasily suspicious of Gurdjieff on this account, describing him as not only a brilliant mystic but also an "Oriental carpet dealer"). During the fund-raising speech, G gleefully recounted how, travelling through Transcaspian Russia before the turn of the century as an itinerant "repair everything" repairman, he never hesitated—while carrying out his repairs impeccably—to exploit his customers for all of their money he could get.

Ashish's views on money, however, were not at all in accord with my businessman's wariness:

A.   On the matter of money I adhere to the Indian attitude that any giving has to be complete, with no strings attached. There are many illustrative anecdotes of gurus promptly giving away something they have received, to the chagrin of the donor. G's behavior with money is recognizably similar. When you give for the Work, think of it as given to G himself—and expect him to take it without a thought of what your intentions were. [June 20, 1990]

Be all that as it may: I continued to be fascinated by Gurdjieff, and, whether it was partially for reasons of the flight from going inward or not, in the late 1980's I got very much into original research on G, producing a number of articles about my mysterious, mystical, mentor. The first had to do with whether Madame

Blavatsky, in predicting that the next great teacher of Eastern ideas in Europe would be an instructor in Oriental dancing, had Gurdjieff in mind (in most European circles, Gurdjieff was regarded not so much as a philosopher as one of the greatest living experts on the sacred dances of the East). Mesmerized as I was by *Beelzebub's Tales to His Grandson*, I also wondered if Beelzebub's six descents to Earth over several thousand years did not represent a sort of super-self remembering on the part of G of six of his former lifetimes. These articles are very specialized in nature; for those interested, I direct your attention to the listings, in the Bibliography/Works Cited pages, of where and when they were published.

Of course, during these years I was growing older (I was 44 when I first met Ashish, and now at the time of the writing of this book, I am 67). It's not to be wondered at, then, that my thoughts should turn from time to time to the subject of death (especially as, at the very beginning, it had been the sudden death of my young wife that had launched me, however slowly at first, upon this path). Often, my questions to Ashish on this theme were tangential to the subject of death itself. One example is my questions about *The Tibetan Book of the Dead*.

Q.   Is it of value to take this book literally, as a book of instruction for rites to be held at the bedside of a deceased?

A.   I don't see *The Tibetan Book of the Dead* as being the slightest use to you. You are supposed to be putting your efforts into finding the thing here and now, and not fussing about what is going to happen. What will happen at your death will be determined by how much you have done towards integration and self-awareness in the service of the Spirit. Worry about what will happen to you at the death of the body is worry about your ego integration, and that is what you hope will disappear. [July 7, 1989]

Q.   What words are there we can use today to address the newly-deceased?

A.   On the one hand, I feel like saying: Stuff Jung and his opinions about Catholicism! Stuff the Cabala! Stuff *The Book of the Dead*! The very idea that a last-minute pious ritual can rectify the evils of an impious life is nonsense, and a nonsense that derives, I believe, from the deathbed phenomenon where the process of dying leads back through the *dhyan* state natural to the Self, and then out. In that state, the most evil person can momentarily appear to be a saint.

The other side of the coin is that anyone who, during life, has had some sort of aspiration or has made any sort of effort, can benefit by being reminded of his aspiration at the moment of death. The disorientation at dying, from pain, weakness, etc., can cause forgetfulness of an as yet uncrystallized effort. A reminder brings the dying person back to it. But this is on the basis of his having done something. It is not the attempt to compensate for a lifetime of neglect. Even *The Book of the Dead* is properly understood as the basis for study/effort during life—not just the deathbed ceremony into which it has degenerated.

Words can help by association, rather then by direct meaning—as with any sort of mantra with which the person is deeply familiar. More important than this is the state of mind the helper is in. Knowing that the dying person may be confused by events, the helper should make every effort to hold himself in that state he believes he would want to be in at death. By imagination, the state is transferred to the dying person. This means that the helper must not be himself confused, anxious, hoping that the person will recover, etc. He must be helping the person to let go and leave the body—rather difficult if in a hospital surrounded by doctors, nurses and the apparatus of the intensive care unit.

The dead person does not hang around where the ashes are. He is more likely to start by going home. But no effort should be made to keep him at home. Indeed, as much as possible of personal effects—clothes, bedding, particular articles to which he is attached—are better disposed of as soon as possible. On no account keep his/her place sacrosanct, holy to the memory of. It keeps the person back. [May 3, 1992]

A. I have great respect for *The Tibetan Book of the Dead*, so much so that I dislike its terminology being turned into jargon. [Sept. 5, 1992]

Q. Does any experience we may have with dreams and meditation help prepare us for what we can expect to encounter after death?

A. Dream and *bardo* states are effectively the same. One has to remember that, prior to Freud and Jung, there was very little understanding of the psychic mechanism of projection in dream and vision. Lacking the means of working on the psychic components of emotional reactions, the Tibetan meditators would have to face nightmarish visions—the wrathful deities—when they broke through into the inner states of vision. This can still happen but the more one has worked on the psychology of one's fears, compulsions, etc., the less one has to face later.

As in meditation, there has to be a combination firstly of analytical probing into the roots of fears, etc., which make thought uncontrollable, and secondly an overall perception of the ephemeral nature of all the seeming realities onto which one projects one's fears and anxieties and ambitions. The second is basic. The first is an aid toward the second's de-identification with phenomena. [May 3, 1992]

A. I may have taken a negative stand against someone's treatment of it, but (*The Tibetan Book of the Dead*) itself is quite important, and one often refers to it and quotes from it. I do not know the new translation. I have been disappointed in so many modern translations of many books that I am now suspicious of all such things. The modern scholar likes to go for semantic exactitude, whereas the best of the old ones who produced the classic translations tried to get at the essence of the meaning. So until I have seen it, I reserve judgment. Incidentally, Lama Govinda in conversation confirmed what I had guessed, that *The Tibetan Book of the Dead* is intended to be the basis of a life's *sadhana* [spiritual practice], and not just something to be read over a dead body. When so read, it is effective/helpful only if the person has worked with it in life. [Nov. 9, 1994]

My question on Carl Jung was also a question about death.

Q.   I just finished reading Jung's *Mysterium Coniunctionis* in some detail. You must know the book. After reading through all the pages where he masterfully connects alchemy and psychology, and speaks so often of higher things, I see that he seems to end up by backing away from the recognition of any transcendental reality. What do you think? Did Jung know of the transcendent reality but decline to state so for professional reasons?

A.   You have selected a damning piece of evidence against Jung. It confirms the worst that Gopalda and I ever thought of him—and even worse than that, because he is writing arrant nonsense. No amount of masterly capacity to relate the symbols of alchemy to the symbols of psychology can substitute for an understanding or grasp of what it is that both sets of symbols refer to. The passage you have marked is particularly revealing, for it suggests that Jung's problem stemmed from the fear of annihilation which mystical experience demands. He rightly sees it is a threat to his empirical ego—and to all his famous learning. There is a lesson for you, also, in all this, for your dreams are dealing with the same problem of avoiding egotistic identification with what you "know" and what you KNOW. Like everyone, including Jung, you have doubts. Jung feeds people his own doubts and is therefore an unreliable and rather dangerous guide to the psyche, in spite of his tremendous insights. One might say that his being was not equal to his perceptions. [May 23, 1990]

A.   Yes, Jung was a very great man. From our point of view, however, he might have been more than that—a mahatma or great soul. Again from our viewpoint, that would have been a greater event for Europe than his contribution to psychology.

One has to say that one's opinions were formed on the basis of his writings. People who knew him personally say that he admitted to much more in private than he would venture in writings for the public. And he seems to have developed over the years, though it would take an effort to dig this out of the collected works which are not separated by date. His trouble seems to have been a basic lack of confidence which led to dependence on his public image or reputation.

Our annoyance with Jung was at the way he could lead his readers up to a point where the next sentence should have affirmed the reality of the Spirit, but then back down. 'These things are real; real in the sense that they are human experiences, and all human experience is real experience. Not in the sense that they have reality in themselves,' is an example. True, he eventually accepted the reality of ghosts—from his experiences in the haunted house in England—but that is not what I am talking about.

His vision when he nearly died is much more to the point— one of the most remarkable death experiences on record. He is high up in space, looking down on the world. He turns away and sees (to the south, the region of the dead) a rock temple with oil wicks burning in niches surrounding the entrance door (each lamp represents a soul or a life). He felt everything sloughed away— "Everything I aimed at, or wished for, or thought, the whole *phantos majoria* of earthly existence...—an extremely painful process. Nevertheless, something remained; it was as if I now carried along with me everything I had ever experienced or done....it was with me and I was it. I consisted of all that...I consisted of my own history and I felt with great certainty: this is what I am. I am this bundle of what has been and what has been accomplished."

In the attainment or self-realization, it is seen that this is precisely what one is not. In the Buddhist teaching, the word "bundle" is used exactly by translators for the Buddha's words, "I am not this bundle of conditioned things." In Jung, this transcendental component obliterating the ego-identity is missing.

He goes on to say: "I had everything that I was, and that was everything." But one cannot read that in a transcendental context, for "as I approached the temple, I had the certainty that I was about to enter an illuminated room and would meet there all those people (represented by the lamps around the entrance) to whom I belong in reality. There I would understand...what historical nexus I and my life fitted into....There I would learn why everything had been thus and not otherwise. There I would meet the people who knew the answer to my question about what had been before and what would come after." Then there is an interruption, and he is re-called to life.

Had he entered the temple, he would have met his "group soul" consisting of the memory images of the persons of his previous lives represented by the lamps around the entrance. They would have told of where they came from, but there would be doubts to where they were going to. They would decide to send a representative to earth to discover more. Jung would have gone—into a new birth. Yes, he was recalled because of the importance of his work. By then there was no question of his changing his direction, though the experience may have altered his views. His work does stand as an important contribution to the human understanding of the psyche. Indeed, one often has the impression that his "patients" sometimes took the understandings and went further than Jung himself. That happens.

His attitude to the doctor whose life was taken in exchange for his own—"He was a good doctor"—reminds one of the dénouement in the last lines of Tennyson's *The Lady of Shalott*, when Lancelot, crossing the bridge to Camelot, looks down to see the body floating past underneath, and says, "She has a pretty face. God in his mercy give her peace." An ingenuous attitude.

In short: He was an outstandingly remarkable man. But he had not approached that step into what lies beyond the ego-integration. Note that the ego is not merely: "I want"—money, fame, etc. It is identification: "I am"—my body, my feelings/thoughts, my experiences. Basically it is an assertion that "I" am one thing and "God" is another. I may be his creature, but I look at him. This is why the "I" has to be annihilated before the transcendental identity can be found.

I wonder whether people will be able to see the point? Do you recall my analogy of the rough diamond, with one face chipped, disclosing its diamond nature, as in a simple *sadhu*? "It is better to be a diamond with but one face chipped, than to be highly polished glass." [Dec. 5, 1995]

Gurdjieff himself had many striking and even wholly original thoughts on the nature of death. At the beginning of this tale, I wrote that as an eleven-year-old child I believed my so-called teachers had made up children's fairy tales about God because they were desperately afraid of their own impending deaths. To situate their feelings in the context which I would learn many years later from Ashish: They were seeing themselves as their egos, egos which are by definition mortal and which disintegrate with the passing of the physical body. In this sense, my teachers' conception of themselves was of that part of themselves that was only relatively real, not objectively real, and certainly not real in the sense of what Gurdjieff calls objective consciousness, the fourth and highest state of human consciousness.

There is a Greek word, *metanoia*, for which there is no exact English equivalent, which Gurdjieff used to describe what we must do to change our perspective from that of the relatively real to that of the objectively real. *Metanoia* means "change of mind," and in the Gurdjieffian spiritual sense it means a change of mind or change of outlook so that we no longer see ourselves as the ego. We turn around, as it were, and begin to see ourselves as the Self, the timeless, eternal Self, within which all consciousness and the entire physical universe can be said to float.

But, according to Gurdjieff, *metanoia* does not happen of itself. For this, work on oneself is required to observe all of the characteristics of the ego, all that it identifies with, and to engage in the process of freeing oneself from that ego identification. It is for this reason that Gurdjieff called his teaching the Work.

But, says Gurdjieff, the thought of our death, that is, of the death of the ego at the disintegration of the physical body, can serve us in this Work. In *Beelzebub's Tales to His Grandson*, Gurdjieff tells us that the only hope for humanity is if we can somehow be caused to *constantly sense and be cognizant of the inevitability of [our] own death as well as the death of everyone upon whom [our] eyes or attention rests* [italics mine]. If this could happen, if we could always be so reminded, then we would begin to behave differently. We would then no longer promote the separatism that has been the unfortunate but primary characteristic of human civilization since its inception. This characteristic, Gurdjieff tells us, is the result of our improper education, an education into which we are conditioned from earliest infancy by our parents and by our teachers—an improper education that is continually passed down from one generation to the next.

For me, the most important idea Gurdjieff presents in *Beelzebub's Tales to His Grandson* is that we have only truly entered into what he called objective consciousness or objective reality, and which Ashish called the unitive vision, when we are able to put ourselves in the position of another being. When we are able to do this completely, we actually enter into that other being. We are able to look out through the eyes of that being, to see all that that being sees, to feel all that that being feels, to know all that that being knows. In that way, we have overcome for a moment our own death, for we are no longer just ourselves. At that moment, we may actually begin to do something effective in the world.

It took me a good many years to begin to understand the spiritual concepts by which Ashish pointed the way toward the unitive vision. I hope the reader has been able to get a taste of those teachings through his letters which I have set into this spiritual adventure. In November, 1992, Ashish was invited to give a talk on the subject of spirituality at the Conference of Indo-European Neurosurgeons in New Delhi. This was a broadly-based group of highly educated people, some of whom were quite familiar with esoteric spiritual concepts, others less so. In his talk, Ashish attempted with broad brush strokes to paint a picture that could be quickly grasped by these intelligent people. He shared that talk with me, and I want to share it with the reader. It comprises the next chapter of this book. Following upon that chapter, the reader will discover a chapter entitled "What Can Be Taught." A few years before he gave his talk on "A Return to Intelligent Inquiry," Ashish had become involved through the pages of *The American Theosophist* in an ongoing discussion on what can be taught about spiritual ideas such as those espoused by the Theosophical Society. He expressed his views in an article in which he was particularly anxious to emphasize the necessity not only of theoretical teaching, but also of practical teaching, such as methods by which self-awareness can be enhanced, the mind quieted, and the outflows of desire turned back. That article, which comprises Chapter Fifteen, I also think the reader will enjoy.

Gurdjieff, *Meetings*, 247-303.
Jung, *Memories, Dreams, Reflections*, 321.

14

A Return to Intelligent Inquiry
By Sri Madhava Ashish

I have been asked to talk on the subject of spirituality. It is not an easy subject to introduce because, as with politics, everyone thinks his own opinion is as good as anyone else's, while in fact there is more confusion about it than about almost any other subject.

The main confusion rather naturally derives from the way every religious sect dogmatically asserts its difference from every other sect, and each projects its own image of what the Spirit is. The images are then imprinted in children's minds, with consequences that range from bigotry to reactions into various forms of disbelief and cynicism.

If I say that there are probably more people in India with greater clarity on the subject of spirituality than elsewhere, you may think I am biased in favour of my adopted country. Perhaps I am; but that is beside the point. The great European Sanskritists and Indologists of the early years of this century who helped revivify India's awareness of its spiritual heritage might have said the same thing. Indeed, I hope that those of you who come from Europe may have inherited some of their respect for Indian thought and their evident feeling that it throws valuable light on the human predicament. India was then, and to a lesser extent still is, a land where the mystery of existence is seen as having spiritual and not material roots, where the perspective of the world view is framed in spiritual coordinates, and where the search for spiritual experience is still a socially accepted life aim.

The reason for the relatively undistorted preservation of spirituality is that Hinduism is not a highly institutionalised religion, and the priestly caste has very little, if any, power to impose particular beliefs or practices. The profusion of cults permits a high degree of religious freedom, and the priesthood's lack of temporal power has protected the mystical schools from the sort of oppression typified by the Catholic Inquisition and by the fate of the Sufi Mansur.

Thus, mysticism in India has had a relatively unharassed existence for some three thousand years. This may account for why the Sufi schools of Islamic mysticism have had a sympathetic reception and have had a widespread influence. My point in emphasizing mysticism in this context is that it is the nearest thing to straight spirituality that any culture can produce, though it is colored by the local culture and is distorted by persecution where it occurs.

Use of the word mysticism runs me into a problem. Both the Christian and the Islamic churches look on mystics as a source of heresy, while the western scientific community use the word mystic to denigrate anyone whose ideas are not orthodoxly materialistic. Often, also, the word mystic is confused with visionary. I intend to use it in its root sense of a person who is concerned with a mystery, in this case the mystery of existence.

Scientists are also concerned with the mystery of existence. But there is a difference. The scientist seeks answers within the objective universe, or from inferences he can draw from his observations. Many religionists are also inveterately outward turned, thinking, as Meister Eckhardt put it, "to see God as they would see a cow." By contrast, the mystical approach to the mystery is inturned, introspective, tracing the self-awareness which is the root of personal identity back to its source.

As is written in the *Kathopanishad*: "Some wise man, seeking deathlessness, with inturned gaze beheld the *Atman*."

I like to regard this verse as an account of how the intelligent inquiry into the roots of consciousness and being began. It did not precede religion, for religion begins as the primitive projection of as yet unintegrated potentials with the human soul onto rocks, mountains, animals and eventually, the heavens in modes that we now call animism, fetishism and theism. Those projected images are perceived as powerful, orderly, harmonious, unifying and, in short, spiritual. Perhaps the Trickster gods precede even this level of emerging rationality. The gods are perceived as the source of such moral codes as the ten commandments.

In this sense, religion is essentially superstition—seeing the indwelling spirit as an external god with tinsel trappings, when the real gold of the spirit is within. Rational inquiry into the spiritual roots of consciousness is not necessarily connected with religion; it can stem from the direct perception, "I am the observer of sense images, of feeling and of thoughts. What is the nature of the observer?"

Implicit in all that I have been saying is the idea that something quite real is being projected into religious forms, and that it is something the mystic can trace to its source. This is denied by the materialist and behaviorist philosophies, a denial which is as stupid (and as tragic) as it would be for a color blind person to deny that others see a color to which he is blind, or for someone to deny the reality of love because he/she has not experienced it.

I am not going to modify the seeming arrogance of that last statement. If I was not certain of the reality of the Spirit, I could be charged with what one of those early Indologists called the besetting sin of the Hindus, namely, "the elaboration of sciences whose subject matter is imaginary." Reality is the crucial issue in any discussion of the Spirit.

What convinces anyone of the Spirit's reality? I am not sure that it is worth trying to formulate an answer. The crux of the matter is whether the spirit in me calls forth a response from the spirit in you—or *vice versa*. I affirm the spirit's reality. At best, you accept my affirmation as second-hand information—it is my experience, perhaps not yours. At worst, it is some sort of monk making the usual lying exhortations. Meanwhile, I run the risk of insulting all of you, some by suggesting that you may not accept the reality of the spirit, others by suggesting that you might.

I must explain my quandary. When people take the trouble to visit me in my mountain retreat, I can assume they are either already convinced or want to be convinced. Here, the situation is different. I can only assume that neuroscientists may be interested in matters relating to the vexed question of brain and mind. From my viewpoint, since Spirit is real, then mind has to be real. But if Spirit were not real, then the whole question would be utterly unimportant, for nothing would have any significance.

What are the questions? Is mind a real entity with some sort of material or energetic being—not necessarily of the sort we class as physical? Is the brain the source of consciousness, or is it the interface between the observing powers of the soul and the electrochemistry of neuron stimuli? I cannot go into other fascinating matters, such as the seeming indestructibility of long-term memory and the psychologists' evidence that every sense impression is recorded and is retrievable, irrespective of our paying attention to it. In this context the computer theory of the brain and the hologram theory of memory appear as rather desperate attempts to hold onto the materialist theory of consciousness in the face of evidence to the contrary. Those could be urgent questions for brain surgeons, deeply affecting attitudes towards patients. Are your patients in some sense embodiments of the Spirit with immensely significant human potentialities, or are they just lumps of animated tissue on the operating table? Or are they both? Truly speaking, the answers do not lie in your views of patients, but in your understanding of yourselves. You cannot see a patient's soul; you cannot excise it with a scalpel; you cannot repair it with a graft. But if you are aware of the reality of your own soul, psyche, Self, *atma*, or whatever name you care to give it, it helps you to take into consideration the whole of the man who is in your care, especially when faced with decisions of life and death, when to operate and when to let the patient go, what advice to give to the relatives and many such matters.

Can any surgeon not feel the burden of responsibility at such times? Would not it ease the burden and make the whole situation more acceptable if you knew for certain that the death of the body does not constitute the end of the person's existence? Life becomes more meaningful. Death loses its finality, and is no longer something to be feared and fought off at all costs; it is a necessary event in the soul's progress.

Then there is the growing list of controversial issues—organ transplants, abortion, foetus tissue—on which clear decisions are not emerging because of the loss of certainty of ethical values. While religious sentimentalism is interfering with abortion laws in the United States, India is soullessly allowing the rich to buy kidneys from the living bodies of the poor.

All this relates to the well-worn theme that the present state of world chaos stems from the loss of religious faith. One has not noticed that the resurgence of fundamentalist religion in the Middle East and India has reduced the chaos; rather, it has aggravated it. I would emphasize that our salvation does not lie in religious dogma deriving from essentially superstitious cults. It lies in our waking up to the fact that the Spirit is experientially present, "closer to us than breathing, nearer than hands and feet," available to all of us, shining through human eyes and brightening human intelligence. It urges us to accept the challenge of growth into full manhood, not behaving like children begging God for his favors, nor behaving with the hubris of those fools who claim that man has conquered nature, and then give us global warming and the destruction of the ozone layer.

The human being who has completed the evolutionary course knows in full consciousness that it is the Spirit that "looks through the eye, but the eye does not see," and takes inspiration from its unshakeable certainty when making whatever decision is appropriate to the moment. If one is to make sense of this business about the Spirit in man and man's place in the universal order, one needs to relate it to a metaphysical view which takes account of the whole mystery, neither just the material or objective aspect of existence, which is what science is concerned with, nor only the subjective awareness by which we perceive the objective world. The subjectivity of awareness often appears as a solipsistic aspect of mysticism which is repugnant to compassionate people.

To appreciate this metaphysical view, one must abandon any such idea as that the physical brain secretes consciousness, and instead entertain the idea that consciousness pervades the universe, as if lighting it from within. Imagine a state of being prior to the manifestation of the universe—prior to the Big Bang, if you prefer it—in which there is no differentiation between subject and object; it is a universally diffused blend of subjectivity and objectivity. There is no focus of awareness to which anything could appear as an object. So there is no I and no It, no here and no there, no now and no then. It is uniform, all over at once. Mystics describe it as nothingness, or as being-consciousness-bliss.

Any such account is inadequate, and there is always an unexplainable element—which is why it always remains a mystery. No one can say why anything began, what made this unmanifest being change to manifest, except by suggesting that the desire to know itself inheres in being. It is, it knows that it is, and its being is blissful. But there is neither a distinct knower, nor anything to be known, nor any means of knowing. Yet it is what Plotinus described as "This Divine Mind, this lovely abundance so abundantly endowed." The sixteenth-century European mystic, Jacob Boehme, expressed the idea that the first cause is a desire to know: "We understand that an eternal will arises within the nothing, to introduce the nothing into something, that the will might find, feel and behold itself....For in the nothing the will would not be manifest to itself. Wherefore we know that the will seeks itself, and finds itself in itself, and its seeking is a desire, and its finding is the essence of the desire..." (*Signatura Rerum*, II 8 & 9).

It bursts out into manifestation, manifesting itself to itself. Only when subject is differentiated from object, when awareness is differentiated from the content of awareness, can the content of Divine Mind, all that is potentially present within it, be unfolded across the fields of space and time. Only then can form, color, life, intelligence and meaning be known to the witnessing consciousness. Yet the witnessing consciousness has itself to be embodied in a manner that permits specific foci in awareness to relate to specific forms and qualities. Thus, mystical vision discloses that every simple entity in some sense consists of a focus in the universal awareness, distinguished by the field of energy which surrounds it, identifies it, separates it from others, and relates it to others. It is imaged as a dim glow in the mineral world, intensifying as it moves up the evolutionary ladder, and becoming incandescent in man. Thus it is that each one of us can be aware of others as animated forms, but our sense powers can never show us the core of awareness which is our essential identity, for the subjective can never become objective to sense.

However, we have direct knowledge of our own awareness, for we are, or can be, aware that we are aware. This corresponds to the image of consciousness becoming incandescent in man. And it is this that the mystical inquiry pursues to its source in universal awareness, re-unifying the individualized point of subjective perception with its divine origin. It is in this sense that what we call Spirit knows "his" manifest form through the eyes of man. "Not I, the I that I am, knows these things," said Jacob Boehme, "but God knows this in me."

Many who have attained to that realisation have been so overwhelmed that they have separated themselves from mankind. Others have attempted to convey its truth to anyone prepared to listen. Others, again, have accepted a greater involvement in the affairs of the world, trying to establish here the harmony they have seen there.

It is characteristic of Indian philosophies that many of them stem from mystical perception and not from intellectual speculation. One of the most influential philosophies is the *Advaita Vedanta*, with its doctrine of illusion (*maya*) and of the utter emptiness of worldly pursuits. One has to understand that this is but one interpretation out of many possible interpretations of the seer's experience. Every man/woman who attains has to interpret the experience in relation to the limitations of the personal nature, mental equipment, and the state of mundane knowledge at the time. While one seer emphasizes the insignificance of this world in comparison with the glory of that one, another will emphasize the compassion which is the feeling-togetherness of unitive being. What is experienced as unity in unmanifest being is experienced in the manifest universe as the unifying power of love, which is why love is said to be the self-nature of the divine.

Let us now leave these exalted states of being and return to more proximate matters, to where the mystery confronts us at every moment of our waking lives. For, if we have not been personally graced with tangible evidence that the universe we live in is spiritual through and through, we should at least try to identify evidence which suggests that our lives are not restricted to the closed box of purely physical existence which is all the materialists have to offer us. The brain/mind mystery is what is with us at every moment. I need not detail the series of events which occur when light waves strike the retina of the eye and give rise to neuron stimuli. The full explanation is immensely complicated, and we can ignore the awkward questions of how the total visual system could have evolved without a prior intention to see. Together with neuron stimulation, something quite extraordinary happens. Neuron excitation, which is a state of the physical brain, gets converted into an image in consciousness, which is a state of the psyche. Color is an experiential correspondence to a particular stimulus of known frequency. The stimulus and the experience belong to different categories of being: while the first can be described in purely physical terms, the second involves the presence of a self-conscious observer. Indeed, we can put aside the questions about mind, memory and thought processes, and concern ourselves only with the observer.

It is worth mentioning here that Descartes's famous dictum, *cogito ergo sum*, "I think, therefore I am," in the mystical context is seen as a fallacy. The mystic says, "I observe both the thoughts and the thinker. Therefore, I am not the thinker," and he has to proceed to what in India is called "the house without support," which is a state of the awareness of being aware, lacking any other content to the awareness, such as "I am aware of being aware of a sensation."

This is the point where the spiritual inquiry meets the neurosciences. Whether they meet and agree, or meet and disagree may already have been determined by your earlier thinking on the subject, and on how far you may insist on applying the criteria of the scientific laboratory to the science of the soul. It is entirely understandable that the scientific movement had to struggle against mythological and superstitious explanations of events and to establish criteria for objective reality. But in spiritual matters we are concerned with reality of a different order and with events that must be judged by different criteria.

The British philosopher, A. N. Whitehead, emphasized the distinction between a state of the nerves and a state of the psyche—he called it the difference between a neurosis and a psychosis—and he understood that some people seem unable to grasp it. To anyone who can grasp it, it seems to be so obvious that there has to be a deficiency in anyone who cannot grasp it. The question then arises as to which is mad, the one who sees or the one who does not. As with the common agreement that we all see the same world, the question is decided by the majority. Mystics have always been in the minority and, in consequence, have been considered mad. Personally, I prefer madness to the sort of sanity that cannot distinguish the qualitative difference in the excitation of neurons and the subjective observer's perception of an image.

Extrasensory perception is another common range of human experience which indicates that there is a lot more to existence than what is encompassed by the physical co-ordinates. The way that we are always picking up each other's thoughts could have some sort of physical explanation, though nothing convincing has yet been found. I imagine that surgeons hear even more stories than I hear about patients floating around the operating theatre and later giving veridical accounts of events as seen from ceiling height; they can be brushed away as due to the psychedelic effects of modern anesthetics. There are any number of well-authenticated prognostic dreams, and all sorts of curious events, from ghosts to mediumistic phenomena. Any one of them by itself seems so trivial in comparison with the seemingly stable and predictable course of everyday life that we tend to ignore it, and we certainly hesitate to talk about it, lest our reputations for reliable objectivity get tarnished. But if we assemble all these trivial events that have happened to ourselves and to our friends—and there are very few people to whom nothing of the sort ever happened—we find a body of evidence for there being "something more" which is difficult to ignore. Trivial though they be in themselves, they constitute cracks in the walls of materiality through which we see gleams of light on the other side. However slight the glimmer, it indicates another dimension to reality. For a prisoner, it is a beacon of hope.

Such things would be a ridiculously fragile base on which to build a spiritual philosophy. Yet the colloquial joke that if there are no ghosts, then God is an impossibility, makes the point that even a spiritual philosophy requires some sort of subtle linkage between the gross materiality of this state and the utter immateriality of the unmanifest divinity. So one should not be too disdainful of these trivia. After all, it was the spontaneous manifestation of psychic power in early man that gave rise to shamanism, and one may speculate that it was one of the shamans who became the first mystic.

One can imagine that "wise man" of the *Kathopanishad* who "with inturned gaze beheld the *Atman*," finding himself in this mysterious world of, to him, unexplainable events, coming to the conclusion that the greatest mystery lay in the way that something in him, something he felt to be most essentially himself, was not only conscious of an external world, but was also aware that he was conscious, aware of specific sensations, aware of emotional responses to sensations, and aware of thinking, feeling, reasoning and questioning both about the world known to him through the avenues of sense and about himself, the Knower.

The *Kathopanishad* refers to something of this sort. It is an intelligent and rational inquiry into the roots of a mystery on the basis of data available to man as man. The inquirer is not dependent on how other people understand themselves; he is not dependent on his social upbringing, on his cultural traditions, or on the dogma of local religions. All of that is information at second hand. Anyone who pursues such a direct inquiry into the experience of awareness at first hand may indeed discover what it is in himself and in all mankind that is "deathless"—deathless, because it is essentially in identity with the unborn, unmanifest, eternal Being from which the whole manifest universe has arisen.

In the modern world, intelligent men and woman turn away from dogma and superstition. But they should not turn away from any mystery which opens to intelligent inquiry.

15

What Can Be Taught

By Sri Madhava Ashish

Felix Layton's excellent question, "What should we teach?" in *The American Theosophist* for Spring, 1988, raises other questions: What has been taught? What remains to be taught? If anything, is it something that can be taught? Is any teaching complete if it fails to provide a method for its confirmation?

What has been taught corresponds to what the "Tibetan Precepts of the Gurus" (in *Tibetan Yoga and The Secret Doctrine* by Dr. Evans-Wentz) regards as indispensable, namely, "A philosophy comprehensive enough to embrace the whole of knowledge." The society has been teaching about the spiritual nature of the universe for over one hundred years. This should have helped members to adopt the much more ancient yet ever valid metaphysics of Theosophy in place of the dominant materialist metaphysic of today.

In consequence, all Theosophists may now agree that there really is something more to the universe than what is perceived by the physical organs of sense, and that the nature of this "something more" may be something like what the teachings have described. They may also believe that the definition of man is not confined to the physical coordinates of body and brain, the human consciousness can obtain knowledge of the subtle universe by direct perception, and that the limited, egocentric viewpoint can be transcended by discovering the identity of the individual's self-awareness with the universal awareness. Such beliefs may have been built into a worldview which governs personal behavior, throws light on human behavior in general, and lends significance to both.

So long as all this remains on the level of "head learning," it is like a theoretical introduction to a practical course which lacks a practical component—like a course in the theory of swimming whose students are never taken to the water and whose teachers do not claim to be able to swim.

It is not denied that much can be learned about swimming (and about the spirit) from the blackboard. What cannot be taught, but must be learned through practical experience, is the feeling of buoyancy in the water which engenders trust in the new element. Such trust is not transferable, even by a teacher's demonstration of floating. Similarly, neither teaching nor demonstration can substitute for personal experience of the higher states of consciousness. To quote again from the "Precepts of the Gurus," "One should acquire practical experience of the Path by treading it..."

However, such acquisition of knowledge is not to be equated with being thrown in at the deep end and left to flounder. There is much that can and should be taught. There are methods and disciplines by which self-awareness may be enhanced, the mind controlled and quietened, the outflows of desire turned back, and the ego-reassuring stimuli of the senses transcended; all of which help to bring the seeker face to face with the crucial question of what, if anything, lies beyond out-turned waking consciousness. Shall we find confirmation of what we were taught in class, or shall we find only a prognosis of that blank annihilation our materialist upbringing leads us to suppose must follow the death of the body and dissolution of the brain? The teaching must be put to the test. Theosophists should graduate from theory to practice.

One of the early strengths of the Theosophical Society was that there was less concern with people becoming "Theosophists" than with their finding allied teachings in the mystical components of their own religions and cultures. To this we owe many of the translations of and commentaries on ancient texts—and, perhaps, the society's reluctance to adopt any specific discipline. But times have changed. The need of the moment is not the revitalization of ancient beliefs (with their fundamentalist snares) but a direct inquiry into the mystery that is Man—a mystery that lies at the root of human awareness—as being the single point at which each of us has firsthand knowledge of anything at all.

Methods and disciplines are like a craftsman's tools that can be used to build church, mosque, temple, or scientific laboratory. For example, anyone attempting to quieten the mind as a preliminary to meditation may be helped by repetition of "mantra," whose use by all the great religions argues for its efficacy in the purely human predicament, irrespective of specific claims for sectarian purposes. If the aim is right, the appropriate use of such tools becomes apparent.

What constitutes a "right" aim? If we enter the admittedly dangerous path of practice, what safeguards have we against abuse of the teaching for ignoble ends—the sorts of abuses listed by Felix Layton? Perhaps the only safeguard, apart from a burning self-dedication to the Path of the Spirit, lies in adopting the highest aim of self-transcendence. To get from "here" to "there," one has to traverse the intermediate worlds with their glittering and deceitful attractions. But if the pilgrim's gaze is on the peaks of lofty mountains, he will not be waylaid.

16

The Passing of a Great Soul

By the early 1990's, Ashish had developed skin cancer. I had sent him a hat with a specially made extra-wide brim to help keep the sun off his face, but this hardly prevented the need for medical treatment. He was content to have his condition treated at Delhi, but his pupils, especially those close to him, urged him to go to England for treatment. He agreed to do this.

Part of his decision to go to England was, I think, a desire to see the England he had left behind some fifty years before when he came out to India during World War Two. While his older sister Penelope, who lived in England, came to India to visit him periodically, and while she and others attempted to keep him abreast of changes in the West, he wanted a first-hand look. Some of his interest was due to western pupils like myself, who referred him through our correspondence and through dream images to conditions in the West of which he had no first-hand knowledge. Many of these things were the mundane conditions of ordinary western living, like shopping centers, motorways and fast food restaurants— things which had only just begun to appear in India, and then in a very non-western form.

Although I was quite unhappy about Ashish's medical condition, his visit to England afforded me an opportunity to visit him more easily than by journeying to the Himalayas, and I took advantage of it. As strange as it had been for me to meet a tall Englishman in monk's robes striding down a hillside in India in 1978, I found it equally strange to see this same tall Englishman striding in his monk's robes along the high street of the traditional English village in which his sister lived. I met him in England only the one time, briefly; then, no letters were exchanged back and forth between us for some months.

Within two years, Ashish's skin cancer, which the doctors had been able to control, had been replaced by prostate cancer. As over the months to come I watched his condition begin slowly but surely to deteriorate, I thought sadly about what little good my gift of an extra-wide brimmed hat had done for him, and of all the great good he had done for me over the years as opposed to—how much?—good I had done for him. It was impossible not to think of all the great good he had done for so many others over the years, and to wonder how much good one had done for the world oneself. Over those years, Ashish's decline also became a spiritual teaching for me and for many others—a teaching that took us well beyond the confines of our lesser selves.

It was almost as if Ashish's decline were reflected in the events around us. In the summer and autumn of 1994, two disturbances took place in India that disrupted my plans for an annual visit. The first was the rioting "for political purposes" in the Kumoan hills where Mirtola is located. These "disturbances," as they are euphemistically called in India, have been a feature of the country for many years. In the past, they were minor and did not interfere with one's travel plans. But in 1994 they took on an ominous tone. In past years, Ashish had made light of such disturbances. The joke was that the students who often led the riots would only barricade the roads during the hours convenient to them, usually between 10:00 a.m. and 5:00 p.m. On two earlier journeys where local rioting was a factor, I had gotten around the problem by making the taxi trip from Delhi to Mirtola at night so that we were past the areas of road blockage by the time dawn came. Now I was surprised to receive a letter from Ashish, posted from New Delhi, in which he voiced considerably more concern.

A.   I doubt that the American news has concerned itself with disturbances in the whole of the U. P. hills, [disturbances which are] partly as a protest against government policy and partly as an effort to get the hills made a separate state from the huge plains position of the U. P. For over a fortnight there was almost total stoppage of all roads and traffic. Banks, post offices, government offices and schools were closed. In one or two towns there was violence, mainly caused by over-reaction by the police who shot several people. However, we did see tourist buses and taxis being allowed through. At present, we hear that the situation is "normal." But with the way both the state government and the central government are behaving, trouble could start again any day.

I do not want to frighten you off. But not to warn you that you might get delayed in the hill portion of the trip would be unfair. I personally expect the whole question to be settled in the next week or so, long before you are due. You could check by phone with your embassy in Delhi, but one would expect them to be over-protective and therefore unreliable. Dave and I got down here during a lull. A friend who followed next day was held up for six hours in Haldwani. I came here for a medical check-up. We expect to start back in a few days. [Sept. 22, 1994]

The medical check-up to which Ashish referred was part of treatment for the prostate cancer he had contracted. The disease, eventually metastasizing into bone cancer, would eventually claim his life. Compared to the skin cancer for which, at the insistence of his pupils, he had gotten treatment in England in 1991, his attitude about medical treatment seemed to me to have changed. Some years earlier, in talking about incarnations, Ashish had told me he would be "getting out" before he was eighty. This would have been before the year 2000. Whether this was insight or mere speculation on his part, I don't know. Although in the earlier instance of cancer he had seemed interested in curing himself for the benefit of his pupils, it struck me that his attitude about this new cancer, going forward, was one of simply accepting the inevitability of physical death.

A week later, I received a second letter.

A.   Just after writing to you about the hill disturbances (now relatively quiet) the plague scare began. It seems more serious than the government will admit. They say that tourists who stick to the five-star (hotel) circuit are under no risk, but one can't believe the views of people with interests in the tourist industry. However, it is possible that the thing will peter out in a week or two. Hope to see you—if not now, then later. [Sept. 30, 1994]

The second event to disrupt my travel plans that autumn was this outbreak of plague in India. Unlike the local riots in the Uttar Pradesh (the Indian state within which Mirtola is located) that were barely mentioned in the western press, the plague in India made world headlines. It caused me and Nick Tereshchenko, with whom I'd intended to make the trip, to rethink our plans. We cancelled the visit, and I wrote to Ashish to inform him. I followed this up with a second letter. He replied:

A.   Your welcome letter of October 25. Yes, one gathers the plague is over—for the present—and a cover-up is going on, trying to prove that it wasn't really plague but another nasty bug. The hill situation is improving, but could blow up again at any moment. There are half-a-dozen groups all agitating, and no central organization. [Nov. 9, 1994]

On Dec. 16, I received another, alarming letter from Ashish.

A.   Nice to be greeted by your letter on arrival at Noida on the 14th. Today I am in hospital for a minor operation tomorrow, and should be back at Noida on Monday. [Dec. 16, 1994]

Though he always made light of his physical condition, specifically of the cancer that had taken hold of his body, I was sure things weren't going well at all. This was confirmed through letters I received from some of Ashish's other pupils.

In early 1995, Nick Tereshchenko, myself, and another friend from England began to think about arranging an international Gurdjieff conference. The manuscript of a new book, *Gurdjieff: Cosmic Secrets* by Russell Smith, had come to our attention, along with several unpublished papers on Gurdjieff's teachings. These recent writings challenged certain long-held assumptions about what Gurdjieff meant in some sections of *Beelzebub's Tales to His Grandson*. The three of us made the decision to get together to discuss these papers and invite several other friends whom we thought would be interested in such a meeting. We planned the conference for February, 1996, in England. I wrote to Ashish about this just after Nick had visited me in Florida and our plans had begun to crystallize.

But I couldn't drum up much enthusiasm for telling Ashish about the conference. Although Gurdjieff and his *Beelzebub's Tales to His Grandson* continued to fascinate me, and I was excited about the coming congress, somehow none of this seemed important beside the fact of Ashish's impending death. His health was steadily deteriorating. He was traveling with increasing frequency to Delhi for medical treatment but, despite that, the cancer was slowly and surely overtaking him. In his next letter, he wrote to me stoically if movingly about how we should face death.

A.   To me it is clear that a man who fights to survive against death, but fails and death wins, is in a terrible position. Last thought: the mind was full of the intention to live. He will likely return to birth rather quickly and is unlikely to get a good birth in terms of the Work. I doubt that the fact of winning the fight with death leads to remarkably better results in the long run.

I confess to being in a bad mood. Everyone of these so-called "dedicated" disciples, after thirty or more years of teaching, on getting anything like a terminal disease, opts for physical survival with an intensity that never went into the inner work. Just what am I doing here? In the language of an engineering workshop, "playing at silly buggers." By all means go to a doctor. But you yourself decide whether to go along with him or not. Has the threat frightened you? If so, that is the priority work to attend to. Yes, I am going to a doctor, but not in a panic. [Nov. 25, 1995]

On one of my many visits to Mirtola, I had been accompanied by Jacqueline, my close friend and the native French speaker of our Gurdjieff group. I've forgotten now whether it was she or I who put the question to Ashish, but we asked: "Is there really a chain of lives, a kind of string of personalities, of which our current incarnations are the latest?"

I was still voicing skepticism about this theory of reincarnation, especially since Gurdjieff had said that reincarnation does not exist for everyone, that if you are not adequately conscious then there is no reincarnation, at least not in any useful sense.

Ashish replied, "Of course, there is a string of lives."

"How can we know that?" I asked.

Ashish laughed. "Well, you'll just have to wait until you die to find out."

I was reminded of one of Krishna Prem's articles, "The Forgotten Land," in *Initiation into Yoga,* in which Prem writes:

"Rebirth there is, but whether he who is reborn is you is for yourself to judge. The stream of life is one, ebbing and flowing, weaving through many lives, with other streams, the Pattern of the Whole. That stream which was yourself, which, if you like, is still yourself, flows forth....Memory remains in me alone, the memory of lives too numerous to count. That memory is yours, if, during life, you learn to enter me. If not, I keep it for you till we meet again once more....Thus does the cycle of nights and days turn on, until the pattern is complete, and pattern blends with pattern in a vast and wondrous whole, too great for you to grasp with finite mind....in all things seek for me who am your friend, your life, your very Self."

In the letters I received from Ashish from about 1990 on, a more urgent note was beginning to be sounded. He was urging me—all of us—to enter farther into the depths of the Self. I think he was concerned that the full measure of his teachings should soon be felt.

IN SEARCH OF THE UNITIVE VISION

A.   Mankind is faced with a problem of identity. We do not know who we are, where we came from or why we are here. We are led to see that the root of the mystery lies at the root of our own being, somewhere in our awareness. We discover that by being aware, we become more aware; our self-awareness becomes "real" and we "wake up." We ask: What is this awareness in itself? When the mind is not full of thoughts and the sense not filled with stimuli, what remains? [June 20, 1990]

A.   So long as "you" are there to feel bored, you have not got beyond yourself—beyond your limited personal integration. Even the highest individualized state you can know is but a spark of the universal fire. What you are in fact seeing is that the states you are familiar with are not and cannot be the final illumination. You have to go further by dropping the remaining identification with the self, [but] that ego-self will oppose you. You are forgetting that your work is an inquiry into what, if anything, is at the root of your self-awareness. [May 3, 1992]

A.   What you have groped for...is the process by which you increasingly find your identification with the Spark, in place of the usual identification with "Sy." [Sept. 5, 1992]

A.   The root of the mystery of being lies at the root of the awareness which perceives the universe. Every human being is human by virtue of that awareness. Every human being is or can be aware that he is aware. When that self-awareness is traced to its inner source, then only can the identity of the individual with the universal be found, then only can the mystery of being be solved. And only when there are enough such individuals can sanity return through them to our troubled world. [April 22, 1996]

On August 24, 1996, I received a distressing letter by Fax from Ashish. It had been sent from Delhi, and in it he said that the cancer from which he suffered had metastasized throughout his body. He wrote, "[No] one is ready to guess whether I have only weeks, months or years." He had gone back to Delhi for medical treatment sooner than anticipated, and was remaining in Delhi for further treatment. I hadn't made my 1996 visit yet, but I had been planning to see him at Mirtola in October. In view of his deteriorating condition and what seemed to be the urgency expressed in his Fax, I decided to go to India immediately, and thus visited with him that September.

He was staying at the home of two of his pupils in Noida, a suburb of Delhi, and had very much weakened by the time I arrived. Paradoxically, it was during this period of a week's visit that I saw more of him and conversed more with him than would normally have been possible at the Mirtola ashram. The week was filled with emotion for me. Although on parting we talked about my visiting again, I knew that this was the last time I would see Ashish. I'm sure he knew this as well.

I wrote to him next in November. I'd been thinking a great deal about the nature of the bond which had originally drawn me to him and which had continued to strengthen over the years. I asked him, "Given our more-than-eighteen-year relationship and that I am, with one exception, your only regular American pupil, do you think we might have had a past life connection?" I also asked about the possibility of our visiting again, though I knew, and he knew, that we had already seen each other for the last time.

A.   I don't know that there was a past life connection specifically with me. It seems more probable that you were previously connected with the TS and were sent here to pick up the inner connection again. The early TS had the connection. G was from the same source. Yes, the personal connection with me has now grown strong—and it means a lot to me. I continue to pray that G and others like him will grace you with their recognizable presence. But they won't do it while there is danger of your taking it to your ego. Therefore, strive to center yourself in what is beyond the ego. I imagine that a visit in early March would be only for a two- or three-night stay. At this distance in time, I can only say O.K. [Dec. 17, 1996]

Ashish's final letter to me was dated February 10, 1997. I had written to him about my forthcoming marriage to Dorothy, a woman I had known twenty-three years earlier. Dorothy and I had finally gotten back together toward the end of 1996. That she and I had come back together after being apart for more than twenty years was something I saw as a miracle in itself. Ashish responded to my letter:

A.   This is wonderful news. But it has always appeared to me that even real love, wonderful though it is, needs the inner work including meditation to make it last and to make it grow from something that is "given" into something that is being consciously worked on. For God's sake, be careful about pushing the teaching. You have as much to learn from her as she has from you, though it is of quite a different sort. You have found something that is of immense significance to you and you naturally want to share it with the beloved, but it is a sharing, not an assertion of superiority on the path.

     In the long run I feel that all this stuff about groups is far less important than how you handle your relationship with Dorothy. This requires far greater personal courage. Remember one of my favorite Sufi quotes, "Love is the guide and love is the goal. Where e'er love's camels turn, the one true way is there." [Feb. 10, 1997]

My last visit with Ashish had taken place in September of 1966. It was only in the following month of October that Dorothy and I renewed our relationship. It was as if the great ache in my heart at the imminent loss of Ashish was to be mended by the renewal of love between Dorothy and myself.

Ashish passed away at Mirtola, at 10:35 a.m. on April 13, 1997. His body was cremated that same afternoon. He had died of complications from the bone cancer, which, I am told, can be very painful. I am grateful to Ashish's sister, Penelope Phipps, for permission to share with the reader parts of a letter she had written earlier but which she sent to me from England on April 13, 1997, the day of Ashish's passing. She had visited him at Mirtola some weeks earlier.

"Ashish spends the day on a specially made bed with adjustable back with a sheepskin type cover, in the front of his two rooms, looking out over the view. There are upright chairs for people he is seeing. I'm told he summons up his strength to give a good show to visitors, says when he is tired, and whoever is there goes. There are rails to the bathroom which he may still be able to use. He has a special limited diet including marrow, coconut juice and weak porridge. David and Shekar look after him beautifully, and he has two bells beside him. Doctors want to do more tests but he says, 'No.' A ten-hour car journey—six in the heat—when they cannot cure it is not worth it. New medication is obtained by someone driving to Almora, faxing Shekar, in Delhi, a friend and head of a pharmaceutical company, who faxes Dr. Michael Kearney in Cork, Ireland, who runs a hospice and who wrote *Mortally Wounded*, who faxes back the correct medication and Shekar drives it up every two weeks.

"I said to Ashish, 'What shall I tell people who ask?'

"He said, 'Tell them I'm very well.'

"No one knows how long he has in his body. But his spirit is splendid. All intellectual discussion seems to fade into insignifcance, bringing us no nearer to 'Self-Realization.' One only wants to absorb 'THAT' and lose one's ego.

"I think our party was allowed to stay, as we had been told six months before that we might. Some are staying in Almora and coming out on the bus or taxi. I don't think Ashish or anyone else has any idea how long he has got, but [this is] a great lesson in complete acceptance—the Christian 'Thy will be done.'

"There is an Indian saying, 'There is always a comet in the sky when a great *rishi* dies.' There was at Gopalda's death—and now Hale-Bopp. We shall see.

"How very lucky we are—and shall have been—to know him."

Penelope Phipps also sent me the following letter, which was sent to her by Mala, another pupil of Ashish, who was present at his death:

"Ashish was conscious till his last breath, this in considerable pain. He gave a full look into Shekar's eyes, a slight smile, and then heaved a sigh and was gone. After bathing the body and dressing it, as is the ritual, he was laid on a sheet outside the *mandir* (temple sanctuary) and, according to instructions, his body was handed over to the villagers. They performed their *puja* and then, with Dave and Shekar at the helm, lifted the simple bamboo structure on which his body was laid and carried it eleven miles down to Dandeswar, the cremating ground, where Gopalda was also cremated. There they sat, till the pyre was cold. The bones and ashes were strewn into the river. A little bit of ash has been kept to be put into the shrine in front of the temple—a memorial to Yashoda Mai and Gopalda before him."

All this while, the comet blazed in the skies.

Prem, *Initiation*, 87-88.

A Short Compendium

This section contains answers to questions that, however great their intrinsic value, did not easily fit within any of the various categories covered in this book. The order is alphabetical by theme. Questions are italicized. The "**A.**" customarily introducing Ashish's answers has been omitted.

Ancestor Worship (Parents)

How does one pray for parents or engage in ancestor worship? Pastor spoke about this, and Gurdjieff says it is important.

Parents: Help is given by the use of imagination. Summon them by conjuring up their image in the mind. Direct the mind to the highest concept/feeling of the spirit you know. "Send" them there. An anniversary is a good time. Do it only once a year. If you feel they are already gone on to another birth, the help can be given, but is probably less necessary. [July 7, 1989]

Consciousness

Difficulties over consciousness are often due to semantic confusions. In the way I use the word it is immaterial by definition. But when we talk of the awareness of being aware, some sort of integration of energies (materiality) is implied so long as it is an integration. Even the universal mind appears to be an integration—the cosmic egg in undimensioned "space." The heart of the onion is aware of all its skins. When the last skin is off, what remains? Consciousness. [Oct. 23, 1983]

IN SEARCH OF THE UNITIVE VISION

A Course in Miracles

What do you think of the book A Course in Miracles? (In the letter in which I'd asked this question, I enclosed a pamphlet I'd picked up on the Course).

I am a little puzzled by this *Course in Miracles*. There is very good stuff in the booklet, but it seems too much like an intelligent reformulation of Christianity with psychological insight, and not enough of true perception. I could call it a conscious attempt to get back to the teachings of Jesus, and away from what the church did to it with its doctrines of sin, the devil and evil. It is unfair to say more without reading the book itself. And I don't feel it worth my while to plough through 1,200 pages just to confirm or deny my first impressions. But I have to repeat what I said about the Charlaine communications, that the psychic provenance adds nothing to the worth of the book. However, I am sure it will help the sorts of people who are screwed up over their being "miserable sinners." But while it is perfectly true that the whole universe is bound into a unity by love, I am not sure that the sort of Christian sentimentalism that passes for love helps anyone. [Nov. 6, 1990]

Diet

Although people have varying motives for being vegetarian, some of them insist that it aids one's inner development. Yet Gurdjieff was known to be an enthusiastic meat eater. I realize that too much meat eating is not healthy. But does it really matter in terms of spirituality? I intuit that it does. For the time being I have given up eating red meat.

Intuition, yes. But it isn't easy to get oneself balanced in this matter. Certainly one must have adequate protein. But what is "adequate"? Western (and Punjabi) standards of vigor and virility place unnecessary stress on the stuff, often making the psychological effects of deprivation worse than the physical ones. It's a complicated matter. Let's talk about it. Your present idea of avoiding only red meat is fine. [Aug. 25, 1979]

270

Entities, Alien and Other

One of the things about which I remain uncertain is that of the reality of entities appearing to people either physically or psychically on other planes. In relation to the Absolute, with which we each seek to realize our identity, do these supposed entities have any objective reality? Can demons be conjured up into physical form as apparently happened through the Enochian magic uncovered by Dr. John Dee?

Two recently published books by a Harvard professor add credibility to the possibility of alien visitations, but I gather his academic colleagues are not at all happy about these published accounts. And I have never seen the supposed Mirtola ghost.

You have asked a question to which there is no simple yes or no answer. Gopalda used to say that an interest in the occult is a necessary part of a neophyte's equipment. I personally found that certain sorts of interest were encouraged, while others were rejected—"Stop playing around and get on with your job"—when one was supposed to be meditating.

Intellectualizing about occult symbols is not the point. Can you work yourself to the pitch of intensity where things start happening? Can you get out of your body? Can you put ideas into people's minds? Do anything of this sort, but also intensify your meditation which goes beyond it all.

Conjuring up demons?

Isn't that like the Tibetans and their Angry Deities? To my mind those are simply personifications of the subconscious fears, uncertainties, doubts, ungratified desires, insecurities, angers, weaknesses etc., etc., etc. I prefer to deal with them directly as factors in the psyche which can be "conscioussed." The other method sees them as alien to oneself—until the very end where the *Tibetan Book of the Dead* says, "They are but the creations of your own mind." This is the school which fears "Sickness, madness or death" as the dangers of the path because they all seem to be utterly real and objective beings which actually attack one. There is a total projection of psychic content. All the evil is outside one. It undoubtedly works for people who are like that.

This is relevant to the Professor who claims that aliens come to people in their sleep. Isn't it another case of projection of the unconscious? He thinks they are real beings, just as the Tibetan thinks there are real Angry Gods.

I would see this sort of thing as dangerously liable to bring about a collective neurosis—a panic syndrome. Think of the panic caused by the radio broadcast of H. G. Wells, *The War of the Worlds*, where Martians landed on earth.

Incidentally, I have also read the original story of Dr. John Dee and I do not think highly of him. The *Beelzebub* congress sounds to be fun. Beware of all the types who will want to muscle in on your show and claim G's mantle for themselves.

And why are you feeling inadequate because you have not seen that wretched headless *dhotiyal* (ghost) at Mirtola? Who else has seen him, other than Ma and perhaps me? [June 29, 1995]

Guidance, Spirit

There seem to be many examples of a kind of "higher guidance" in my life. What might be the "spiritual dynamics" behind this kind of higher guidance, whether it exists for me or not?.

I see very little point in trying to pinpoint the source of such guidance. There are the Masters and their helpers, but I doubt that their personal intervention is the only source. As with synchronicities, there is something else at work. When one pays attention to the Self, the Self pays attention to one. Long before one becomes aware of the Self as a reality, its inherent affinity with the harmony of being brings one into touch with people, events, books which one needs to bring one towards the Self. Jung referred to "the autonomous nature of the psyche," meaning that the psyche acts and leads one from a level that is higher than and independent of the waking integration. As we see in dreams, our dream-making power knows more about us and our needs then we ourselves consciously know.

I believe that one must be content to live within a mystery whose workings can be intuited but seldom analyzed in detail. Unlike the physical world, where its stability allows respectable demonstrations, the inner worlds are fluid, with one thing running into another. Attempts to pin it down usually result in crude, mechanistic models of things which are better seen as a shimmering matrix of conscious powers, the energies of creation.

So, receive the help reverentially. Don't suggest by your questioning that you must, "know who shot the arrow....before allowing it to be pulled out"—before accepting and being grateful for the help. The need to "understand" how it happens, other than in the general terms I have mentioned, implies that in some sense you want to remain in control. That "you" is still the separate individual, wanting to remain distinct from the universal life, whereas your effort should be to get that separate "you" out of the way so that the one life is undistorted by egotism, and the Self takes charge. [May 3, 1992]

Kailash, Mount

Is there any spiritual significance to Mount Kailasa?
Kailash (Mt. Kailasa)! A mountain in Tibet, a place of Hindu pilgrimage, north of Nepal's western border with India, beyond Lake Manasarovar. You'll find it on the map. It's a curious, specially shaped geographic formation. Pilgrims circumambulate. But the joke is, you know, it's also the name of a little hill near Ranikhet. Ranikhet is thirty miles west from Almora.

The famous Lahiri Mahasaya, the man you've read about in Yogananda's book, *Autobiography of a Yogi*, he claimed to have done his daily worship on Mt. Kailash. Yogananda did not mention the fact that the Mt. Kailash he refers to is in Ranikhet, whereas the reader immediately thinks of the Mt. Kailash up in Tibet. So Lahiri Mahasaya presumably, sort of magically went up to Tibet and back again every morning. It's one of these confusions. [Dec. 22, 1979]

Nature Images

In recent meditation, I observed an image of the center of the galaxy and another of a barren landscape, almost like a moonscape. You once said that we need to pay attention to images that appear in extended meditation, but that we must first get past the nature images that appear. Are what I observed nature images?

Nature Images. There has been some garbling. I told you that, as one withdraws towards the state of dhyan, images/visions are apt to appear (not always). Such images are often (not always) of the hypnagogic type which seem to have an affinity with the powers of nature – as symbolized by gnomes, sylphs, undines, salamanders. If they come, observe them, get used to them, read any message they may seem to give...and pass on. [Dec. 7, 1989]

Nothingness, Bare

If in the ultimate reality there is nothing, bare nothingness, than how does one account in the external world for evidences of subtle planes, such as what is coming through Charlaine, for example?

Your "burning question": Stay in the state of "bare nothingness" long enough, and it soon becomes evident that what you are experiencing is not the liberation all the saints talk about. Then you begin looking for what will carry you further. Agreed that from the ultimate viewpoint G and his brothers are also "bare nothingness". But that ultimate viewpoint is not Sy Ginsburg philosophizing on the logic of nothingness. [Sept. 18, 1989]

Psychological Aspects

As a group leader, I'm concerned that, if someone really opens up in a psychological way, either through bringing a dream or just talking about their inner state, I do not have the presence to read them and handle the situation rightly. If one doesn't actually stand in the unity, then "psychological wisdom" winds up coming from personality.

As for your group, how can you learn except by doing the job. And if it pushes you to do more yourself, so much the better. Learn to be sensitive to inner promptings. You may also find your dreams prompting you with advice about particular people, often enough mixed with things that apply to you.

Dreams have always been treated as significant in the inner work. The so-called "primitive" peoples still pay great attention to them, but their interpretations (and the dreams themselves) relate to affairs which concern them, and are largely contained within their world view.

The psychological theory of dreaming has, of course, been popular since Freud. This still holds good. What is lacking in most current dream theory, as it is lacking in the current world view, is the presence of a spiritual centre and a universal view to which the personal psychic patterns can be related, and which gives significance to the person and his struggles with his nature.

The only person who approaches this problem is C. G. Jung. His followers would say that he did more than approach it, that his concept of the center is the same as what all mystics have talked of. But he never seems to have felt that what he talked of is far, far greater than the individual. This reduces it to something to be added to the person—a sort of super personality—instead of transcending individuality. The power that shapes dreams adjusts them to the level of interpretive understanding they will meet. Even if they often do say more, the person interpreting will not see it until he is ready for it Indeed, it often seems to be the case that one can see the meaning only if one already knows the sort of thing the dream must be saying. Presumably this is why so few people can handle them. However, this does not mean that one has to be a realized man to understand dreams in this fashion. A sufficient familiarity with a comprehensive world view will be enough. Another fact is that even if one misinterprets a dream, provided one's motives are true, the result will work out positively. The theme will also be repeated until the message is understood.

Repetition of a theme in dream often implies either that one has not understood, or that one has not gone deep enough. The feeling of dismay or annoyance at the repetition of a theme one thought was finished, is itself an indication that there is more to discover and good reason for discovering it. [July 3, 1985]

IN SEARCH OF THE UNITIVE VISION

Ramana Maharshi

I have lately become interested in the teaching of Ramana Maharshi, which seems to be the same in essence as Gurdjieff's teaching.

I am glad you are on to Ramana. His is about the straightest approach possible. [July 3, 1985]

Ritual Magic

I have read enough to see that there could be a way through this method, if one can get past their personification of powers, just as there is a way through tantric teaching. But in nearly all the Tantric and Occult schools the accent tends to fall on power, and this in turn tends to strengthen egotistic motives to the detriment of the spiritual aim. The ego gets hardened rather than transcended. [May 6, 1987]

Sex on the Path

I continue to come across references to sexual energy being of importance in the inner work. What can you tell me about this? Does this energy somehow give Sathya Sai Baba his powers?

We all know something of the connection between sexual restraint and "the production of substances necessary for the Work" or "building the Kesdjan (astral) body."

We all know that in order to attain to the vision of the unity (Nirvana, or anything else one likes to call it) the "outflows" have to be withdrawn, and that since all outflowing interests are derivatives of eros, withdrawal of the major erotic interest, sexual interest, is a major step in the process. Most of us are now aware that to interpret these requirements in terms of celibacy is mere literalness, and that a balance has to be found such that the fires of the external passions can themselves be harnessed to serve our self-transcending aim.

A difficult, dangerous doctrine, in which it is only too easy to deceive ourselves.

If this is true for the seeker, why should it suddenly become untrue for the man who attains? If the seeker finds the fires of the spirit burning in sex, why should the mahatma find them extinguished? The compulsions must be extinguished, not the fires themselves. Mahatmas cannot be classified according to their sexuality. There have been men, like Ramana Maharshi, who, so far as we know, never had any sort of sexual life. But Nisarga Datta was married and had children. Gurdjieff was married and had children. [July 6, 1979]

Teacher

There are people in leadership positions in Gurdjieff groups who hold their groups together, but do not appear to have developed something real in themselves. Is this possible as the result of highly developed personality characteristics and not a highly developed level of being?

Holding groups together: I am not talking about popular movements and group leaders who jolly their members along with false promises and mystery-mongering. I am talking about actual "schools" in G's sense. The requirements are different and should not be confused. The main requirements are the character and status of the teacher. He can be a pupil teacher, in the sense that he has not yet attained but is, at least, sure of what he is doing and where he is going. His main task is his own work, and he must not judge himself by the quality and number of his group members. He serves and learns through service. As you rightly suppose, you are acting as a pupil teacher. From what I have heard, the instructors in the G groups put on an air of authority and learn to order their pupils around and to knock them about. That is the accepted system, and its dangers have to be guarded against—the dangers of ego-inflation and self-fooling, enjoying the power of the position. One should remember how G treated Orage in New York, possibly because he was getting inflated. Someone in the group has to have the capacity to see when such dangers are affecting the instructors and take appropriate action. [Jan. 24, 1989]

Appendix

MASTERS

During the mid-1990's, the subject of the reappearance of an avatar, called the Lord Maitreya, came to my attention. He presumably had taken human form in a Pakistani body, and was apparently able to appear and disappear at will before crowds of people. I knew that these recent claims about the appearance of an avatar would not impress Ashish. But, when a friend of mine in England told me he was interested in this phenomenon, I suggested he write to Ashish, sending him published materials on the matter. He did so, and Ashish replied. My friend sent me a copy of the letter, which recapitulated Ashish's views on Masters.

I have read the papers and, frankly, am not happy about this particular "Master." I am certainly not going to accept any such claims just because the presumptive Master or his side-kick solemnly tells me he is calling a press conference to announce himself. Nor will I accept the "instant recognition" of a hyped-up crowd.

Then how does one recognize a Master? What is a Master, anyway? Someone who has fulfilled the evolutionary purpose and is Complete or Perfected. Fine words! What has he actually done? Raised his kundalini? I know dozens of people to whom that has happened and they are certainly not Masters. Seen God? What a vague definition! A vision of one's particular deity does not turn one into a Master, as I know very well from personal experience. Perhaps the nearest one can get to it is to say he has found the root of his individualized being, and has found how that individualized point of self-awareness relates to the universal awareness so that he stands in the unity.

One can add here that in this respect all Masters are one, and that there is no hierarchy of Masters, one being greater than another. The person who founded this ashram, when asked about the Masters of Blavatsky, replied, "They are the forms in which the Lord showed himself to her." That is the essence of the matter.

In this context it should be clear that one cannot recognize the Master by his looks, his words, or his behavior, for it is none of these things that constitute his attainment. So, if the sensible characteristics are not the Master, he cannot be recognized by sense perception.

Then what "recognizes?" I know only that when one seeks for the truth where it lies, in one's own "heart," then one's own heart resonates when it meets its likeness in the worlds of form.

Even in our specialized spheres of action we develop a fine sense for whether another man is speaking from real knowledge, or is pretending to a knowledge he does not have. Anyone on the inner path needs to develop the same capacity in this field—a capacity that requires one to develop the touchstone of the heart. If one does not, then what protection does one have from the charlatans who batten on the simple minded? Charlatans commonly take the line of "How can we inferior beings dare to assess those great Beings whose feet we are unworthy to touch." The seeming humility catches one if one has not learned to trust one's own perceptions, and one will be led down a dangerously wrong path and be fleeced into the bargain.

"Believe and be saved" has never been a valid doctrine because it assumes that the person so exhorted has no means of assessing the person exhorting him. So it is a matter of chance whether one is exhorted by a true teacher or a pretender.

If one is to become a full man, one must accept responsibility for one's decisions, and so responsibility for understanding the criteria of thought and feeling by which true decisions are made. In the context of the Spirit, the criteria must be spiritual, not material. The one taste of Spirit given to all men is the self-awareness that one finds at the root of one's being—one's "heart."

Let me give an example from real life. At one period we had a series of visitors, mostly foreigners, who had come to India in search of a Guru, and had all been cheated and felt disillusioned. They had gone to famous gurus, learned gurus, gurus with thousands of disciples, gurus whose bodies conformed to the criteria for Mahatmas given in the *shastras*, gurus who sang devotional songs with emotion, gurus reputed to raise kundalini. All publicly claimed to be enlightened Gurus, and some called themselves World Teachers. It had cost the visitors quite a lot in terms of damage to their faith and loss of money before they came to my guru to ask what they should do. They came to him because he was English by birth, he had gone straight to a guru who had not deceived him, and, as one says, he had gone a long way on the path. But he never called himself a guru. He called himself a pupil teacher.

Later, we discussed what differentiated us from them so that we had been led straight to our teachers, while they had tried all sorts of supposed gurus and had been deceived. We could not lay claim to being "special," yet there must be some crucial difference.

What we arrived at was that while these people had been hunting the guru outside themselves on the basis of reputation and public claims, we had from the start been seeking at the root of our beings. In some sense, therefore, we assessed the status of avowed gurus in relation to the touchstone that had formed in our hearts. Did his words ring true in relation to whatever little bit of certainty our inner effort had yielded?

So when one met a person whose whole being so harmonized with what one was seeking inwardly that there was a great peal of inner bells, one had found the man who corresponded to what one was seeking, and one was not deceived.

Another thing is working here. When one goes straight to the Self, Soul, *Atman* or whatever, long before one has any direct experience of it, it is, as it were, activated. It is this which is responsible for those times when one puts out a hand, takes up a book, opens it at random, and finds the answer to the question of the moment. One finds oneself taken to the books, places and people where one will find the instructions and experiences one needs. And, because Self responds to Self, one 'finds' and 'recognizes' one's guru.

"Lo here! Lo there!" How many bogus teachers there have been! And if not actually charlatans, certainly not World Teachers. There was a period when there were at least six claimants to being reincarnations of H. P. B. around the world. A member of this ashram on a trip to London was invited to two tea parties on the same afternoon where two distinct bogus Comtes de Saint Germain were manifesting, one of whom was reputed to appear and disappear at will.

False coin cannot circulate unless there is true coin somewhere. But the true coin does not have "true coin" stamped on it. One has to be able to recognize it. How? I must repeat: find it in one's own heart, and one will recognize it wherever it appears outwardly. The true Teacher is always within one, for even if one hears the truth spoken, it is true only if one's inner being recognizes it. The same applies to the well-worn saying that true words ring false in the mouth of a man who speaks from his head but has not experienced them in his heart, for it is in the heart of the hearer that the words ring false.

It is true that the Masters take any opportunity to help mankind move in the right direction. They make use of any vehicle or "channel" that is available. But for reasons connected with the make-up of persons capable of acting as channels, these vehicles are inherently unreliable. Bits of teaching come though undistorted, and the rest may be distorted beyond recognition.

People who believe that God or the Masters ought to change the world, but are unwilling to start the job by changing themselves, are quite common. This appears to me as the sort of immaturity that wants a super father figure to take responsibility for growth out of the hands of the individual and to make everything easy for him. The real Masters urge us to work on ourselves. They certainly do not encourage us to sit back, relax, and let them handle things.

All this leads me to the simple conclusion that public claims on behalf of the Lord Maitreya and his supposed emergence do not mean a thing to me. Nor do the phenomena of appearing and disappearing. Nor do the predictions. As one of the Masters said: "Any fool can do them."

You asked for my reaction to the papers and I have given it on the basis of what my guru made me learn. He would throw a book or pamphlet across to me: "Is the Thing there?" he would ask. And I would have to tell him whether it was written from first hand experience of the Spirit, or whether it was just second-hand book-learning. Once when I evaded the issue by saying, "Some of the things he says seem true," he replied, "One can't write anything on this subject without saying something that is true. Charlatans mix enough truth with their claims to catch unwary people."

It is evident that, as a reaction to the collapse of all the old cultural standards and the resulting chaos in human affairs, more people than ever before are turning away from the false promises of technology and towards inner solutions, turning away from the second-hand teachings of conventional religion and towards direct inquiry into the nature of being.

So is it the coming of an avatara that changes the world, or is it that changes in the world make it possible for the teaching of an avatara to be accepted by human society? When this double sided question gets garbled, one tends to get the sort of muddled thinking that says the physical world will get spiritualized, that the mere coming of the avatara will change the world, and that all the ordinary man need contribute is to "recognize" and believe. The hard work and the suffering requisite for individual growth is sought to be avoided.

This business of the self-corrective nature of life, such that mistakes mankind makes give rise to consequences which tend to turn man back to the true teachings is something I feel very strongly about. It would be a great sorrow if potential seekers were to be led off on another set of false trails.

The root of the mystery of being lies at the root of the awareness which perceives the universe. Every human being is human by virtue of that awareness. Every human being is or can be aware that he is aware. When that self-awareness is traced to its inner source, then only can the identity of the individual with the universal be found, then only can the mystery of being be solved. And only when there are enough such individuals can sanity return through them to our troubled world. [April 22, 1996]

Works Cited/Bibliography

A. E. *The Candle of Vision*. New York: University Books, 1965.

Anderson, Margaret. *The Fiery Fountains*. New York: Hermitage House, 1951.

---. *The Unknowable Gurdjieff*. New York: Samuel Weiser, 1972.

Ashish, Sri Madhava. "The Guru as Exemplar of and Guide to the Term of Human Evolution." *Time and the Philosophies*. Paris: UNESCO, 1977. 211-236.

---. *Man, Son of Man*. Wheaton: Theosophical Publishing House, 1970.

--. "The Moral Stream," *Seminar*. Jan. 1985: 305.

---. *Relating to Reality*. New Delhi: Banyon Books, 1998.

---. "A Return to Intelligent Inquiry." Address. Conference of the Indo-European Neuro-Surgeons. New Delhi, Nov. 1992.

---. *An Open Window: Dreams and the Inner Reality*. Unpublished manuscript, 1997.

---. "The Value of Uncertainty." *The American Theosophist* Vol. 67 No. 1 (Jan. 1979): 10-13.

---. "What Can Be Taught." *The American Theosophist* Vol. 7 No. 2. (March-April 1989): 51-53.

Attar, Farid ud-Din. *The Conference of the Birds*. Trans. C. S. Nott. London: Routledge & Kegan Paul, 1954.

Bailey, Alice A. *Initiation Human and Solar*. New York: Lucis, 1922.

---. *The Unfinished Autobiography*. New York: Lucis, 1951).

Barker, Trevor, comp. *The Mahatma Letters to A. P. Sinnett*. Adyar, Chennai (Madras): Theosophical Publishing House, 1962.

Benjamin, Harry. *Basic Self-Knowledge Based on the Gurdjieff System of Development with Reference to the Writings of Krishnamurti*. York Beach, ME: Weiser, 1971.

---. *Everyone's Guide to Theosophy*. London: Theosophical Publishing House, 1969.

Bennett, J. G. *Gurdjieff: Making a New World*. New York: Harper & Row, 1973.

Besant, Annie, and C. W. Leadbeater. *Occult Chemistry*. Adyar/Madras: Theosophical Publishing House, 1908.

Blavatsky, H. P. *The Collected Writings of H.P. Blavatsky*. Comp. Boris de Zirkoff. 14 vols. Wheaton: Theosophical Publishing House, 1966-1985.

---. *Isis Unveiled*, 1877. Pasadena, CA: Theosophical University Press, 1988.

---. *The Secret Doctrine*. 1888. Los Angeles: The Theosophy Company, 1974.

---. *The Voice of the Silence*. 1889. Facsimile reprint. Wheaton: Quest-Theosophical Publishing House, 1991.

Bowen, P. G. *The Occult Way*. London: Rider, 1936.

Brook, Peter. *Meetings with Remarkable Men.* Corinth Films. 1978.
Film on Videotape. New York: Remar, 1978.

---. *Threads of Time.* New York: Perseus Books, 1999.

Castaneda, Carlos. *The Teachings of Don Juan: A Yaqui Way of Knowledge.*
Berkeley: University of California Press, 1968.

Collin, Rodney. *The Theory of Celestial Influence.* London: Watkins, 1954.

---. *The Theory of Conscious Harmony.* London: Vincent Stuart, 1958.

Collins, Mabel. *Light on the Path.* 1888. Pasadena: Theosophical University
Press, 1976.

Cranston, Sylvia. *H.P.B.: The Extraordinary Life & Influence of Helena Blavatsky,
Founder of the Modern Theosophical Movement.* New York: Tarcher/Putnam,
1993.

Daumal, René. *Mount Analog.* New York: Pantheon, 1960.

de Hartmann, Thomas and Olga. *Our Life with Mr. Gurdjieff.* London: Penguin,
1992.

Douglas, Nik, and Penny Slinger. *Sexual Secrets.* New York: Destiny, 1979.

Evans-Wentz, W. Y. Trans. *The Tibetan Book of the Dead.* London: Oxford, 1960.

---. *The Tibetan Book of the Great Liberation.* London: Oxford, 1954.

---. *Tibetan Yoga and Secret Doctrines.* London: Oxford, 1958.

---. *Tibet's Great Yogi Milarepa.* London: Oxford, 1928.

Frye, Northrop. *Anatomy of Criticism: Four Essays.* Princeton: Princeton
University Press, 1957.

Ginsburg, Seymour B. "Examine Thoroughly Gurdjieff s Teaching." *The
American Theosophist* Vol. 76 No. 9 (Nov.-Dec. 1988): 239-242.

---. "Gurdjieff s Contribution to Theosophy." *The American Theosophist* Vol. 75
No. 11. (Dec. 1987): 406-410.

---. "H.P.B., Gurdjieff and *The Secret Doctrine.*" *The American Theosophist* Vol. 76
No. 5 (Special Spring Issue May 1988): 147-155.

Gurdjieff, G.I. *All and Everything, First Series: Beelzebub's Tales to His Grandson.*
New York: Harcourt Brace, 1950.

---. *All and Everything First Series: Beelzebub's Tales to His Grandson.* New York:
Viking/Arkana, 1992.

---. *Meetings with Remarkable Men.* New York: E. P. Dutton, 1963.

---. *Textes et Témoignages Inédites.* Paris: Question de No. 50 1989.

---. *The Third Series: Life Is Real Only Then, When "I Am.*" New York: Triangle
Editions, 1975.

---. *Views from the Real World,* New York: Triangle Editions, 1973.

Herrigel, Eugen. *Zen, in the Art of Archery.* London: Routledge & Kegan Paul,
1953.

Hodson, Geoffrey. *The Kingdom of the Gods.* Wheaton: Theosophical Publishing
House, 1981.

Joyce, James. *Finnegan's Wake.* New York: The Viking Press, 1967.

Jung, Carl G. *Man and His Symbols.* London: Aldus Books, 1964.

---. *Memories, Dreams, Reflections.* New York: Pantheon Books, 1973.
---. *Mysterium Coniunctionis.* Princeton: Princeton University Press, 1970.
Keynes, Geoffrey. Ed. *Poetry and Prose of William Blake Complete in One Volume.* London: Nonesuch Press, 1956.
La Berge, Stephen. *Lucid Dreaming.* Los Angeles: Jeremy Tarcher, 1985.
Liber Mutis. 1677. Edinburgh: Magnum Opus Hermetic Source Works, 1982.
Lutyens, Mary. *The Years of Awakening.* Varanasi: Krishnamurti Foundation, 1975.
Mahabharata of Krishna-Dwaipayana. Trans. Kisari Mohan Ganguli. 4 vols. New Delhi: South Asian Books, 1991.
Mead, G. R. S. *Apollonius of Tyana.* 3 vols. London: Theosophical Publishing House, 1901.
---. *Thrice Greatest Hermes.* 1906. Detroit: Hermes Press, 1978
Merton, Thomas. *New Seeds of Contemplation.* New Ed. New York: Penguin New Directions, 1962.
Monroe, Robert A. *Far Journeys.* New York: Doubleday, 1985.
Moore, James. *Gurdjieff. The Anatomy of a Myth.* Shaftesbury, UK: Element, 1991.
---. "A Footnote on Maud Hoffman and A. T. Barker." *Theosophical History* Vol. 3 No. 3 (July 1990): 77-78.
Muldoon, Sylvan J., and Hereward Carrington. *The Projection of the Astral Body.* New York: Samuel Weiser, 1970.
Nectar of Chanting, The. South Fallsburg, NY: SYDA Foundation, 1978.
Needleman, Jacob, and George Baker. Eds. *Gurdjieff: Essays and Reflections on the Man and His Teachings.* New York: Continuum, 1997.
Nicoll, Maurice. *Psychological Commentaries on the Teaching of G. I. Gurdjieff and P. D. Ouspensky.* 5 vols. London: Robinson & Watkins, 1952.
Nisarga Datta. *I Am That.* Mumbai: Chetana, 1973.
Nott, C. S. *Teachings of Gurdjieff: A Pupil's Journal.* New York: Samuel Weiser, 1962.
Ouspensky, P. D. *In Search of the Miraculous.* London: Routledge & Kegan Paul, 1950.
---. *The Psychology of Man's Possible Evolution.* New York: Knopf, 1954. Vintage Books, 1974.
Pastor. *La Conscience Cosmique ou L'Homme Transfiguré.* Paris: Editions Fernand Lanore, 1990.
Patterson, Frank Allen. Ed. *The Student's Milton.* New York: Appleton-Century Crofts, 1957.
Peters, Fritz. *My Journey with a Mystic.* Laguna Niguel, CA: Tale Weaver, 1980.
Prem, Sri Krishna. *Initiation into Yoga: An Introduction to the Spiritual Life.* Wheaton: Quest-Theosophical Publishing House, 1976, 1989.
--- "Outline Sketch of Buddhist Philosophy." Journal Name Unknown. 1925.
---. *The Yoga of the Bhagavat Gita.* Baltimore, MD: Penguin Books, 1973.

Prem, Sri Krishna, and Sri Madhava Ashish. *Man, The Measure of All Things.* Wheaton: Theosophical Publishing House, 1969.

Reymond, Lizelle. *My Life with a Brahmin Family.* New York: Knopf, 1972.

---. *To Live Within.* New York: Knopf, 1971.

Roy, Dilip Kumar. *Yogi Sri Krishnaprem.* Bombay: Bharatiya Vidya Bhavan, 1975.

Schukman, Helen. *A Course in Miracles.* Tiburon: Foundation for Inner Peace, 1976.

Scott, Walter. *Hermetica.* 4 vols. London: Dawsons, 1968.

Seabrook, William. *Witchcraft: Its Power in the World Today.* New York: Harrap, 1940.

Smith, Russell A. *Gurdjieff: Cosmic Secrets.* Sanger, Texas: The Dog, 1993.

Speeth, Kathleen. *The Gurdjieff Work.* London: Turnstone Books, 1977.

Stevenson, Ian. *Twenty Cases Suggestive of Reincarnation.* Charlottesville: University Press of Virginia, 1974.

Taylor, Paul Beekman. *Gurdjieff and Orage: Brothers in Elysium.* York Beach, ME: Weiser, 2001.

Thurman, Robert A. F. Trans. *The Tibetan Book of the Dead.* New York: Bantam/ Doubleday, 1994.

Trismosin Solomon. *Splendor Solis.* 1582. Des Plaines, IL: Yogi Publication Society, 1991.

Wachmeister, Countess Constance. *Reminiscences of H. P. Blavatsky and The Secret Doctrine.* Wheaton, IL: Quest, 1976.

Walker, Kenneth. *A Study of Gurdjieff's Teaching.* London: Jonathan Cape, 1957.

Washington, Peter. *Madame Blavatsky's Baboon.* London: Martin, Seeker and Warburg, 1993.

Weiss, Brian L. *Many Lives, Many Masters.* New York: Fireside, 1988.

White, Charles S. J. "The Sai Baba Movement: Approaches to the Study of Indian Saints." *The Journal of Asian Studies* Vol. XY-XL No. 4 (Aug. 1972): 863-867.

Whitehead, A. N. *Process and Reality.* London: Macmillan, 1967.

Wilson, Edmund. *Axel's Castle: A Study in the Imaginative Literature of 1870-1930.* New York: Charles Scribner's, 1969.

Woodroffe, Sir John. *The Serpent Power.* Chennai/Madras: Ganesh, 1978.

Yogananda, Paramahamsa. *Autobiography of a Yogi.* Los Angeles: Self Realization Fellowship, 1979.

ABOUT THE AUTHORS

Seymour B. Ginsburg was born in Chicago, IL, in 1934, and graduated from Northwestern University with degrees in accountancy and law. A founder of the predecessor business and the first president of *Toys R Us*, he was for many years involved in commodities trading. He met Sri Madhava Ashish while on a private visit to India in 1978. He was a co-founder of the Gurdjieff Institute of Florida, and currently divides his time between South Florida and Chicago.

Sri Madhava Ashish was born Alexander Phipps, in Edinburgh, Scotland, in 1920, graduating from Chelsea's College of Aeronautical Engineering. He served in India during World War Two as a Spitfire engine repairman, meeting the guru Krishna Prem during a visit to Almora in 1946. He immediately adopted Sri Krishna Prem as his teacher, and, at the death of the guru in 1965, took over the direction of the Mirtola ashram. At his death in 1997, he had written extensively on spiritual subjects and on farming reforms in northern India.

Index